Collins *Gem*

BABIES'
Names

Julia Cresswell

HarperCollins*Publishers*

Julia Cresswell is an authority on first names, and has written a number of books on the subject

HarperCollins*Publishers*
Westerhill Road, Bishopbriggs, Glasgow G64 2QT

First published 1967
Fifth edition published 2002

Reprint 10 9 8 7 6 5 4 3 2 1 0

© HarperCollins*Publishers* 2002

ISBN 0 00 712785-5

Printed in Italy by Amadeus S.p.A.

Contents

Using this book

Today's parents have an enormous pool of names to choose from, probably more than at any other time in history. Alongside the traditional stock of names from the Bible, the classical world and the old Germanic names brought over by the Anglo-Saxons and the Normans, we now have names from all over the world, both Continental versions of traditional names and names from cultures with which our grandparents had little or no contact. This has led to a change in the attitude to what a 'real' name is, and as a result people now feel free to create a wonderful range of new names, many unique to their child. The danger here, of course, is that the child will have a lifetime of explaining what their name is, and how it is spelt, but many of these names pass into general circulation, particularly those that are blends; that is, combinations of sounds from other names. In addition, a much wider range of spellings of any given name is used by parents, perhaps to distinguish their child from others of the same name. I have tried to include as many of these different spellings as is reasonably possible, under the standard or traditional form of the name. I have also included a wide range of short forms. This is not only to show the range available, but also so that parents can check that all possible forms of a chosen name go harmoniously with the surname. For however determined a parent might be to use one particular form of a name, someone will at some time use a pet form of the name. I have also given a lot of information about naming habits in America. In part, this is because so many new names come from America, particularly from the African-American communities, which are particularly rich coiners of new names. But it is also because of America's dominance of the entertainment world. I hope that those curious about the unusual names they find used by actors and musicians will find the answer here.

Most of the variant names in this book have been cross-referenced to the name you can find it under. But in order to squeeze as many names as possible into this small book, if the cross reference would come near the headword, then it has been left out. Please look for the name you want under alternative spellings, and check under overlapping sounds such as 'C' and 'K', or 'sh' and 'ch'.

The first edition of this book was compiled in 1967. Since then I have revised it at regular intervals to bring it up to date. Leslie Dunkling has added names from Arabic and from the Indian Sub-continent.

I hope that this book will help you find just the right name for your child.

JULIA CRESSWELL, 2001

Registering your baby's birth

If you have your baby in a hospital in England or Wales, there is a good chance that your local registrar's office will have a branch there. It is worth taking advantage of this facility, rather than having to cope with a new baby and getting down to the registrar's office later on. If nothing is said at the hospital, ask one of the nurses. Unfortunately, this facility is not available in Scotland where the regulations concerning the registration of births vary slightly from those in England and Wales.

By law, you have to register the birth of your child within 42 days of his or her birth, or within 21 days in Scotland. If you have not used a hospital office, you can go to any registrar's office, although the procedure is slightly simpler if you use your local one, the address of which should be in the phone book. Registration centres round the mother. If the baby's parents are married either parent can register the birth. If they are not married, they can register the birth together if they go to the registrar together, or else the father must get special forms from the registrar's office in advance which, when filled in, will enable his details to go on the birth certificate. Otherwise, the father's details will be left blank, although it may be possible to fill these in later – talk to the registrar about this. There is no need to take the baby with you to the registrar, but only a parent can register the birth; a friend or relative will not do.

At the registrar's you will be asked to give the following information. The place and date of the baby's birth (the time of birth will only be needed if you have twins or more, although in Scotland it is always required). You will also need to state his or her sex, and will be asked for the names you intend to give your child. If the father's details are to go on the form you will need to give his full name, his date and place of birth and his occupation. The mother will be asked to give her full name, her maiden name if she has changed her surname and her place and date of birth. If she wishes, an occupation (current or previous) can be filled in. She has to give her usual address at the time of the birth and, if she is married to the father, the date of marriage will be asked for. She will also be asked for the number of other children she has had.

All this information will be entered into a register, which you should then check carefully – it will be difficult to correct mistakes later – and then sign. You will then be given a free short birth certificate which is all you need. You can also get full copies of the information on the register if you would like to have them, and spare copies of either type of certificate. There is a charge for birth certificates which varies depending on the type you get, but it is always more expensive to get extra copies later than at the time of registration. It is probably worth considering an extra copy so that each parent can have one, or so that one can be sent off with something like an application for a passport and you can still have one to hand.

If you still have not decided on a name for your baby by the time the limit for registration is up, you must still register the birth, but the name can be left blank. You then have up to one year from registration to make up your minds, although in Scotland any correction to the records after registration is likely to attract a fee. If your baby is baptised, the baptismal certificate can be produced at the registrar's office as evidence of the child's name. (Extra names given at baptism can also be added in this way.) Otherwise you need to ask the registrar's office for a Certificate of Naming, and use this to have the names inserted. You can give your child any forenames or surname that you like. In Scotland the registrar has the power to refuse to record a name if he or she deems it to be potentially offensive, although in practice a name is rarely objected to. In England and Wales, the registrar has no right to refuse your choice, although if your choice is too outrageous you may find that you are asked to think of the effect on the child before confirming it is what you want. Modern registrars are trained to be friendly and helpful, and you can always phone your local office for any advice you need; alternatively, contact The General Register Office, Smedley Hydro, Trafalgar Road, Birkdale, Southport PR8 2HH (tel. 0870 2437788) or The Registrar General's Office for Scotland, New Register House, Edinburgh (tel. 0131-334 0380).

Aakash *see* **Akash**

Aaliyah *see* **Ali**

Aamena, Aaminah *see* **Amina**

Aaron *m.*

In the Old Testament, Aaron was the brother of
MOSES and the first High Priest of Israel. The
traditional interpretation links this name to the
Hebrew for 'high mountain', but like Moses, Aaron
is probably an Egyptian name of unknown meaning.
It is connected with the Arabic names **Harun** and
Haroun, and has been in use since the Reformation.
In the past it was pronounced with a first sound as
in 'air', but now it is also found with a short 'a',
a pronunciation reflected in the spelling **Ar(r)on**.

Abdullah *m.*

A Muslim name from the Arabic for 'servant of
Allah'. The short form **Abdul** also occurs.

Abe, Abie *see* **Abel, Abraham**

Abel *m.*

In the Old Testament, Abel was the second son

ADAM and **EVE** and murdered by his brother Cain. The name may come from a Hebrew word for 'breath', but like so many of the earliest names, its meaning is doubtful. The name has been used in England since before the Norman Conquest. The short forms include **Abe** and **Abie**.

Abigail *f.*

From the Hebrew, meaning 'father rejoiced'. It was the name of one of King David's wives and was much used in England during the 16th and 17th centuries when many Old Testament names were popular. It was so popular for working-class women that it degenerated into a term for a lady's maid and so became unfashionable; but it has now come back into favour. It is sometimes spelt **Abagail** or **Abigal**. The short forms include **Abbie, Abb(e)y** and **GAIL**.

Abner *m.*

From the Hebrew words for 'father of light'. In the Bible it is the name of King Saul's cousin, who was commander of the army. In England it came into common use, together with other biblical names, after the Reformation in the early 16th century. It is still found occasionally in North America.

Abraham *m.*

This is the name of the Old Testament patriarch who, for the first 90 years of his life, was called **Abram**, 'high father', but then was told by God that he should be called Abraham, 'father of many nations'. It was used in England regularly after the Reformation and became popular in North America where the abbreviation **Abe**, as in President Abe Lincoln (1809–65), was widely used. Other short forms are **Abie, Ham** and **Bram**. (See IBRAHIM)

Ada *f.*

A name which started life as a pet form for **ADELA**, **ADELAIDE** and **ADELINE**, and so means 'noble'. It was fashionable in Britain in the late 18th and 19th centuries, but is now rare. Adah is often confused with Ada, but is in fact derived from the Hebrew word for 'ornament' or 'brightness'.

Adam *m.*

From the Hebrew, meaning 'red', possibly referring either to skin colour, or to the clay from which God formed the first man. The name was adopted by the Irish as early as the 7th century, when *St Adamnan*, 'Little Adam', was Abbot of Iona. It was very common in the 13th century and has been in use ever since, particularly in Scotland. It is currently one of the most popular boys' names. **Adamina** is a rare feminine form.

Adeel *see* Adil

Adela *f.*

From the Old German, meaning 'noble'. It was

common among the Normans, who brought it to England. One of William the Conqueror's daughters had this name. It died out but was later revived and became fashionable in the French form **Adèle**. **Addie** or **Addy** is used as a pet form for the names derived from this root (see also **ADELAIDE** and **ADELINE**). Adela can also be spelt **Adella**, which gives us the name **DELLA**, now more popular than its source.

Adelaide *f.*

Derived from the Old German words meaning 'noble and kind'. The name was common for centuries on the Continent but only came to Britain in 1830 when Adelaide of Saxe-Coburg became queen. Adelaide, the capital city of South Australia, was named after this popular queen. It can be shortened to **ADA**, and **ALIDA** is a Hungarian pet form (see also **HEIDI**).

Adeline *f.*

Like **ADELAIDE**, this name is derived from the Old German for 'noble'. It was first cited in England in the Domesday Book and was common during the Middle Ages. After that it disappeared until the Victorian Gothic revival. It is best known from the song *Sweet Adeline*. **ADA** is sometimes used as a pet form, and **Alina** and **Aline**, now used as separate names were also once short forms.

Adil _m._

An Arabic name meaning 'just, honest'. It is also spelt **Adeel**.

Adnan _m._

An Arabic name of uncertain meaning. According to tradition, Adnan was the ancestor of the North Arabians.

Adrian _m._, Adrienne _f._

From the Latin meaning 'man from Adria', and a form of the name of the Roman Emperor **Hadrian**, who built the wall across northern England. It has been used since Roman times; a St Adrian was the first British martyr in the 4th century. Adrian and **Adrien** are now sometimes used as girls' names. **Adriana** is a rare female form, the French Adrienne being more popular. **Adria** and **Adrianne** are also found.

Aeneus, Aengus _see_ Angus

Afra _see_ Aphra

Agatha _f._

From the Greek for 'good woman', this was the name of a 3rd-century martyr and saint. The short form is **Aggie**.

Agnes _f._

From the Greek meaning 'pure'. There was an early

Christian martyr called Agnes, whose symbol is a lamb, since the name also sounds very like the Latin *agnus*, 'lamb'. Old forms still occasionally used include **Annis, Annice** and **Annes**. **Agneta** is the Swedish form and **Inez** is the anglicised form of the Spanish **Inés**. Agnes was popular in Scotland where it also became **Nessie** and **Nessa**. In Wales it became **Nest** and **Nesta**. **Aggie** is a short form shared with AGATHA (see also INA).

Ahmad *m.*

This Arabic name is often spelt **Ahmed**. It is one of the names applied to the Prophet Muhammad and means 'more praiseworthy'.

Aidan *m.*

An ancient Irish name which means 'little fire'. It was the name of a 7th-century Irish missionary who founded the monastery of Lindisfarne in Northumbria. The name was revived during the 19th century and is popular at the moment in Ireland. It is sometimes anglicised as **Edan**.

Ailbhe *see* Elvis

Aileen *see* Eileen

Ailis, Ailish *see* Alice, Eilis

Ailsa *f.*

From the Scottish island, Ailsa Craig. First used in

Scotland where it can also be a pet form of **ALICE**, it has now spread through Britain.

Aimée *see* **Amy, Esmé**

Ainsley *m. and f.*

A place and surname used as a first name, this comes from the Old English and probably means 'lonely clearing'. It is also spelt **Ainslie**.

Aisha *f.*

From the Arabic meaning 'alive and well' or 'prospering'. A favourite name in the Arab world, originally borne by the third (and favourite) wife of the Prophet Muhammad. In Britain and the USA the name is found in many forms, including **Aiesha, Aishah, Ayisha, Asia, Aysh(i)a, Ieasha, Ieesha, Iesha** and **Isha**. H. Rider Haggard used the form **Ayesha** in his novel *She*, where the meaning was given as 'she who must be obeyed'.

Aisling *f.*

The commonest form of a name also found as **Aislinn, Isleen** and the phonetic **Ashling**. It is an old Irish name meaning 'a dream, vision' and has been popular in Ireland since the 1960s.

Ajay, Ajit *m.*

Popular Indian names from the Sanskrit for 'invincible'.

Akash *m.*

This Indian name is sometimes found as **Aakash**.
It is from the Sanskrit and means 'the sky'.

Akhil *m.*

An Indian name from the Sanskrit meaning 'whole, complete'.

Akshar *m.*

An Indian name from the Sanskrit meaning 'imperishable'.

Alan *m.*

An old Celtic name of unknown meaning.
It has appeared in various forms from early times.
In England it first became popular after the
Norman Conquest as **Alain** or **Alein**, the French
forms. These developed into Alleyne which is
preserved as a surname. Alan, **Allan, Allen** and
Alun (strictly speaking, a Welsh river name used as
a first name) are in use today. **Alana**, the feminine
form, is also spelt **Allana, Alanah** and **Alanna**, and
in the USA has developed the form **Alaina** or
Alayna. The actress **Lana** Turner made the short
form well known.

Alastair *m.*

Also spelt **Alasdair, Alistair** and **Alister**, this is the
Gaelic form of **ALEXANDER**, 'defender of men'. It is
shortened to **Al, Ali, Alli** or **Ally, Alec** and **Alick**.

Alban *m.*, Albina *f.*

From the Latin *Albanus*, meaning 'man from Alba' (a Roman town whose name means 'white'), and the name of the earliest British saint. The town of St Albans, where he was martyred, is called after him. **Albin** and **Albinus** are variants which appear occasionally, and Albina and **Albinia**, 'white', are used as feminine forms.

Alberic *see* Aubrey

Albert *m.*

An Old German name meaning 'noble and bright'. The Old English form was **Ethelbert**, the name of the Kentish king who welcomed Augustine to Canterbury when he came to convert the Anglo-Saxons to Christianity. This was replaced after the Norman Conquest by the French form, Aubert. Albert became so popular after the marriage of Queen Victoria to Prince Albert of Saxe-Coburg that it became over-used and so went out of fashion. BERT and BERTIE are short forms. **Alberta, Albertina** and **Albertine** are forms of the name used for girls.

Alby *see* Elvis

Aldous *m.*

From the Old German Aldo, meaning 'old'. It has been used in the eastern counties of England since the 13th century and has given rise to various surnames like Aldhouse and Aldiss. **Aldo** is still used in North America. The writer Aldous Huxley (1894–1963) is the best-known British example.

Aldwyn *m.*

This Anglo-Saxon personal name, meaning 'old friend', has been revived in modern times. Some parents prefer the spelling **Aldwin**.

Alec *see* **Alastair, Alexander**

Aled *m.*

The name of a Welsh river used as a first name. There is a female form **Aledwen**, 'fair Aled'.

Alessandra *see* **Sandra**

Alethea, Aletia *see* **Althea**

Alexander *m.*

Currently one of the most popular boys' names, this comes from the Greek meaning 'defender of men'. It was made famous in the 4th century BC by Alexander the Great, and was very popular in England in the Middle Ages. **Sandy** is a pet form, particularly in Scotland. **Alex** is the most common of the many short forms, others being **Al, Alec, Ali, Lex, Xan** and **Xander** or **Zander**. SACHA is another form of the name.

Alexandra *f.*

The feminine form of **ALEXANDER**, and like it, currently popular. **SANDRA** was originally an Italian form, but has become established as a name in its own right. It shares pet and short forms with **ALEXANDER**, along with **Alix** or **Alyx** (also from **ALICE**) and **Alexa** (see also **ALEXIS**). **Alexandria** and **Alexandrina** are also found.

Alexis *f. and m.*

From the Greek word meaning 'helper' or 'defender', Alexis is the name of one of the great saints of the Orthodox church. Originally a man's name, it is now more frequently used for women. Alternative forms are **Alexie, Alexus**, and for girls **Alexia, Alexa** and short forms such as **Lexi(e)** and even **Lexus**.

Alfred *m.*

From two Old English words, meaning 'elf' (hence 'good') and 'counsel'. It is also a possible development of the Anglo-Saxon name Ealdfrith, meaning 'old peace'. It is sometimes written **Alfrid**. When Alfred was written down in old Latin, the name was spelt **Alured** and developed into **Avery** (now used for both sexes). **Alf, Alfie** and **Fred** are diminutives. There is a feminine form **Alfreda**, and **Elfrida**, although it technically comes from a slightly different name meaning 'elf-strength', is also used as a female version of Alfred.

Algernon *m.*

From a Norman French nickname meaning 'with whiskers'. It was popular in the 19th century but is not much used today. The usual diminutive is **Algie** or **Algy**.

Ali *f. and m.,* Aliyyah *f.*

When used as a boy's name Ali is a popular Arabic name meaning 'exalted, noble', and as one of the terms used of Allah, invokes God's protection for the child. The feminine form is Aliyyah (also found as **Aliyah, Aliah, Alia** and **Alya**). This has been well used in the USA, particularly in the Swahili form **Aaliyah**, popularised by the singer Aaliyah Houston (1974-2001). As a western name Ali is a pet form of names such as ALICE, ALISON or ALASTAIR.

Alice *f.*

From the Old German word for 'nobility'. It originally had the form **Adelice** or **Adelise**. A number of forms remained popular from the Middle Ages until the 17th century, when it went out of favour. It was revived again in the 19th century together with the variant **Alicia**. Nowadays these have developed additional forms such as **Allice, Allyce** and **Alyssa, Alysia, Alis(s)a, Alisha** or even **Elis(s)a** or **Elys(s)a** although these are also pet forms of ELIZABETH. ALISON is a variant. **Alys** is the Welsh form and Irish forms are **Alis, Ailis** or the phonetic **Ailish**. **Ali**, **Allie** and **Alley** are used as pet forms, while **Alix** and **Alyx** can be used either as forms of Alice or **ALEXANDRA**.

Alick *see* Alastair

Alida *see* Adelaide

Alina, Aline *see* Adeline

Alis, Alisa, Alisha *see* Alice

Alison *f.*

Originally a diminutive of **ALICE** that was adopted in the 13th century, this was soon treated as a separate name. It was at one time a particularly Scottish name. Pet forms include those used for **ALICE** and **ELSIE**. **Allison** and **Al(l)yson** are standard forms in the USA.

Alistair, Alister *see* Alastair

Alix *see* Alexandra, Alice

Allan, Allana, Allen *see* Alan

Allegra *f.*

An Italian word meaning 'cheerful, lively', given by the poet Lord Byron to his daughter and still used occasionally as a result.

Alli, Ally *see* Alastair

Allice, Allie, Allyce *see* **Alice, Alison**

Alma *f.*

There are many opinions about the origin of this name. It could be derived from the Hebrew word for 'maiden', the Latin for 'kind' or the Italian for 'soul'. Most importantly, the name became very popular after the Battle of Alma during the Crimean War, and is still found occasionally.

Alondra *f.*

Alondra is the Spanish for 'lark'. It is a common American place name, but more importantly in the 1990s it was the name of a successful Mexican-made television series, named after its heroine. Its broadcast led to increased use among Spanish-speaking Americans.

Aloysius *m.*

This is the Latin form of Aloys, an old Provençal form of **Louis** (see **Lewis**). There was a popular Spanish saint of this name in the 16th century and Roman Catholics continue to use the name in this country. Aloys or Aloyse was the female form of the old name, and is a possible source of **Eloise**.

Althea *f.*

From the Greek for 'wholesome', this was the Greek name for the marsh mallow plant, still used as a healing herb. It seems to have been introduced to England with various other classical names during the Stuart period, and appeared in the charming lyric by Richard Lovelace *To Althea from Prison*. The similar-sounding **Alethea** (**Alethia**, **Aletia**) comes from the Greek for 'truth'.

Alun *see* **Alan**

Alured *see* **Alfred**

Alvin *m.*

From two Old English names, Alwine, 'friend of all' and Athelwine, 'noble friend'. **Aylwin**, **Alvan**, **Alvyn** and **Alvy** are alternative forms. There is a rare feminine, **Alvina**. The similar-sounding **Alvar** means 'elf army'.

Alys, Alyssa *see* **Alice**

Alyson, Alysson *see* **Alison**

Alyx *see* **Alexandra, Alice**

Amabel *f.*

From the Latin meaning 'lovable'. It has been in use in England in various forms since the 12th century. The short form, **MABEL**, became established as an independent name at an early date.

Amalia *see* **Amelia**

Amanda *f.*

From the Latin for 'deserving love'. It appears first in Restoration plays, where many classical or pseudo-classical names were introduced or fabricated. It has remained in use since then and is still popular. **Mandy** is a pet form also used as a name in its own right.

Amaryllis *f.*

Originally from Greek, probably meaning 'sparkling', and used by Greek poets as a name for a country girl. It served the same purpose for Latin poets, and was introduced to Britain via English poetry in the 17th century.

Amber *f.*

The name of the gemstone, used as a first name. It was not used before the 20th century.

Ambrin *f.*

From the Arabic for 'ambergris', a substance renowned for its sweet odour. It can also be spelt **Ambreen**.

Ambrose *m.*

From the Greek for 'divine'. There was a 4th-century St Ambrose who was Bishop of Milan. The name is found in the Domesday Book and has been used occasionally ever since. The Welsh name **Emrys** is derived from the Latin form of the name. There is a rare feminine form, **Ambrosine**.

Amelia *f.*

From an Old German name possibly meaning 'work', its form is perhaps influenced by **Emilia** (see **EMILY**). **Amalia, Amalie, Amaline** and **Amalita** are forms of the name. It can be shortened to **Milly**.

Amin *m.*, **Amina** *f.*

From the Arabic for 'honest', 'trustworthy' or 'reliable'. **Amina**, the feminine form, has always been much used by Muslim families, in honour of Amina bint-Wahab, mother of the Prophet Muhammad. It is sometimes spelt **Aamena, Aaminah** or **Amena. Iman**, 'faith, belief' comes from the same root. The model who uses this name has made it widely known, and it sometimes appears as **Imani** or **Imana**.

Aminta *see* **Araminta**

Amit *m.*

An Indian name from the Sanskrit for 'without limit'. It is also a simplified pet form of names like **Amitbikram** ('limitless prowess') and **Amitjyoti** ('limitless brightness').

Amitabh *m.*

A name of the Buddha, from the Sanskrit meaning 'limitless splendour'. The spelling **Amitav** is also used.

Amos *m.*

A Hebrew name, possibly meaning 'he who carries a burden'. It was the name of an Old Testament prophet and was adopted by English Puritans after the Reformation, when saints' names fell out of favour. Popular until the 19th century, it is at present uncommon.

Amrit *f. and m.*

In the Vedic epics of the Hindus, this Sanskrit name refers to immortality or that which confers it, such as the 'water of life, soma juice, nectar, [or] ambrosia'. Amrit can be used for both sexes, although the form **Amrita** can also be used for a girl.

Amy *f.*

From the French, meaning 'beloved'. Sir Walter Scott's novel *Kenilworth*, about Amy Robsart, the tragic wife of the Earl of Leicester, made the name fashionable in the 19th century, and it has been popular again in recent years. **Aimée** is the French original of this name, which can also be found in forms such as **Aime(e), Ami(e)** and **Amye**.

Amynta *see* **Araminta**

Anaïs *f.*

A French name which comes from the Greek word for 'fruitful'. There has been a small increase in its use since it became the name of a perfume.

Anand *m.*, Ananda *f.*

From the Sanskrit for 'happiness', 'joy' or 'bliss'.
It is the name of a god in the *Veda*, sacred book of
the Hindus. Variants of the girl's form include
Anandamayi ('full of joy'), **Anandi** and **Anandini**
('joyful').

Anastasia *f.*

From the Greek meaning 'resurrection'. The name
of a 4th-century saint and martyr, it became
fashionable in England in the 13th century, though
it was usually abbreviated to Anstey or **Anstice**,
which mainly survive today as surnames. It has
always been very popular in Russia, and a daughter
of the last Tsar of Russia, called Anastasia, is said to
have escaped from the massacre in which the rest of
her family died in 1918. **STACEY** and **Tansy** started
as pet forms of this name. **Nastasia** is a Russian pet
form and the emerging name **Tassia (Taja, Tasia)** is
probably a shortening of this.

Andrew *m.*, Andrea *f.*

From the Greek for 'manly'. Andrew is the name of
the Apostle who is patron saint of Scotland, Russia
and Greece, and first appears in England in the
Domesday Book. It has been used in Britain
continuously and has enjoyed particular favour in
Scotland. The pet forms include **Andy, Dandy**
(Scots) and **DREW**, which is also used as an

independent name. The Italian form, Andrea, is actually a boy's name in Italy, but is used as a girl's name in this country. The French boy's form, **André**, is likewise sometimes used for girls, although the more correct form **Andrée** is also used. Other female forms include **Andrene, Andrena** and **Andreana**, while **Andra** is both a traditional Scots form of the boy's name and used for girls.

Aneka, Aneke, An(n)ika *see* **Anne**

Aneurin *m.*

This name is traditionally interpreted as the Welsh form of Latin Honorius, meaning 'honourable', and is one of the oldest names still in use in Britain. It also appears in the form **Aneirin**. Short forms are **Nye** and **Neirin**.

Angela *f.*

From the Latin *angelus* originally derived from the Greek word meaning 'messenger', hence our word 'angel'. It is shortened to **Angel** and **Angie**. Other forms of the name include the French **Angelique**, and elaborations such as **Angelica, Angelia, Angeline** and **Angelina**, as well as spellings with a 'j' instead of a 'g'. Masculine forms of the name died out at the Reformation, but the Italian boy's name **Angelo** and the Spanish **Angel** are now found in the USA.

Angharad *f.*

A Welsh name meaning 'much loved'. It is an

important name in early Welsh literature, and has been in use since at least the 9th century. The stress is on the second syllable.

Angus *m.*

From the Gaelic **Aonghas**, meaning 'one choice'. It appears in Irish legend in the form **Aengus** or **Oengus**, but is more common in Scotland. The name became associated with the classical myth of **Aeneas** (which is close to the Irish pronunciation) in the 15th century, and this form was also used.

Anil *m.*, Anila *f.*

The name of the wind-god in the Hindu Vedic epics. It is derived from the Sanskrit meaning 'air' or 'wind'. Anil is the driver of Indra's golden chariot, which is pulled by a thousand horses. **Anila**, the feminine form, is used mainly by Hindu families.

Anish *m.*, Anisha *f.*

A Sanskrit name, one of the thousand borne by the Hindu god Vishnu. Its meaning is possibly 'without a master'.

Anita, Ann, Anna *see* Anne

Annabel *f.*

Together with **Annabelle** or **Annabella**, this is probably from the Latin *amabilis* meaning 'lovable', a variant of **AMABEL**. It is found in Scotland earlier than **ANNE**, so it is unlikely to be a form of that name, though it is now sometimes thought of as a compound of **Anna** and the Latin *bella* meaning 'beautiful'. Diminutives include **Bel**, **Belle** and **Bella**.

Anne *f.*

From the Hebrew **HANNAH**, meaning 'God has favoured me'. The French form Anne or **Ann**, traditionally the name of the mother of the Virgin Mary, was introduced into Britain in the 13th century and the name has enjoyed great popularity since. Anne is currently slightly more popular than Ann, but the form **Anna** is now much more popular than either. Pet forms include **Nan**, **Nanette**, **Nana**, **NANCY** and **Annie**, as well as the variants **Anita**, **Annette** and **Anona** (although this, with its pet form **Nona**, can be Welsh in origin). Ann(e) has often formed part of compounds such as **Mary Ann(e)** or **Annalise**. **Anneke** is the Dutch pet form, more often spelt **Anneka** in this country to reflect the Dutch pronunciation; **Aneke**, **Aneka** and **An(n)ika** are also found. **Anya** is from the Spanish pronunciation of the name and **Anouk** is a Russian form.

Annes, Annice, Annis *see* Agnes

Annette, Annie *see* Anne

An(n)ora *see* Honoria

Anona, Anouk *see* Anne

Anoop *see* **Anup**

Anstice *see* **Anastasia**

Anthea *f.*

From the Greek *antheos*, meaning 'flowery'.
This name seems to have been introduced by the
pastoral poets of the 17th century and it has been
in use ever since, although it was not until the
20th century that it became very widely known.

Ant(h)ony *m.,* Antonia *f.*

A Roman family name. Its most famous member
was Marcus Antonius, the Mark Antony of
Shakespeare's *Julius Caesar* and *Antony and
Cleopatra*. The name was very popular in the
Middle Ages as a result of the influence of St Antony
the Great and St Antony of Padua. The alternative
and commoner spelling **Anthony** was introduced
after the Renaissance, when it was incorrectly
thought that the name was derived from the Greek
anthos meaning 'flower', as in **ANTHEA**. The usual
short form is **Tony**, which is also used for the
female forms **Antonia** and the French **Antoinette**.
Feminine short forms **Toni** and **Tonya** are also
found, and **Toinette, Net** and **Nettie** are pet forms
of Antoinette. **Anton**, a Continental form of the
name, is now also used for boys. In the USA
Antonio (shortened to **Tonio**) and **Antoine** (often in
phonetic spellings such as **Antwan** or **Antuan**) are
often used.

Anup *m.*

An Indian name, from the Sanskrit meaning 'without comparison'. The spelling **Anoop** is also used.

Anusha *f.*

The name of a star in Hindu astrology.

Anya *see* **Anne**

Aoife *see* **Eve**

Aonghas *see* **Angus**

Aphra *f.*

From the Hebrew word for 'dust'. It is best known from the novelist, playwright and spy Mrs Aphra Behn (1644–89), said to have been the first woman in England to earn her living as a writer. It is also spelt **Afra**.

April *see* **Avril**

Arabella *f.*

A possible variant of **AMABEL**, though it could be derived from the Latin for 'obliging'. It used to be a predominantly Scottish name, particularly in the forms **Arabel** and **Arabelle**. It can be shortened to **Bel**, **Belle** and **Bella**.

Araminta *f.*

This name appears to have been invented by Sir John Vanbrugh (1644–1726) to use in one of his

plays. It may have been influenced by **Aminta** or
Amynta, an ancient Greek name meaning
'protector'. They all share the short forms **Minta**
and **Minty**.

Archibald *m.*

From Old German words meaning 'truly bold'.
The Old English form was used in East Anglia
before the Norman Conquest. Thereafter, it was
primarily Scottish and was associated particularly
with the Douglas and Campbell families. The most
usual diminutive is **Archie**, now sometimes given to
a child rather than the full name.

Ardal *m.*

This is an Irish name of disputed meaning, either
'high valour' or coming from the word for 'bear'.

Arianna *f.*

This is an ancient Greek name meaning 'the very
holy one' which probably originally belonged to a
goddess. In Greek mythology **Ariadne** was the
daughter of King Minos of Crete and helped
Theseus to escape from the labyrinth. Arian(n)a is
an Italian form of the name. **Ariane**, the French
form, is also used.

Ariel *f. and m.*

The name Ariel has two different origins. The
masculine form is a Hebrew name, traditionally said

to mean 'lion of God', which is popular in Israel and sometimes used in the USA. As a girl's name it has been popular in the USA ever since it was used as the heroine's name in Disney's *Little Mermaid* film and TV series. This name, which is also found in forms such as **Arial** and **Arielle**, presumably owes at least something to Ariel, the airy spirit in Shakespeare's play, *The Tempest*.

Arjun *m.*

A Hindu name from the Sanskrit for 'white' or 'bright'. It was the name of a famous Pandava prince, son of the god Indra.

Arlene *f.*

Arlene, **Arleen** or **Arline** is a modern name which probably comes from the final sounds of such names as CHARLENE or MARLENE.

Armand, Armin, Arminel, Arminelle *see* Herman

Arnold *m.*

From the Old German Arnwalt, meaning 'eagle's power'. It appeared in various forms, both Germanic and French, in the Middle Ages, but dropped out of use from the 17th century until the late 19th when it had a revival.

Aroon *see* Arun

Artemisia *see* **Diana**

Arthur *m.*

The origin of this name is disputed. Possible sources are the Celtic word for 'bear' and the Roman name Artorius. Whatever its source, its use comes entirely from the fame of its first known bearer, King Arthur. Victorian interest in things medieval made it popular in the 19th century when Queen Victoria gave the name to one of her sons. Over-use in the late 19th and first quarter of the 20th centuries led to a decline, but there are now distinct signs of a revival in popularity. **Art** or **Arty** is used as a short form, particularly in America.

Arun *m.,* Aruna *f.*

An Indian name from the Sanskrit for 'reddish brown', a colour associated with the dawn. It became the name of the mythical personification of the dawn, charioteer of the sun. **Aroon** is an alternative spelling for boys, while for girls **Arumina** is also used.

Asa *m.*

From the Hebrew word meaning 'physician'. In the Bible it is the name of a king of Judah, noted for his piety.

Asha *f.*

An Indian name from the Sanskrit for 'hope, desire, aspiration'.

Ashanti *f.*

The name of this Ghanaian people has had a certain popularity among people of African origin wanting to honour their roots. It is often shortened to **Shanti** (**Shante, Shaunti**).

Asher *m.*

The name of one of the tribes of Israel. It means 'happy'. Although it is an unusual name, there are signs that its use is on the increase, along with other names from the Bible. It is, of course, also a common surname meaning 'ash tree', and some uses may be from this.

Ashish *m.*

A relatively modern Indian name, probably derived from the Sanskrit for 'prayer' or 'benediction'.

Ashley *f. and m.*

A place and surname meaning 'ash field' which has become very popular throughout the English-speaking world. The spelling **Ashleigh** is rather more common for girls, and the variant **Ashlyn(n)** is used as a girl's name in the USA. The related surname **Ashton**, meaning 'ash farm', is also found as a first name for both sexes in the USA.

Ashling *see* **Aisling**

Ashraf *m.*

A popular Muslim name, from the Arabic for 'more noble' or 'more honourable'.

Asia *see* Aisha

Aslam *m.*

A Muslim name, from the Arabic meaning 'safer' or 'sounder'.

Asma *f.*

A popular Muslim name, from the Arabic for 'more eminent' or 'more prestigious'. Asma was the daughter of the caliph Abu-Bakr. She courageously helped the Prophet and her father escape from Mecca when their lives were threatened.

Astrid *f.*

From the Old German words meaning 'god' and 'beauty'. The name of the wife of St Olaf of Norway, it has long been popular in Scandinavia, and has been used in Britain in the 20th century.

Athene *f.*

This is the name of the Greek goddess of war, crafts and wisdom. In Britain, it has been used occasionally as a girl's name, as has the Latin form of the name, **Athena**. The Roman equivalent, **Minerva**, is also found.

Athol *f. and m.*

Athol or **Atholl** is the Scottish place name, used as a first name. The place name means 'New Ireland'.

Aubrey *m. and f.*

From the Old German meaning 'elf ruler'.
In medieval romance the diminutive **Auberon** was used and Shakespeare adopted it as **Oberon** in *A Midsummer Night's Dream*. The German form, **Alberic**, developed first into Albery and later into Aubrey. Aubrey is now to be found as a girl's name in the USA.

Audrey *f.*

A shortened form of **Etheldreda**, Old English for 'noble strength' and one of the sources of **ETHEL**. St Etheldreda was a 7th-century Anglo-Saxon princess who founded at Ely a religious house which later developed into the cathedral that now stands on the site. She was a popular saint and many churches are still dedicated to her.

Augusta *f.,* Augustus *m.*

From the Latin for 'venerable'. Augustus was a title given to the first Roman Emperor and Augusta is its feminine form. **Augustine**, the name of two important saints, one of whom converted the English to Christianity, is another form of the name. It was so popular in the Middle Ages it developed the shorter forms **Austin, Austyn** and **Austen**, a name which has been popular in the USA for some years. **Augustina** is a feminine form of Augustine. **Gus** and **Gussie** are pet forms.

Aurelia *f.*

From the Latin *aurelius* meaning 'golden'. It has been used since the 17th century, and recently a short form, **Auriol, Auriel, Oriel** or **Oriole**, has shown some popularity. The boy's form is **Aurelius**.

Aurora *see* Dawn

Austen, Austin, Austyn *see* Augusta

Autumn *f.*

This season is growing in popularity as a girl's name in the USA. **Spring** and **Summer** are also used.

Ava *f.*

This name is of obscure origin, but probably started life as a pet form of names beginning Av-. It was made famous by the film star Ava Gardner, and is more commonly found in the USA than Britain.

Aveline *see* Evelyn

Averil *f. and m.*

Probably from the Old English *eofor* ('boar') and *hild* ('battle'), which appears as **Everild** and **Everilda** in the 7th century. It was regularly in use until the 17th century, since when it has been less common. Averil is often confused with **AVRIL** which originally was an entirely different name.

Avery *see* **Alfred**

Avril *f.*

The French for **April**. The name has been popular in the 20th century, mainly for girls born in that month (see also **AVERIL**).

Ayesha, Ayisha *see* **Aisha**

Aylmer *see* **Elmer**

Aylwin *see* **Alvin**

Aysha, Ayshia *see* **Aisha**

Azim *m.,* Azima(h) *f.*

This Arabic name means 'determined'.

Aziz *m.*

This Arabic name means 'friend'. **Azeez** is a common alternative spelling, and **Aziza** or **Azeeza** are feminine forms.

Bab, Babs *see* **Barbara**

Babette *see* **Barbara, Elizabeth**

Bailey *f. and m.*
This surname, which comes from the job of steward or bailiff of an estate, has recently been fashionable as a girl's name in the USA.

Bairre *see* **Barry**

Bala *f. and m.*
An Indian name, from the Sanskrit for 'young child'. The boy's form can also appear as **Balu** and **Balan**.

Barbara *f.*
From the Greek *barbaros*, meaning 'strange' or 'foreign', and associated with St Barbara, a 3rd-century martyr. The name was little used after the Reformation, but in the 20th century it became popular again. Abbreviations include **Bab, Babs, Barbie** and sometimes **Bobbi**. The variant form Barbra was publicised by the singer **Barbra** Streisand. **Babette** is a French form of the name.

Barnabas *m.*

From the Hebrew meaning 'son of exhortation or consolation', it is best known as the name of the New Testament companion of St Paul. The diminutive, **Barnaby**, is rather fashionable at the moment, more so than the full form. **Barney** is a short form which is also shared with **BERNARD**.

Barney *see* **Barnabas, Bernard**

Barry *m.*

The English form of a variety of Celtic names, most prominently **Bairre**, a pet form of the Irish **Finbarr** (**Finnbar, Fionnbharr**) meaning 'fair-haired'. Barry can also be spelt **Barrie**, the usual spelling in the name's infrequent use for girls.

Bartholomew *m.*

From the Hebrew, meaning 'son of Talmai', Talmai meaning 'full of furrows'. It was the surname of the Apostle **NATHANIEL** and was very popular in the Middle Ages when the cult of St Bartholomew was at its height. St Bartholomew's Hospital in London was founded in the 12th century, and a riotous annual Bartholomew Fair held in the city to provide funds for it, was suppressed only in the 19th century. The name is still in use, and has short forms **Bart**, made famous by the cartoon character Bart Simpson, and **Barty**.

Basil *m.*

From the Greek *basileios*, meaning 'kingly'. It was probably brought to England by the Crusaders, and it has remained in use ever since. Diminutives include **Bas** or **Baz**, **Basie** and **Bazza**, and there are two feminine forms, **Basilia** and **Basilie**. These were common in the Middle Ages, but are hardly ever found today.

Bastian, Bastien *see* Sebastian

Bathsheba *f.*

This name derives from Hebrew words which mean 'daughter of opulence'. In the Old Testament Bathsheba was the beautiful wife of Uriah and was seduced by King David who arranged to have Uriah die during a battle. Bathsheba married David and became the mother of Solomon. The name was formerly used in Cornwall in the form **Bersaba** and appears also in its pet form **Shoba**. Bathsheba Everdene is a central character in Thomas Hardy's *Far From the Madding Crowd*.

Baz, Bazza *see* Basil

Beatrice *f.*

From the Latin **Beatrix**, meaning 'bringer of happiness'. It has strong literary associations. Dante's Beatrice is probably best known, but Shakespeare also used the name in *Much Ado About*

Nothing. Recently, both forms of the name have shown signs of returning to popularity, no doubt helped by the publicity given to it as the name of one of the Duke and Duchess of York's daughters. Short forms include **Bea** or **Bee, Beata, Beatty, Triss** and **Trixie**. There is also a Welsh variant, **Bettrys**, and a Spanish form **Beatriz**.

Becky *see* **Rebecca**

Bel *see* **Annabel, Arabella, Belinda, Isabel**

Belinda *f.*

From an Old German name, the latter part of which means 'a snake' (see **LINDA**). The first part of the name is obscure, but is commonly thought of as representing the French 'fair'. Its popular use began in the 18th century when it was used in plays by Congreve and Vanbrugh, and in Pope's poem *The Rape of the Lock*. Short forms include **Bel** and all forms of **LINDA**.

Bella, Belle *see* **Annabel, Arabella, Isabel**

Ben *see* **Benjamin**

Benedict *m.*

From the Latin *benedictus*, meaning 'blessed', and most familiar as the name of St Benedict, founder of the Benedictine Order. It was common in medieval England in the forms **Bennet** and **Benedick**. The latter is the name of a character in Shakespeare's *Much Ado About Nothing.* There are feminine forms **Benedicta** and **Benedetta**, and a Spanish-American form **Benita**.

Benjamin *m.*

From the Hebrew, meaning 'son of the south' or 'right hand', which might imply strength and good fortune. The Old Testament story of Benjamin, son of Jacob, gave the name the added implications of a favoured youngest son. The commonest pet forms are **Ben, Bennie, Benny, Benjie** and **Benjy**. It is currently a very popular name.

Bennet *see* **Benedict**

Berenice *f.*

From the Greek Pherenice, meaning 'bringer of victory'. It was spread by the imperial conquests of Alexander the Great over Europe and Asia. It was especially popular in Egypt, during the period of Macedonian rule, and its use spread also to the family of Herod of Judea. **Bernice** is a modern form of the name, and **Bunny** is sometimes used as a pet form (see also **VERONICA**).

Bernadette *f.*

The commonest female form of **BERNARD**. Its use has spread due to the fame of St Bernadette of Lourdes, who lived in the mid 19th century and whose visions started the pilgrimages of healing to that town. The Italian **Bernardetta** has been shortened to **Detta**, which can be used as an independent name. **Bernadine** is another form of the name, and **Bernie** the short form.

Bernard *m.*

A Germanic name meaning 'brave as a bear'. It was very popular in the Middle Ages. Two important saints bearing the name were St Bernard of Menthon after whom St Bernard dogs are named, and St Bernard of Clairvaux who inspired the Second Crusade. It has remained in use ever since. The most usual short forms are **Bernie** and **Barney**, which is shared with **BARNABAS**.

Berry *see* **Bertram**

Bert, Bertie *m.*

A pet form of a large number of names including **ALBERT**, **BERTRAM**, **BERTRAND**, **GILBERT**, **HERBERT**, **HUBERT**, **ROBERT**. In all these cases, the '-bert' part of the name is a Germanic element meaning 'bright'. The name is sometimes used as a given name, when it may take the form **Burt**.

Bertha *f.*

From the Old German word *beraht*, meaning 'bright'. The first famous English Bertha was the wife of King Ethelbert of Kent who welcomed

St Augustine to England on his mission of conversion. In the Middle Ages both Bertha and **Berta** were popular, and the name has been regularly used ever since, although it is rather uncommon at present.

Bertram *m.*

From the Old German meaning 'bright raven', the bird associated with the god Odin. The name has been used in England since the early Middle Ages, and has the short forms BERT and **Bertie**, and the less common **Berry**. **Bertrand**, meaning 'bright shield', is often treated as the French form of Bertram and shares with it the short forms BERT and **Bertie**.

Beryl *f.*

From the gemstone, whose name is related to the Arabic for 'crystal'. It appeared in the 19th century, and was popular in the early part of the 20th century.

Bess, Bessie, Beth *see* Elizabeth

Betha *see* Bethia

Bethany *f.*

A popular name taken from a New Testament place name, the village where Lazarus lived. The short form **Bethan** is used independently, and is also a short form of ELIZABETH which has spread from Wales.

Bethia *f.*

Bethia or **Bethea** can be interpreted in three different ways. It can be thought of as a pet form of ELIZABETH, as a use of the Old Testament place name Bethia, or as an English version of a Gaelic name also found as **Betha**, meaning 'life'.

Betsy, Bettina, Betty *see* Elizabeth

Bettrys *see* Beatrice

Beverl(e)y *f. and m.*

From an Old English surname meaning 'of the beaver-meadow'. It is shortened to **Bev**, and is now only rarely used for boys.

Bevis *m.*

This is a French name, possibly meaning 'bow', introduced into England at the Norman Conquest. It was popular in the Middle Ages and revived again after Richard Jeffries' *Bevis, The Story of a Boy* was published in 1882.

Bharat *m.*

This was the name of several famous heroes in the Hindu epics, and derives from the Sanskrit for 'being maintained'. India officially became Bharat when it achieved independence.

Bharati *f.*

A Hindu name identified with the goddess of speech and learning.

Bhaskar *m.*

A Hindu name from the Sanskrit for 'the sun'. Bhaskara, the famous 12th-century Indian astronomer and teacher, shows an earlier form of the name.

Bhavana *see* **Bhavna**

Bhavini *f.*

A Hindu name meaning 'illustrious, beautiful', a term for the goddess Parvati, wife of the god Siva.

Bhavna *f.*

An Indian name, from the Sanskrit meaning 'wish', 'desire' or 'thought'. The form **Bhavana** is also used.

Bianca *see* **Blanche**

Bidelia, Biddy *see* **Bridget**

Bill *see* **William**

Billie, Billy *f. and m*

This pet form of the boy's name **WILLIAM** is being used increasingly as a girl's name particularly in America, often in combinations to produce names such as **Billie Jean** or **Billy Joe**.

Birgitta *see* **Bridget**

Björn *m.*

A Scandinavian name which means 'bear'. The name has become widely known in modern times through the Swedish tennis champion Björn Borg.

Blaise *m.*

From the French, meaning either someone from the Blois region, or derived from the Latin for 'stammerer'. It is also spelt **Blase** or **Blaze**.

Blake *f. and m.*

A surname, from the Old English meaning 'black, dark-complexioned', used as a first name.

Blanche *f.*

This is a French name which was brought to England in the 13th century. It means 'white' or 'fair-skinned'. The Spanish and Italian form **Bianca** was used by Shakespeare, and is now rather more popular than the older form.

Blodwen *f.*

From the Welsh for 'white flower'. It is rarely found outside Wales. **Blodeuwedd**, 'flower form', is the name of a beautiful but unfaithful woman in Welsh medieval romance, while **Blodyn** or **Blodeyn** is the more simple 'flower'.

Blossom *see* **Fleur**

Bob *see* **Robert**

Bobbi(e), Bobby *f. and m.*

These pet forms of **ROBERT**, **ROBERTA** and **BARBARA** are used as names in their own right, and in combinations such as **Bobby Joe**.

Bonnie, Bonny *f.*

A Scots word for 'pretty' used as a name. Like many modern names, it probably owes its spread to its appearance in *Gone with the Wind*.

Boris *m.*

From the Russian word for 'fight'. It was used in Britain and North America in the 20th century, possibly due to cultural influences such as Moussorgsky's opera *Boris Godunov*, the film actor, Boris Karloff, and the author of *Dr Zhivago*, Boris Pasternak, as well the large number of Slavic immigrants who have come to the West.

Boyd *m.*

From a Gaelic word meaning 'yellow', referring to the colour of the hair. It is the name of a Scottish clan, though the surname can also derive from 'isle of Bute'. Boyd became more widespread outside Scotland after its use in Margaret Mitchell's *Gone With the Wind*.

Bradley *m.*

A surname from the Old English, meaning 'wide meadow', now popular as a first name. **Brad(d)** is a short form.

Brady *m.*

An Irish surname, possibly meaning 'broad-chested' now found as a first name.

Bram *see* **Abraham**

Bran see **Brenna**

Brand see **Brenda**

Brandan, Brandon see **Brendan**

Brandi *f.*

This name, which seems to come from the vocabulary word 'brandy', has been a popular girl's name in the USA for some years. It is also found spelt **Brandy, Brandee** and **Brandie**, and probably serves as a feminine form of **Brandon**.

Brannan see **Brenna**

Breanna *f.*

This new name, which has developed in the USA, can either be seen as a blend of the names **Bree** (a pet form of **BRIDGET**) and **Anna**, or as a development of **BRIANNA**, a feminine form of **BRIAN**. It is also used in the form **Breanne**, and found in spellings such as **Breeanna** and **Brieanne**.

Bree see **Bridget**

Bren see **Brenna**

Brenda *f.*

Probably a feminine form of the Norse name **Brand**, meaning 'a sword', found in the Shetlands. It was used by Walter Scott in his novel *The Pirate*. However, in practice, it has been used more frequently as a feminine form of **BRENDAN**.

Brendan, Brandon *m.*

An Irish name meaning either 'with stinking hair', or, according to one authority, from the Welsh word meaning 'prince'. It is most famously found in the 6th-century Irish St Brendan the Navigator, credited in legend with the discovery of America. It is today particularly popular in Ireland, Australia and the USA. The form **Brandan** or **Brandon** has a long history as an alternative form of Brendan, but can also come from an Old English place and surname meaning 'a hill where broom grows'. The name is also spelt **Brandin, Brandyn, Brenden** and **Brendon**.

Brenna *f.,* Brennan *m.*

Brennan is a pet form of the Irish name **Bren**, which probably means 'tear, sorrow', with **Brenna** a modern feminine form. Since the earliest records this name and **Bran**, 'raven', and its pet form **Brannan** have regularly been confused, and it is not always possible to tell which form of the name has come from which source.

Bret(t) *m.*

From an Old French word meaning 'a Briton' or 'a Breton'. It is currently well used in the USA.

Brian *m.,* Brianna *f.*

A Celtic name, the origin of which is obscure, though it may be derived from words meaning 'hill' or 'strength'. It was known mainly in Celtic areas until the Norman Conquest, when it was introduced to England. Brian Boru was a famous Irish King of the 11th century, who defeated the invading Vikings. The name continued to be popular in England until Tudor times, but after that it disappeared until it was reintroduced from Ireland in the 18th century. Today the spellings **Bryan, Brien** and **Brion** are found, and **Bryant** or **Briant**, originally a surname developed from the name Brian, is also found. **Brianna, Bryan(n)a** and **Brianne (Bryanne)** are used as feminine forms, as is BRYONY.

Brice *m.*

Brice, possibly meaning 'speckled', is an old Gaulish name, the name of a 5th-century French saint and bishop of Tours, which is now well used in the USA, often in the form **Bryce**. The surname which developed from the first name, **Bryson**, is also found used as a first name.

Bridget *f.*

Brigit was the ancient Irish goddess of poetry whose name meant 'strength'. Her name was borne by 5th-century St Brigit of Kildare, the most revered of the Irish female saints. The Irish name also appears in the forms **Bri(d)gid** and **Bride** (which reflects the Irish pronunciation of the name, with a long 'ee' sound and no 'g'), with the diminutives **Bridie, Biddy, Bree** (now sometimes **Brea**) and the older elaboration **Bidelia**. There is also a Swedish saint **Birgitta** or **Brigitta** whose feast day falls on the same day as St Brigit's, and her name has influenced the most common English form of the name, Bridget. **Britt** is a pet form of the Swedish name.

Brien *see* Brian

Brigid, Brigit, Brigitta *see* Bridget

Brin *see* Bryn

Brion *see* Brian

Briony *see* Bryony

Britt *see* Bridget

Brittany *f.*

This French place name began to be used as a name for American girls in the 1960s, for reasons which are unclear. The sound of the name rather than its meaning seems to be important, as it also occurs as **Britanee, Britani, Britney** (made famous by Britney Spears) and **Brittney**. In the 1980s a sudden surge in popularity took it to the top of the American name charts and use is growing in the UK.

Bronwen *f.*

From the Welsh words meaning 'white breast'. This name has long been popular in Wales where it has strong associations with ancient legend.

Brooke *f.* and *m.*

The surname meaning 'a brook', used as a first name, made famous by the actress Brooke Shields. The American place name **Brooklyn**, most famously used in the UK for a boy, Brooklyn Beckham, is more often used for girls in the USA, and is treated as if a blend of Brooke and LYN in forms such as **Brooklynne**.

Bruce *m.*

A French surname which came to Britain at the time of the Norman Conquest. Members of the family moved to Scotland where a descendant of one, Robert Bruce, became King of Scots, and was the ancestor of the Stewart or Stuart Kings. Bruce has only been used as a first name since the 19th century, but it proved so popular in Australia in the mid 20th century that it is almost a nickname for an Australian man. **Brucie** is a pet form.

Bruno *m.*

This is a German name meaning 'brown', probably imported to the UK via the USA where it has been established for longer.

Bryan *see* Brian

Bryce *see* Brice

Bryn *m.*

A Welsh name, originally describing where someone

lived, meaning 'hill'. It can be found as **Brin**, and **Brynmor** ('large hill') is also used.

Bryony *f.*

Bryony, or **Briony**, is the name of the climbing hedgerow plant used as a girl's name. It is a rather insignificant plant, although it has pretty berries, and the name probably owes its popularity to the fact that it can be used as a female equivalent to **BRIAN**.

Buddy *m.*

This word for a friend is occasionally used as a first name, but is usually a nickname. The singer Buddy Holly, for example, was christened Charles.

Buffy *see* **Elizabeth**

Bunny *see* **Berenice**

Bunty *f.*

This was a traditional name for a pet lamb, which came into use for girls after 1911, when it was featured in a very successful play called *Bunty Pulls the Strings*. However, it is used more commonly as a nickname.

Burhan *m.*

An Arabic name meaning 'evidence' or 'proof'. **Burhanuddin** means 'proof of faith'.

Burt *see* **Bert**

Byron *m.*

A name more frequently used in America than Britain, though it honours the English poet Lord Byron (1784–1824). Byron comes from the word 'byre', which means a cow-shed or barn. The name may have originally indicated someone who lived near a barn.

Caddy *see* **Caroline**

Cahal *see* **Carol**

Cai *see* **Caius**

Caitlin *f.*

This, like **Kathleen**, is an Irish form of **KATHARINE**. It is currently popular in the UK, and it has been one of the most popular names in the USA for some years. The Irish pronounce it with the sound of 'cat' but the American pronunciation is reflected in the spelling **Katelynn**. Forms such as **Caitlyn(n)**, **Kaitlyn** and **Katlin** are also found.

Caius, Gaius *m.*

A Roman first name, meaning 'rejoice', which is still used occasionally. The Welsh name **Cai, Kai** or **KAY**, well known as the name of Sir Kay, King Arthur's foster-brother, is derived from this.

Caleb *m.*

From the Hebrew *kalebh*, meaning 'dog' or 'intrepid'. It first appeared in England in the 16th century and is now coming back into fashion. It is shortened to **Cale** and can be spelt with a 'K'.

Callie _f._

Callie or **Cally** was originally a short form of several names, but is now used as a name in its own right. It is an old pet form of **CAROLINE**, or it can come from any name beginning Cal-, particularly those containing the Greek element for 'beautiful', such as **Calliope**, 'beautiful face', the name of the ancient Greek muse of epic poetry, or **Calista**, 'most beautiful' a name that may become more popular with the success of the actress Calista Flockhart. It is also found spelt **Kally** or **Kalli(e)**.

Callum _m._

Callum comes from the Latin _columba_, 'a dove'. When the Irish St **Columba** went as a missionary to Scotland in the 6th century, he introduced the name there and it became a typically Scottish name, along with **MALCOLM**, which comes from it. It has recently become increasingly popular in the rest of the UK. It is found spelt **Calum** and **Colum**, while the form **Colm** is particularly popular in Ireland.

Calvin _m._

From the surname of the 16th-century French religious reformer Jean Cauvin or Chauvin, which was latinised to Calvinus, and adopted as a first name by Protestants. The surname may mean 'bald'. It is most commonly found in North America and Scotland, and can be shortened to **Cal**.

Cameron *f. and m.*

From the Gaelic meaning 'crooked nose' this is the
name of a Scots clan. Its popularity as a boy's name
has spread from Scotland. It is now being used for
girls as well.

Camilla *f.*

A name from Roman legend. Camilla was Queen of
the Volsci, a great warrior and exceptionally swift
runner. The name may be Etruscan, and possibly
means 'one who helps at sacrifices'. It was recorded
in Britain as early as 1205 and is popular at the
moment. **Camille** is the French form which can be
used for either sex, and **Milla**, **Milly** and **Millie** are
used as short forms.

Candice, Candace *f.*

This is an ancient title of the Queen of Ethiopia.
It is also spelt **Candis**; **Candy** is a short form.

Candida *f.*

From the Latin meaning 'white'. The name was not
used in Britain until the early 20th century and its
introduction was probably due to G.B. Shaw's play,
Candida.

Candis, Candy *see* Candice

Cara *f.*

This Italian word meaning 'dear' came into use as a
first name only in the 20th century and is often spelt

Kara in the USA. Pet forms, used as names in their own right, include **Carissa**, **Carita** and particularly **Carina** or **Karina**. These are found in a number of variant forms such as **Karissa**, **Karena**, **Caryssa** and **Charissa**, and it is not always easy to tell when parents are using forms of Cara, KAREN or CHARIS.

Caradoc *m.*

From the Welsh for 'beloved'. It is common in Wales, but not in other parts of Britain. In the form Caratacus, the name of a Briton who fought against the Romans in the first century, it is one of the earliest recorded British names.

Cari *see* Ceri

Carl, Karl *m.,* Carla, Karla *f.*

These are German forms of CHARLES. The names have been in general use in America for a century, and from there spread to Britain. The feminines **Carla** or **Karla**, **Carlie** or **Carly** can also be found as forms of the names found under CAROLINE.

Carlo *see* Charles

Carlotta *see* Charlotte

Carlton, Charlton *m.*

These names are both forms of an Old English place name and, later, a surname meaning 'countryman's farm'.

Carlyn *see* **Caroline**

Carmel *f.*

From the Hebrew meaning 'garden', and the name of a mountain famous for its lush vegetation near the city of Haifa in Israel. St Louis founded the church and convent on this mountain which, as legend has it, the Virgin Mary and infant Jesus often visited. **Carmen** is the Spanish form of the name, **Carmela** the Italian, and **Carmelita** and **Carmelina** pet forms. Carmen is also the Latin word for song, and some people like to think of it in this sense, hence such modern coinages as **Carmina**, the Latin for 'songs'.

Carol *f. and m.*

The female forms of this name, which include **Carole**, **Carola** and **Caryl**, were originally pet forms of **CAROLINE** or **Carolina**, but are now popular names in their own right. As a boy's name it can be an English form of the Irish **Cathal** or, in its phonetic spelling, **Cahal** ('battle-mighty'). It is also used in central Europe and often spelt **Karol** or **Karel**, deriving from **Carolus**, the latinised form of **CHARLES**, but it is an uncommon male name.

Caroline, Carolyn *f.*

These names come from **Carolina**, the Italian feminine form of **Carlo**. The name was introduced into Britain from southern Germany by Queen Caroline of Brandenburg-Anspach, wife of George II.

Both forms have been used steadily since the 18th century. Derivatives are **Carla** (see CARL), **Carlyn**, CAROL, **Carola, Carole**. Abbreviations include **Carrie, Caddy, Caro** and LYN.

Caron *see* Karen

Carrie *see* Caroline

Carwen, Carwyn *see* Ceri

Cary *m.*

A surname which was only rarely used as a first name until it became famous through the film star Cary Grant. Ultimately, it probably goes back to one of a number of Irish surnames, including ones meaning 'battle-king' or 'dark brown'.

Caryl *see* Carol

Caryn *see* Karen

Carys *see* Ceri

Casey *f. and m.*

This comes from an Irish surname meaning 'vigilant in war'. It can also be a form of the Polish name **Casimir**, 'proclamation of peace'. This has a female form **Casimira**. The name takes various forms, often spelt with a 'K'.

Caspar *see* Jasper

Caspian *m.*

Although at first this looks like the name of the great Asian inland sea, use of Caspian as a first name comes from the character of Prince Caspian in C.S. Lewis's *Narnia* books, particularly the 1951 volume named after him.

Cassandra *f.*

In Greek literature this was the name of a prophetess and princess of Troy. She foretold the truth, but was never believed. The name first became popular in the Middle Ages and has continued in use ever since. It is shortened to **Cassie** and **Cass** and sometimes **SANDRA** or **Sandy**. Cass also occurs as a masculine name, when it may come from an Irish name meaning 'curly-haired'.

Cassia *see* Kezia(h)

Cassidy *f.*

This is an Irish surname, of unknown meaning, used as a first name, mainly in the USA. **Cassie**, also used as a name in its own right, is a short form it shares with **CASSANDRA**. It is occasionally used for boys.

Cathal *see* Carol

Catharine, Catherine, Cathleen, Cathy *see* Katharine

Catriona *f.*

A Gaelic form of **KATHARINE**. It was the title of a
book by Robert Louis Stevenson, and became very
popular in the 19th century as a result of this.
Catrina, **Katrina** and **Katrine** are other forms of the
name, and it becomes **Catrin** in Welsh. **Riona** is an
Irish pet form.

Cecily *see* Cecilia

Cecil *m.*

From the Latin meaning 'blind'. It was the name of
a famous Roman clan and was first adopted into English
as a girl's name. The popularity of the name in its
masculine form only became marked in the 19th
century, probably as one of several aristocratic surnames
which it was then fashionable to use as first names.

Cecilia *f.*

The female version of **CECIL**. It was the name of
a 2nd-century martyr and saint, the patroness of
music. The name was first introduced into Britain by
the Normans. Variant forms are **Cicely**, **Cecily**,
Sisley, **Cecil** and the French **Cecile** (used for boys
and girls in France). The popular shortened form
Celia (which can also be derived from another
Roman name, Coelia) probably came into fashion as
a result of the Celia in Shakespeare's play *As You
Like It*. Other abbreviated forms are **Sis, Ciss** and
Cissy or **Sissy** (see also **SHEILA**).

Cedric *m.*

This name seems to have been a creation of Sir Walter Scott's for a character in the novel *Ivanhoe*. Scott is said to have used it by mistake for Cerdic who was the first king of the West Saxons. However, as there is a Welsh name **Cedrych** ('pattern of generosity'), it may well be from this. Cedric became popular with parents as a result of the book *Little Lord Fauntleroy* (1886) by F.H. Burnett whose hero bore that name, and it may well also owe its fall in popularity to its association with the book and its hero's smugly virtuous image. It does, however, show signs of coming back into fashion, particularly in the USA.

Celeste *f.*

From the Latin meaning 'heavenly'. Pet forms, used as names in their own right, are **Celestine**, **Celestina** and **Celesta**.

Celia *see* Cecilia

Celina, Céline *see* Selina

Cenydd *see* Kenneth

Ceri *f.*

A popular Welsh name, sometimes spelt **Keri** to reflect its pronunciation with a hard 'c'. It comes from the Welsh word for 'love' as do the names **Cerian**, **Cerys** or **Carys** and **Cari**. **Carwen** is 'fair love' and has a masculine form, **Carwyn** (see also **KERRY**).

Ceridwen *f.*

This name probably comes from the Welsh words for 'poetry' and 'white, blessed'. It was the name of a Celtic goddess who was said to inspire poetry and was the mother of the great poet, **Taliesin** ('radiant brow'). It is pronounced with a hard 'c' and is generally confined to Wales.

Cerys *see* **Ceri**

Chad *m.*

The name (of uncertain meaning) of a 7th-century saint who was Bishop of Lichfield. The name became quite popular in America in the 20th century. A famous holder of the name was the Rev. Chad Varah, founder of The Samaritans.

Chae *see* **Charles**

Champak *m.*

The Hindu name of a god, and of a tree bearing yellow flowers.

Chandan *m.*

An Indian name from the Sanskrit for 'sandalwood'. The paste derived from sandalwood is important in Hindu religious ceremonies, when it is used to anoint statues of the gods and to make a mark on the foreheads of worshippers. Chandan occurs as a divine personal name in traditional Hindu texts.

Chandra *f.*, Chander *m.*

An Indian name from the Sanskrit meaning 'the moon'. In the Hindu religion, the moon is a god rather than a goddess, but the name Chandra is nevertheless a popular one for girls. The variant Chander is often used for boys while **Chandrakala** 'moonbeams', can be used for girls.

Chandler *m.*

The success of the television series *Friends* has led to an increased use of the name, originally a French surname meaning 'candle maker'.

Chandrakant *m.*, Chandrakanta *f.*

From the Sanskrit for 'loved by the moon', referring to a mythical jewel mentioned in classical Hindu texts, supposedly formed by the moon's rays. It is also the name of a white water-lily which blossoms at night.

Chanel *f.*

The name of this famous French perfume has been taken up as a girl's name in recent years, especially by Afro-Americans. The perfume was named after Gabrielle 'Coco' Chanel, whose family name derives from an Old French word meaning 'wine jar', indicating an ancestral connection with the wine trade. Chanel is frequently spelt phonetically, taking such forms as **Shanel, Shanell**, **Shanelle** and **Shannel**. **Chanelle** is also used.

Chantal *f.*

This is a French name which has only been in use since the beginning of the 20th century. It was the surname, meaning 'stone', of the 16th century saint, Jeanne-Françoise de Chantal. It has been popular in the USA, where it has developed forms such as **Chantalle** and **Chantel(l)e**. It is pronounced, and sometimes spelt, with a 'sh' sound at the beginning.

Charis *f.*

From the Greek meaning 'grace'. The 'Ch' is pronounced as a 'K'. It was first used as a first name in the 17th century, although in the 16th century the poet Edmund Spenser in the *Faerie Queen* used the form **Charissa**. It has been quite popular in the USA. **Chrissa** can be a short form of this or belong under the **CHRISTINE** group of names. There is some overlap between the names under **CERI**, **CARA** and Charis as they are pronounced so similarly.

Charity *f.*

From the Latin *caritas*, meaning 'Christian love'. Translated into English as charity, it was adopted when it became the custom for Puritans to name childen after the Christian virtues. The name Charity was shortened to **Cherry**, and is the source of this name. Another abbreviation is **Chattie**, used also for **CHARLOTTE**.

Charlene *f.*

A 20th-century, feminine form of **CHARLES**. It may

owe something to **Charline**, a Dutch form of
CHARLOTTE. **Charleen** and **Sharlene** are also used
(see also **ARLENE**).

Charles *m.*

Originally from an Old German word *carl*, meaning
'man', which was latinised as **Carolus** and then
changed by the French to Charles. The Normans
brought the name to England, but it did not become
popular until its use by the Stuart kings of Britain
caused it to be taken up by Royalists in the 17th
century and Jacobites in the 18th century. Its
popularity has continued ever since. The pet form
Charlie is now common as the given form of the
name. **Chas**, originally a written abbreviation, has
now come to be used as a short form. **Chuck** is also
used, and in Scotland **Chae** or **Chay**. **Carlo**, the
Spanish and Italian form, is well used in the USA.

Charlotte *f*

The French female form of **CHARLES**. It was
introduced into Britain from France in the early 17th
century. Goethe's heroine from the romantic novel,
The Sorrows of Werther, and Princess Charlotte,
daughter of George IV, increased its popularity.
Abbreviations are **Lottie**, **Lotty**, **Totty**, **Charlie** and
Chattie, and spellings such as **Sharlott** have been
recorded. It has been one of the most popular girls'
names for a number of years. **Carlotta** is the Italian
form.

Charlton *see* **Carlton**

Charmaine *f.*

A 20th century name of rather obscure origin. It may well be a form of **Charmian**, from the Greek, meaning 'joy'. This was the name of one of Cleopatra's attendants in Shakespeare's *Antony and Cleopatra*. Strictly speaking, Charmian should be pronounced with a hard 'c', but the 'sh' pronunciation is also found. Charmaine is sometimes spelt **Sharmaine**.

Charulata *f.*

A Hindu name meaning 'beautiful'.

Chas *see* **Charles**

Chase *m.*

The rise in popularity of this surname, meaning 'hunter', as a first name in the USA probably owes much to its use for a character in the 1980s television series *Falcon Crest*.

Chasity *f.*

In 1969 the singer Cher and her husband Sonny Bono named their daughter **Chastity**. This name seems to have been misinterpreted, and Chasity developed as a first name in the USA.

Chattie *see* **Charity, Charlotte**

Chay *see* **Charles**

Chelsea *f.*

This name of a fashionable part of London, which originally indicated a 'landing place (on the River Thames) for chalk or limestone', is also a place name in Australia, where its use as a girl's name seems to have begun. The name was introduced to America by a character in the film *On Golden Pond*, and its popularity was secured by the wide-spread publicity it received through Chelsea Clinton, daughter of US President Bill Clinton, who was named after a Joni Mitchell song. It is now well used in Britain. Spelling variants such as **Chelsie**, **Chelsey** and **Chelsi** are also found.

Cheralyn, Cherilyn *see* Cheryl

Cherie *f.*

The French word for 'darling'. The forms **Cheri, Sherry, Sheree** and **Sherrie** are phonetic spellings. **Cher** can be the French for 'dear' or a short form of **CHERYL**. **Cherise** can be regarded either as a development of Cherie, or as a form of **Charisse**, the French form of **CHARIS**.

Cherry *see* Charity

Cheryl *f.*

This is probably a development of the name **Cherry** (see **CHARITY**). Other forms of the name are **Cheralyn, Cherilyn, Sheril** and **Sheryl**, and **Cher** can be a short form (see also **CHERIE**). These names came into general use only in the 1940s, but rapidly became popular.

Chester *m.*

A surname taken from the English city, used as a first name. The word comes from the Latin for 'fort'.

Chetan *m.*

A Hindu name meaning 'consciousness' or 'awareness'.

Chevonne *see* **Sheena**

Cheyenne *f.*

The name of a famous American Indian nation, of unknown meaning. Cheyenne was first launched as a boy's name in a TV series of that name in the USA in the late-1950s. Pronunciation of the name as **Shyann**, in which form it is also found, possibly linked it in parents' minds with the name **ANNE**, suggesting its use for girls. In the USA it continues to grow in popularity.

Cheyna *see* **Shaina**

China *see* **Chyna**

Chintana *f.*

An Indian name meaning 'meditation'. The form **Chintanika** is also used.

Chip *see* **Christopher**

Chloe *f.*

Chloë come from the Greek, meaning 'a green shoot', a name given to the goddess Demeter who protected the green fields. It was a popular name in classical literature which was picked up by the Elizabethan poets. It is very popular at the moment. **Chloris**, 'greenish', is another name from Greek myth, and was again associated with fertility. It is sometimes spelt **Cloris**, to reflect the pronunciation of these names with a hard 'c'.

Chris *see* **Christabel, Christine, Christopher**

Chrissa *see* **Charis, Christine**

Chrissie, Chrissy *see* **Christabel, Christine**

Christabel *f.*

This name was first used in Britain in the 16th century, and is thought to be a combination of 'Christ' and the Latin *bella* to mean 'beautiful Christian'. It is not a common name in Britain, although it is sometimes used in memory of the suffragette, Dame Christabel Pankhurst (1880-1958). It is also spelt **Christobel** and abbreviated forms are **Chris, Chrissy, Chrissie** or **Christie**.

Christel, Christen *see* **Christine**

Christian *f. and m.*

This name, with its transparent meaning, has been

used in Britain since the 13th century. It became more popular after its use by Bunyan for the hero of *Pilgrim's Progress*, but has never been as common as the feminine form, CHRISTINE, although it is currently enjoying some popularity.

Christie *see* Christabel, Christopher

Christine *f.*

The commonest of the many girls' names meaning 'a Christian'. **Christen** is probably the oldest form, followed by **Christiana**. Others are **Christina**, **Christian(n)e**, a feminine form of CHRISTIAN, the Welsh form **Crystin**, and spellings such as **Krystyna**, **Kristina**, **Krista** and **Kristin**. The German form, **Christel,** may have helped the development of the name CRYSTAL. Short forms are **Chrissie**, **Chrissy** and **Chris** and further variants will be found under the Scottish pet form, KIRSTY. **Chrissa**, **Chryssa** or **Kryssa** can be thought of either as a part of this group or as a short form of **Charissa** (see CHARIS).

Christmas *see* Noel

Christopher *m.*

From the Greek meaning 'bearing Christ'. As a first name it is used in honour of the saint who was believed to have carried the infant Christ to safety across a river. Thus St Christopher became the patron saint of travellers. The popularity of the name in Britain has fluctuated since the 13th century when it was first used, but it is presently a popular choice. The Scottish equivalent of the name was **Chrystal** or **CRYSTAL**. Abbreviated forms are **Kester**, **Kit**, **Chip** and **Chris**. **Christie** or **Christy** is a pet form particularly used in Ireland.

Chryssa *see* Christine

Chrystal *see* Christopher, Crystal

Chuck *see* Charles

Chyna *f.*

Based on the place name **China**, the name is particularly associated with the singer **Chynna** Philips, while the form Chyna is associated in the USA with a woman wrestler.

Cian *see* Keenan

Ciara, Ciaran *see* Kieran

Cicely *see* Cecilia

Ciera, Cieran *see* Kieran, Sierra

Cilla *see* Priscilla

Cimmie *see* Cynthia

Cindy *f.*

A short form of names such as **LUCINDA** and **CYNTHIA**, now used as an independent name. It is also spelt **Cindi** and **Cindie**.

Ciss, Cissy *see* **Cecilia**

Clare, Claire *f.*

From the Latin meaning 'clear, famous'. The religious order of the Sisters of St **Clara** or 'Poor Clares', founded in the 13th century, was probably responsible for the rapid spread of the name throughout Europe. The name has been popular for some time. Among the many derivatives are **Claribel** and **Clarinda,** which can be shortened to **Clarrie**.

Clarence *m.*

In the 14th century **LIONEL**, son of King Edward III of England, married the heiress of the town of Clare in Suffolk. He was later created Duke of Clarence, the name Clarence meaning 'of Clare'. This title seems to have been first used as a name in the early 19th century in Maria Edgeworth's novel *Helen*.

Clarissa *f.*

From the Latin meaning 'brightest, most famous'. It was made popular in the 18th century by Samuel Richardson's novel *Clarissa Harlowe*. **Clarice** is an older form of the name. They share the abbreviation **Clarrie** with **Clara**.

Clark *m.*

The surname meaning 'a clerk', used as a first name. Famous users were the actor Clark Gable and in fiction Clark Kent, the everyday name for *Superman*. **Clarke** is also found.

Claud *m.*, Claudia *f.*

From the Roman name, Claudius, itself derived from
the Latin meaning 'lame'. In homage to the Emperor
Claudius, who was ruler when Britain was conquered
by the Romans, the name was used in this country in
the 1st and 2nd centuries. Its use soon lapsed in
Britain though not in France where it is spelt **Claude**
and used for either sex. It was from the French that
it was revived in Britain in the 16th century by the
Scottish family of Hamilton. A derivative is
Claudian, and the pet form **Claudie** can be found.
The female form, **Claudia**, is at the moment the
more popular. Two French diminutives are also
used: **Claudette** and **Claudine**, a name made famous
by the novels of Colette.

Claus *see* Nicholas

Clayton *m.*

Clayton, from a place name, later a surname,
meaning 'settlement on clay', is enjoying some
popularity in the USA as a boy's name, as is the
shorter **Clay**. Both are also found spelt with a 'K'.

Clem, Clemmie *see* Clement, Clementina

Clement *m.*, Clementina, Clementine *f.*

From the Latin, meaning 'mild, merciful'. Clement
was the name of an early saint and of several popes.
Its abbreviated forms are **Clem** and **Clemmie**, which
are shared with the feminine forms Clementina and

Clementine. Clementine was originally a German form, fashionable during the 19th century, and is now showing signs of returning to popularity. **Clemency** is also used for girls.

Cleo *f.*

A shortened form of **Cleopatra,** from the Greek meaning 'glory of her father'. The famous Egyptian queen of this name died in 30 BC and it did not take long for her name to become a byword for sexual allure and tragic love. The form **Clio** is, strictly speaking, the name of the Greek Muse of history.

Clifford *m.*

There are several places named Clifford ('ford by the cliff') in Britain, any of which could become a surname. Towards the end of the 19th century the surname came into use as a first name. It is now most often used in its short form **Cliff. Clifton**, 'settlement by the cliff', is also found.

Clint *m.*

A short form of **Clinton**, an aristocratic surname meaning 'farm by the river Glyme', used as a first name. The short form has been given fame by the actor, Clint Eastwood.

Clive *m.*

A surname meaning 'dweller by the cliff' which has come to be used as a first name, probably in honour of Robert Clive (1725-1774), known as Clive of India, who was prominent in the British conquest of India.

Clodagh *f.*

The name of a river in Ireland. It was first used in the 20th century as a first name by the Marquis of Waterford for his daughter. Its use has now spread beyond Ireland.

Cloris *see* Chloe

Clover *f.*

This is the flower name used as a first name. Its spread may have been helped by its use for a character in the *Katy* books by Susan Coolidge. Names such as **Clova** can be interpreted either as a re-spelling of Clover, or as a feminine form of **Clovis** (see **LEWIS**).

Clovis *see* Lewis

Clyde *m.*

Clyde is an ancient Scottish river name meaning 'the washer', possibly from the name of a local goddess and used since before the Roman occupation. It became a surname, then a first name.

Cody *f. and m.*

This is said to be an Irish surname meaning 'descendant of a helpful person'. It has been popular in the United States, where it is also a place name and well known as the surname of the Wild West hero, Buffalo Bill Cody. **Codey** and spellings with 'K' have also been recorded. **Codi(e)** is the spelling most often used for girls.

Coinneach *see* **Kenneth**

Colby *m.*

An English place name and surname, now used as a first name in the USA where it grew steadily in popularity in the early 1990s. The name originally indicated a farmstead owned by a Norseman called Koli. **Colton**, however, comes from a place name meaning 'farm by the River Cole'.

Colette *f.*

From a French diminutive of NICOLA. It was the name of the 15th-century reformer of the 'Poor Clares' religious order. The name is best known in this country as the pen-name of a 20th-century French writer. It is also spelt **Collette**. The masculine name **Cole** comes from NICHOLAS.

Colin *m.*

This has a similar origin to COLETTE, for it was a French pet form of NICHOLAS. In Scotland, it was also interpreted as coming from the Gaelic word *cailean*, meaning 'puppy' or 'youth'. There are rare feminine forms **Colina** and **Colinette**.

Colleen *f.*

The Irish word for 'girl' used as a first name. The name

is not widely used in Britain, but is fairly common in North America and Australia.

Collette *see* **Colette**

Colm, Colum, Columba *see* **Callum**

Colton *see* **Colby**

Con, Conchobar, Conchobhar *see* **Conor**

Conan *m.*

From the Irish meaning 'hound, wolf'. A famous holder of the name was Arthur Conan Doyle, creator of Sherlock Holmes, but the name is probably best known today from the fictional stories and films of *Conan the Barbarian*. Although the fictional character's name is pronounced in the American films with the same sound as in 'cone', in Ireland the name has a short 'o'. It shares its short forms with CONOR.

Conn, Connor, Conny *see* **Conor**

Connie *see* **Constance**

Conor *m.*

From the ancient Irish name **Conchobar** or **Conchobhar** meaning 'lover of hounds'. It was the name of one of the great kings in Irish heroic stories, and has long been a popular name in Ireland. Its popularity has spread to the UK, where it is usually spelt **Connor**. It can be shortened to **Con** or

Conny and sometimes **Conn**, which is also a separate name, perhaps meaning 'wisdom'.

Conn, Connor, Conny *see* Conor

Conrad *m.*

From the Old German words for 'bold counsel'. The name is found mostly in Germany where in the 13th century Duke Conrad was a greatly beloved figure. Objection to his public execution by the conquering Charles of Anjou led to a widespread use of this name in German-speaking states. Examples of it have been found in Britain since the 15th century. **Curt** or **Kurt** is a short form used as an independent name, now used rather more frequently than the full form.

Constance *f.*

Constance and its Latin form, **Constantia**, mean 'constancy'. It became popular in many parts of Christendom after Constantine the Great ordered the toleration of Christianity in the Roman Empire, AD 313. It was introduced into England at the time of the Norman Conquest. The form **Constancy** was used by the Puritans in the 17th century while **Constantia** became popular in the 18th century. **Constantina** is another form of the name. Constance has been out of fashion since the early 20th century, but there has recently been an increase in its use. Its abbreviation is **Connie**. **Constantine**, the masculine form, comes from the Latin for 'firm, constant'.

Three Scottish kings were named Constantine after a Cornish saint who was believed to have converted their ancestors to Christianity in the 6th century. It became popular in England from the 12th to the 17th centuries, and was the origin of the surnames Constantine, Considine, Costain and Costin. It is not widely used in Britain today. The composer **Constant** Lambert (1905–51) shows an English form of the name.

Cora *see* **Corinna**

Coral *f.*

This name reflects the beauty and value of the substance, and was popular earlier this century. A French form which is also in use in Britain is **Coralie.**

Corbin *m.*

Corbin comes from a surname based on the Old French word for 'raven'. Its spread owes much to the success of the actor Corbin Bernsen.

Cordelia *f.*

This name first appeared as **Cordeilla** in the 16th-century chronicles of Holinshed, from which Shakespeare altered the name to Cordelia for his play *King Lear*. The name is probably a form of **Cordula**, the name of one of the virgins martyred with St Ursula. It probably comes from the Latin word for 'heart'.

Corey *f. and m.*

This is an Irish surname of unknown meaning which has come to be used as a first name. It has been popular in the USA for some years. It is also spelt **Cory**, and in forms such as **Cori** or **Corrie** has been used for girls, especially in combination with other names. Spellings beginning with 'K' particularly **Kori** for girls, are also found.

Corinna *f.*

This name and **Cora** both come from the Greek word *kore* meaning 'girl' or 'maiden', a name given to the goddess **Persephone** who was associated with the coming of spring. The appearance of the name in Ovid's love poetry probably inspired its use among some 17th-century poets, particularly Herrick. The French form **Corinne** is also used. **Corin,** much used in poetry as the name for a love-sick shepherd, is the male form of the name, although it is occasionally also used for girls.

Cormac *m.*

This Irish name is of doubtful meaning, although it is sometimes said to mean 'a charioteer'. It appears frequently in Irish legend, but through its prevalence in early Irish history and the Irish Church the name was accepted as having a Christian character in Ireland and so remained in steady use. A variant is **Cormick**.

Cornelius *m.*, Cornelia *f.*

From the Latin *cornu* meaning 'a horn', these were the male and female forms of the name of a famous Roman clan. The male form was used in Ireland as a substitute for the native **Conchobar** (see **CONOR**). Its abbreviated forms are **Corney**, **Corny** and **Cornie**.

Corrie, Cory *see* Corey

Cosmo *m.*

From the Greek *kosmos*, meaning 'order'. It is the name of one of the two patron saints of Milan and was used by the famous Italian family of Medici in the form **Cosimo** from the 14th century onwards. It was the name of the 3rd Duke of Gordon who was a friend of Cosimo III, Grand Duke of Tuscany, and the name was introduced into several other Scottish families. **Cosima** is the feminine form.

Courtney *f. and m.*

An aristocratic surname used as a first name. It comes from **Courtnay**, a French place name, although the name is often interpreted as coming from *court nez*, the French for 'short nose'. It is currently more used for girls than for boys.

Craig *m.*

The place and surname meaning 'crag', used as a first name.

Cressida _f._

Cressida comes from a misreading of the name
Briseida, 'daughter of Brisis', who appears in
Homer's account of the Trojan War. In the 14th
century, the Italian writer Boccaccio used the name,
and it was adapted by Chaucer in his verse-novel
Troilus and Criseyde, the story of Troilus's undying
love for the fair Cressida, set against the background
of the Trojan War. Shakespeare changed the name
to Cressida for his version of the story. Despite the
fictional character's faithlessness in love, the name
has recently become quite popular. An abbreviated
form is **Cressy**.

Crispin, Crispian _m._

From the Latin _crispus_, meaning 'curled'. The 3rd-
century martyrs Crispinus and Crispinianus were the
patron saints of shoemakers. Crispin was popular in
Britain in the Middle Ages and has recently enjoyed
a revival.

Crystal _f._

While this looks like, and is no doubt mainly used
as, another jewel name (see also **AMBER**, **JADE**),
the spread of this name may have been helped by
Christel, the German form of **CHRISTINE**. Crystal is
also spelt **Chrystal** and the form **Krystal** has become
known through the TV series _Dynasty_. As a man's
name it is a pet form of **CHRISTOPHER**.

Crystin *see* **Christine**

Cudbert, Cuddy *see* **Cuthbert**

Curt *see* **Conrad**

Curtis *m.*

A surname from the French meaning 'courteous', used as a first name. It has been used more frequently in the United States than in Britain.

Cuthbert *m.*

From the Old English words *cuth* and *beorht*, meaning 'famous' and 'bright'. It was in common use both before and after the Norman Conquest, and was the name of a 7th-century saint who was Bishop of Lindisfarne in Northumbria. It sometimes appeared as **Cudbert**, and had the pet form **Cuddy**. The name fell out of use just after the Reformation until the 19th century, when it was brought back by the Oxford Movement. It was a slang term for someone who avoided military service during the First World War, and it may be partly due to this usage that the name is not popular today. The school 'swot' in the *Beano*'s Bash Street Kids is called Cuthbert Cringeworthy.

Cy *see* **Cyril, Cyrus**

Cybill *see* **Sybil**

Cynan *m.*

This is a Welsh name based on the word *cyn*, meaning 'chief' or 'outstanding'. It can also be found spelt **Cynin** or **Cynon**. There are a number of other Welsh names formed from this word, including **Cynyr**, which means 'chief hero'.

Cynthia *f.*

One of the titles of the Greek goddess Artemis (see **DIANA**), Cynthia means 'of Mount Cynthus', reputedly one of her favourite places. It first became known as a name through its use by the Latin poet Propertius, and it was later popular among Elizabethan poets. Mrs Gaskell's character in her novel *Wives and Daughters* brought it back into favour during the late 19th century. Pet forms include **CINDY**, **Cindi** or **Cindie** and the rarer **Cimmie**.

Cyprian *m.*

From the Latin *Cyprianus*, meaning 'from Cyprus'. It was the name of a Christian martyr of the 3rd century.

Cyra *see* **Cyrus**

Cyril *m.*

From the Greek *kyrios*, meaning 'lord'. There were two saints of this name in the 4th and 5th centuries, and it was a 9th-century Saint Cyril who took Christianity to the Slavs, and devised the Russian

Cyrillic alphabet. The name was first used in England in the 17th century, but did not become common until the 19th century. The name shares the abbreviation **Cy** with **CYRUS**, and has been recorded spelt **Syril**. There is a rare feminine form **Cyrilla**.

Cyrus *m.*

A Greek form of the Persian word meaning 'sun' or 'throne'. This is the name of the founder of the Persian Empire in the 6th century BC, as well as a number of other Persian kings. It was first used in Britain in the 17th century among Puritans, probably in honour of the fact that the Emperor Cyrus allowed the Jews to return to Palestine from their Babylonian captivity. They took it to North America, where the short forms are **Cy** and **Cyro**. There is a feminine form, **Cyra**.

Dafydd, Dai *see* David

Daisy *f.*

This probably started out as a 19th-century pet name for **MARGARET**, a pun on *marguerite*, the French word for daisy. However, there is no reason why it should not have come into use as a simple flower name, and few people today would use it otherwise.

Daithi *see* David

Dakota *f. and m.*

The name of this American Indian nation is now being regularly used in the USA. Its use can be compared to that of **CHEYENNE**.

Dale *f. and m.*

The Old English for 'valley'. At first more common as a girl's name, it is now more frequently used for boys. There are a number of other surnames from place names starting with the same sound, such as **Dalton, Dallas** and **Dallin**, that may owe their use as boys' names to the popularity of Dale.

Damaris *f.*

The Greek name in the New Testament of an Athenian woman converted by St Paul. This led to its adoption by Puritans in the 17th century. It is probably a form of a Greek name meaning 'heifer'.

Damhnait *see* Devnet

Damian, Damien *m.*

From the Greek, meaning 'tamer'. There have been four saints called by this name. It was little used in the UK before the 20th century, but became popular in the 1970s.

Damon *m.*

From the Greek, meaning 'to rule' or 'guide'. In Greek legend, Damon and Pythias were inseparable friends, famous for their willingness to die for each other.

Dan *see* Daniel

Dana *f. and m.*

As a boy's name this comes from the surname, the Old English word for a Dane, and is sometimes found in the form **Dane**. The female name is either a Scandinavian girl's form of **DANIEL**, or, in Ireland, can be taken from the pagan fertility goddess, Dana or Ana.

Dandy *see* Andrew

Daniel *m.*, Danielle *f.*

Daniel, meaning 'God has judged', is the Hebrew name of an Old Testament prophet. It was found in England before the Norman Conquest, but only among priests and monks. It became more widespread in the 13th and 14th centuries. In Ireland and Wales it is often found as a version of the Irish **Domhnall** (see **DONALD**) and Welsh **Deiniol**, meaning 'attractive, charming'. Its shortened forms are **Dan** and **Danny**. For girls, **Danielle** is the most common form, but **Daniel(l)a** and **Danette** are also used.

Dante *see* Donte

Daphne *f.*

From the Greek for 'bay tree, laurel'. In classical mythology, it was the name of a nymph who the god Apollo loved. She called on the gods for help to escape his attentions, and was changed by them into a laurel. The name was a traditional name for dogs until the end of the 19th century, when it became quite common as a girl's name.

Dara *f. and m.*

This is an Irish name, a shortened form of Mac Dara 'son of the oak', the name of a popular Connemara saint. It is also spelt **Darragh**. Although traditionally a masculine name, it is now also used for girls.

Darcy *f. and m.*

Darcy can be either from a French surname meaning someone from a place called Arcy, hence the form **d'Arcy**, or an Irish surname meaning 'descendant of the dark one'. For girls it often takes the form **Darcey** or **Darci(e)**.

Daria *f.,* Darius *m.*

Darius was the name of the 6th-century BC king of the Persians who was defeated by the Athenians at Marathon. The name means 'protector'. Daria is the feminine form.

Darian, Darien *see* Dorian

Darlene *f.*

This appears to be a relatively modern invention, made up of the first syllable of one of the names beginning 'Dar-', or perhaps from 'darling', with the -ene ending that is popular with newly created names such as **CHARLENE** and **Kaelene**.

Darrel(l) *f. and m.*

Also spelt **Dar(r)yl**, this is another surname used as a first name. In this case the surname comes from a French village, the village name meaning 'courtyard, open space'. Originally mainly a boy's name, its spread as a girl's name may owe something to Enid Blyton's use of her second husband's surname, Darrell, for the heroine of her *Malory Towers* school stories.

Darren *m.*

A surname of unknown meaning used as a first name. It seems to have been introduced in the 1950s and become popular in the 1960s. **Darran** is also found.

Darshan *m.*

An Indian name from the Sanskrit meaning 'to see'. Darshan refers to being in the presence of, or being near enough to touch and see with one's own eyes, a holy or revered person. It is thought to bestow spiritual enrichment on the observer.

Dashia, Dasia *see* Deja

David *m.*

The Hebrew name of the second king of Israel in the Old Testament, meaning 'beloved'. This name absorbed the Celtic **Daithi**, meaning 'nimbleness' (the 'th' is pronounced 'h'), and became very popular in Wales and Scotland. The patron saint of Wales is a 6th-century David. There were Scottish kings of this name in the 10th and 14th centuries. The name did not appear in England before the Norman Conquest, but it was a common medieval surname in the variant forms Davy, Davit and Deakin. Short forms are **Dave**, **Davy**, **Davie**, and in Wales **Dafydd** becomes **Dai** or **Taffy**, the latter being an English nickname for a Welshman.

Davida, Davina *f.*

These Scottish female forms of **DAVID** are found from the 17th century, but were not much used until the 20th century, when they started to become more popular. They are sometimes shortened to **Vida** and **Vina**, and **Davita** and **Davinia** are also found.

Davie, Davy *see* David

Dawn *f.*

This name came into use in the late 19th century. **Aurora**, the name of the Greek goddess of dawn, had been in vogue slightly earlier and the English translation was probably a literary invention.

Dean *m.*

A surname, meaning 'valley', adopted as a first name. It seems to have become popular in the United States first, but has been widely used in the UK since the 1960s. **Deana** or **Dena** is a feminine.

DeAndre *m.*

One of the names that was highly fashionable among Afro-American families throughout the 1980s. The prefix 'De-' was regularly attached to other names, leading to new forms such as **DeAngelo**, **DeJuan**, **DeMarco** or **DeMarcus**, **DeMario**, **DeShawn** and **DeWayne**. For the meanings of these names, look under the entries for the names which follow the 'De-' prefix.

Deanna, Deanne *see* **Diana**

Dearbhail *see* **Dervla**

Deb *see* **Dev**

Debdan *see* **Devdan**

Deborah *f.*

A Hebrew name meaning 'bee', and the name of a prophetess and poet in the Old Testament. It was first used by Puritans in the 17th century. **Debbie** or **Debby** is a common abbreviation which is sometimes used independently. **Debra** is a modern spelling of the name.

Declan *m.*

The name of an early Irish saint associated with Ardmore. It has recently been popular with Irish parents.

Dee *f. and m.*

This is usually a nickname, given to anyone with a name beginning with the letter 'D', but is occasionally found as a given name. Compounds such as **Deedee** also occur.

Deepak *m.,* **Deepika** *f.*

An Indian name from the Sanskrit meaning 'little lamp'. It is one of the descriptive names applied to Kama, god of love. The spelling **Dipak** is also used for boys.

Deiniol *see* **Daniel**

Deirbhaile *see* **Dervla**

Deirdre *f.*

The Irish name of a character in Irish and Scottish legend, possibly meaning 'raging' or 'sorrowful'. The name became popular after the late 19th-century Celtic revival, and is now enjoying another major revival in Ireland. It often takes the form **Deidra** in the USA.

Deja *f.*

This new name is something of a mystery. It has been linked to the French word *déjà*, 'already', as in *déjà vu*, but this seems unlikely. A more likely source is the character of Dejah Thoris, the beautiful princess in Edgar Rice Burroughs' *Barsoom* novels. Spellings include **Dejah**, **Dasha** and **Dasia**.

DeJuan *see* **DeAndre**

Del, Dell *see* **Delbert, Derek**

Delbert *m.*

This name has been in use since at least the beginning of the 20th century. It is probably formed on the pattern of several surnames such as **Delroy** ('of the king') and **Delmar**, ('of the sea') which are also used as first names, keeping the 'Del-' part and adding '-bert' from the many Germanic names which end in this suffix. The short forms **Del** or **Dell** are also used as first names, and can be pet forms of **DEREK**.

Delia *f.*

This name is derived from Delos, the legendary birthplace of the Greek moon goddess Artemis (see **DIANA**) and a name sometimes given to her. It was popular with pastoral poets in the 17th and 18th centuries.

Delilah *f.*

This is the name borne by the well-known biblical character who betrayed Samson to the Philistines. It derives from a Hebrew name meaning 'coquette' or 'flirt'. It was also the title of a song popularised by Tom Jones, but this failed to persuade many parents to make use of it.

Della *f.*

Originally a short form of **ADELA**, this is now well established as a name in its own right.

Delmar, Delroy *see* **Delbert**

DeMarco, DeMarcus, DeMario *see* **DeAndre**

Demelza *f.*

A place name, meaning 'the hill-fort of Maeldaf', used as a first name in Cornwall. It became more widely known through its use in the *Poldark* books and TV series.

Demetrius *m.*

This is an ancient Greek name which means 'follower' or 'devotee of **Demeter**', the Greek pagan goddess of corn and agriculture whose name in turn means 'earth mother'. It was the name of a highly successful general who died in 286 BC. In the form **Demetrios**, it is the name of a Greek saint and as **Demitrus** it is found in the Bible. **Dimitri** or **Dmitri** is the form the name takes in Russia, where it has been long established. **Demetra**, which can be shortened to **Demi**, as in the actress Demi Moore, is the commonest form for girls. Demetrius was a name little used by English speakers until fairly recently, when it became popular in the United States among Afro-American families because it began with the fashionable 'De-' prefix (see **DeAndre**).

Den *see* **Denis**

Dena *see* **Dean**

Denholm *m.*

A place name, meaning 'island valley', used as a first name. The similar **Denham**, 'home in a valley', is also used.

Denis *m.*, Denise *f.*

A development of the name of Dionysos, the Greek god of wine and revelry. Denis or **Dennis** is the

French form and the name of the patron saint of
France. It occurs in England from the 12th century
on. In Ireland it has long been used as a substitute
for the Irish **Donnchadh** (see DUNCAN). **Den** and
Denny are short forms. Denise, the female form, is
also from French. **Dion** or **Deon**, (*m.*) and **Dionne**
(*f.*) can either come from Dionysos or be a separate
name from the same root, connected with the word
for 'a god', while **Dione** can be thought of either as
a variant of Dionne, or as the name of another
character from Greek mythology whose name
means 'divine queen'. These are growing in
popularity (see also DWIGHT).

Denzil *m.*

In the form **Denzell**, this is an old Cornish surname
derived from a place-name.

Deo *see* Dev

Deodan *see* Devdan

Deon *see* Denis

Derek, Derrick *m.*

This is from the Old German **Theodoric**, meaning
'people's ruler'. It occurs in the 15th century but
only became popular in the 20th century. Its fall
from favour between these two periods is attributed
to a notorious 17th-century hangman of that name.
Variants recently revived are **Deryk**, **Deric** and the

Dutch form **Dirk**, popularised by the actor Dirk
Bogarde. Pet forms are **Derry**, **Rick**, **Rickie** and
Del or **Dell**.

Dermot *m.*

This is the anglicised spelling of **Diarm(a)it** or
Diarm(a)id, the Irish name possibly meaning 'free
from envy', or 'free man'. The legendary character
who bore this name eloped with **GRAINNE** who was
betrothed to **FINN**. Finn pursued the lovers for a
long time and finally brought about Dermot's death.

Derrick, Derry *see Derek*

Dervla *f.*

This is the phonetic form of **Deirbhaile**, an old Irish
name which means 'daughter of the poet'. It is best
known through the travel writer, Dervla Murphy. It
also occurs as **Dervila**, reflecting the Irish
pronunciation. The similar-looking **Dearbhail**,
which can be anglicised **Derval** or **Dervilla**,
meaning 'daughter of Fal' (a figure in Irish legend),
is also popular at the moment in Ireland.

Deryk *see Derek*

Des, Desi *see Desmond*

DeShawn *see DeAndre*

Désirée *f.*

A French name meaning 'desired'. It has been in

use since the beginning of the Christian era in the Latin form **Desideria**, originally for a long-awaited, much-desired child. The French boy's name **Didier**, 'longing', shortened to **Didi**, would be the male equivalent.

Desmond *m.*

From the Irish *Deas-Mumhain*, meaning '(man) of Desmond', an old name for Munster. It was originally used as a surname in Ireland. Later it became a first name, and came to England in the late 19th century. **Des** and **Desi**, **Desy** or **Dezi** are short forms.

Destiny *f.*

This vocabulary word has recently become popular as a girl's name in the USA.

Detta *see* Bernadette

Dev *m.*

An Indian name from the Sanskrit meaning 'god'. Deva is also the term used to address royalty, Brahmins and priests. Dev becomes **Deb** or **Deo** in different parts of India. **Devdan** means 'gift of the gods'. The forms **Debdan** and **Deodan** are also used.

Devnet *f.*

This is the anglicised spelling of the Irish name **Damhnait**, the name of an early Irish martyr meaning 'fawn, little deer'. An older form is **Dymp(h)na**.

Devon *f. and m.*

This name appears to be the name of the English county, but American parents usually stress it on the second syllable. Its use was probably suggested when 'De-' became a fashionable prefix for names among Afro-American families, as in **DeAndre**. The alternative spelling **Devin** is frequent and forms such as **DaVon** are also found.

DeWayne *see* DeAndre, Duane

Dexter *m.*

This is a surname, originally given to a dyer, now used as a first name.

Dezi *see* Desmond

Dhanishta *f.*

An Indian name that derives from the Sanskrit for 'star'.

Di *see* Diana

Diamond *see* Ruby

Diana *f.*

The Latin name of the Roman goddess, equivalent to the Greek, **Artemis**. She was associated with the moon and virginity. She was also the goddess of hunting and protector of wild animals. Its use as a first name dates from the Renaissance, when the

French form **Diane** is also first found. **Di** is the
commonest short form, as seen in the popular
nickname for the late Princess of Wales. Despite her
immense popularity the name is not widely used,
although it was given to rather more babies than
usual in the months following her death in 1997.
The actress **Deanna** Durbin introduced a different
form of the name, and the form **Deanne** is also
found, while Diane has developed forms such as
Dianne and **Dyan(ne)**. DINAH is a separate name.

Diarm(a)id, Diarm(a)it *see* Dermot

Dick, Dickie, Dickon *see* Richard

Didi, Didier *see* Desirée

Diego *m.*

This popular Spanish name is well used in the USA.
It is a form of **JAMES**, through the intermediary
forms Tiego and Tiago, from Sant Iago, 'Saint James'.

Digby *m.*

A place and surname, meaning 'the settlement by
the dike', used as a first name.

Dilip *m.*

The name of several kings in the Hindu epics.
It probably comes from the Sanskrit words meaning
'protecting Delhi'. An alternative form of the name
is **Duleep**.

Dilys *f.*

From the Welsh, meaning 'perfect, genuine'.
The name became current in Wales in the 19th
century, and is now no longer confined to Wales.
Dilly is a short form.

Dimitri *see* Demetrius

Dinah *f.*

From the Hebrew, meaning 'lawsuit' or 'judged'.
It was the name of one of Jacob's daughters in the
Old Testament. It came into use in the 17th century
and was a favourite name in the 19th century, when
it was often confused with **DIANA**. Nowadays it is
often spelt **Dina**.

Dinsdale *m.*

A place and surname used as a first name. It means
'settlement surrounded by a moat'.

Dion, Dione, Dionne, Dionysos *see* Denis

Dipak *see* Deepak

Dirk *see* Derek

Divya *f.*

An Indian name from the Sanskrit for 'divine lustre'.

Djamila *see* Jamila

Dmitri *see* **Demetrius**

Dodie, Dodo, Doll, Dolly *see* **Dorothy**

Doireann *see* **Doreen**

Dolores *f.*

This name was originally a short form of the
Spanish *Maria de los Dolores*, or 'Mary of the
Sorrows', after the feast of the 'Seven Sorrows of
Our Lady'. Spain uses other names from titles of
the Virgin: **Mercedes** (Our Lady of the Mercies)
and **Montserrat**, from Our Lady of Montserrat, a
famous monastery. Dolores became popular in
North America about 1930. Pet forms are **LOLA**,
Lolita and **Lo**.

Domhnall *see* **Daniel, Donald**

Dominic *m.,* **Dominique** *f.*

From the Latin *dominicus* meaning 'of the Lord'.
It probably became more widespread on account
of St Dominic, founder of the Order of Preachers
known as the Black Friars early in the 13th century.
Until this century it was almost exclusively a Roman
Catholic name, but is now widely used. **Dominick** is
also found, and the name can be shortened to **Dom**
and **Nic**. **Dominique**, from the French, is now the
most popular form for girls, although **Dominica**,
the original Latin feminine form, is sometimes used.

Donald m.

From the Irish **Domhnall** or **Donal(l)** (the second reflecting the pronunciation, with a long 'o' as in 'doe') meaning 'world mighty'. It was the name of a number of medieval Irish kings. The name became Donald in Gaelic. Common short forms are **Don** and **Donny**. Various forms of the name were coined in the Highlands to turn Donald into a girl's name, of which **Donalda** and **Donella** have been the commonest.

Donata f.

This name is far more often used than its male equivalent, **Donatus** or **Donat**, both Latin for 'given [by God]'. The Old French equivalent was **Dieudonné(e)**, which is still very occasionally found.

Donella see Donald

Donna f.

This is the Italian word for 'lady'. It became popular as a first name in the 20th century, particularly in North America. **Madonna**, 'My Lady', used of the Virgin Mary, in use in the USA by the 1930s, comes from the same word.

Donnchadh see Denis, Duncan

Donny see Donald

Donovan *m.*

An Irish surname, meaning 'dark brown', used as a first name. It gained publicity as the name of a popular singer from the 1960s.

Donte *m.*

The Italian name **Durrante**, meaning 'steadfast', developed the shortened form **Donte**, and **Dante**, famous as the name of the medieval poet. Donte (pronounced with two syllables) has been well used in the USA in recent years.

Dora *f.*

Originally this name was a short form of **DOROTHY** and **THEODORA**, but it is now a name in its own right. It came into use at the beginning of the 19th century. A pet form is **Dorrie**, shared with other names like **DOREEN** and **DORIS**. **Dorinda** was an 18th-century elaboration of the name.

Dorcas *see* Tabitha

Doreen *f.*

From the Irish **Doireann**, a name sometimes found in English spelling as **Dorren**. Its origin is rather obscure, but in Irish mythology it is the name of at least two supernatural beings. A short form is **Dorrie**, and the name can also be spelt **Dorinne**.

Dorian *f. and m.*

The ancient Greek people known as Dorians came from Doris in the north, but later dominated southern Greece. The best-known group were the Spartans. The word was introduced as a first name in Oscar Wilde's *The Picture of Dorian Gray* (1891). Like so many boy's names, it is now used as a girl's name as well. It is now also spelt **Dorien** or **Dorrien** and for girls **Dorianne** and **Doriana**. Forms such as **Darian** and **Darien** can be seen as either a form of this name, or a blend of such names as **DARIUS** and **DARREN**.

Dorinda *see* Dora

Dorinne *see* Doreen

Doris *f.*

The name of a sea nymph in Greek mythology, possibly meaning 'bountiful', and also a term for a woman member of the **DORIAN** people of Greece. In classical literature it was used as a poetic name for a lovely woman. It came into common use at the end of the 19th century and was popular into the 1930s. A short form is **Dorrie**.

Dorothy, Dorothea *f.*

From the Greek meaning 'gift of God'. The name is found in Britain from the end of the 15th century and has been in use ever since. In the 16th century, it was abbreviated to **Doll(y)**, and was so popular that the toy became known as a doll, Doll being such a likely name for a baby. In Scottish dialect, a doll is sometimes called a **Dorrity**. Later short forms are DORA, **Dot**, **Dottie**, **Dodo**, **Dodie** and **Thea** (see also THEODORA).

Dorren *see* Doreen

Dorrie *see* Dora, Doreen, Doris

Dorrien *see* Dorian

Dorrity, Dot, Dottie *see* Dorothy

Dougal, Dugal(d) *m.*

From the Irish *dubh ghall*, meaning 'dark stranger', a name given to the Danish Vikings. It was a common first name in the Scottish Highlands, and while it still has strong Scottish associations, it now has a more general use.

Douglas *m.*

From the Gaelic *dubh glas*, meaning 'black stream'. It was first a Celtic river name, then the surname of a powerful Scottish family famous for its strength and bravery in fighting, and then, from about the late 16th century, a first name for both girls and boys. It is now restricted to boys. **Duggie** and **Doug(ie)** are pet forms.

Drew *m. and f.*

From the Old German **Drogo**, meaning 'to carry'
or 'to bear', a name which was brought to Britain
by the Normans and later became a surname.
This surname, which like any other, can also be
used as a first name, may also come from two other
sources: as a short form of **ANDREW**, probably the
commonest form of Drew as a first name, and from
an old French word for 'lover'. Parents wishing to
use this name may take their choice. It has recently
been used occasionally for girls.

Drusilla *f.*

A feminine form of the Latin Drusus, a Roman
family name, possibly meaning 'firm'. It occurs in
the New Testament and was adopted in the 17th
century by the Puritans. It is still used occasionally,
mainly in North America.

Duane, Dwayne *m.*

An Irish surname, probably meaning 'black', used
as a first name. Pop star Duane Eddy made the
name better known in the 1950s. More recently it
has developed exotic variants such as **DeWayne**
or **Du'aine**.

Dudley *m.*

Originally a surname from the place name in
Worcestershire. Robert Dudley, Earl of Leicester,

was the favourite of Queen Elizabeth for many years. Like other aristocratic names it came into general use as a first name in the 19th century. **Dud** is a short form.

Dugal(d) *see* Dougal

Duggie *see* Douglas

Duke *see* Marmaduke

Dulcie *f.*

Dulcie is a name coined in the 19th century from the Latin *dulcis*, meaning 'sweet'. There was an earlier name, Dulcibella ('fair and sweet'). Dulcie was very popular in the early years of the 20th century, but now has an old-fashioned ring to it.

Duleep *see* Dilip

Duncan *m.*

The Scots form of the Irish **Donnchadh** (pronounced *don*-ne-ha, the 'h' ideally the sound in Scottish 'loch'), meaning 'brown'. It was the name of two Scottish kings and at one time was almost entirely confined to Scotland, although this is no longer the case.

Dunstan *m.*

From the Old English words *dun*, meaning 'hill'

and *stan*, meaning 'stone'. It was the name of a famous 10th-century Archbishop of Canterbury. It appears from time to time before the Reformation, and was revived by the Oxford Movement in the 19th century.

Durga *f.*

The name of the Hindu goddess, the wife of **Shiva**, when depicted in her terrifying form. Durga is from a Sanskrit word for 'inaccessible'.

Dustin *m.*

Best known from the actor Dustin Hoffman, this name has recently been very popular in the USA. It may be from a place name meaning 'dusty', or could be a form of **Thurstan**, a Norse name meaning 'Thor's stone', i.e. an altar dedicated to the thunder god Thor.

Dwayne *see* **Duane**

Dwight *m.*

Originally an English surname, which may go back to the same source as **Denis**. The use of this name as a first name in the United States probably arose from respect for Timothy Dwight, President of Yale University (1795–1817). US President Dwight D. Eisenhower gave a wider circulation to the name.

Dyan, Dyanne *see* **Diana**

Dylan *m.*

This is the name of a legendary Welsh hero, son of
the sea god, possibly meaning 'son of the wave'.
It was rare outside Wales, but the Welsh poet,
Dylan Thomas, made it more familiar to the general
public. The singer, Bob Dylan, often referred to by
his second name, took his stage name from the poet
and has increased its use.

Dymp(h)na *see* Devnet

Eachan see **Hector**

Eadan see **Etain**

Eamon(n) see **Edmund**

Earl *m.*

From the title, in Old English meaning 'nobleman' or 'chief'. It has been used as a first name for about a century, mainly in North America. **Erle** is a variant spelling, as in the author Erle Stanley Gardiner.

Earnest see **Ernest**

Eartha *f.*

From the Old English *eorthe*, meaning 'earth'. A famous modern example is the singer and actress Eartha Kitt, but the name is rare outside the southern USA, where **Ertha** and **Erthel** are also found.

Ebenezer *m.*

From the Hebrew meaning 'stone of help'. In the Old Testament it is the name of a stone monument set up by Samuel, in memory of the triumph of the Jews over the Philistine army and in thanks for God's help. It was first used as a first name in the 17th century among the Puritans. It is now used mainly in North America, with the shortened form **Eben**.

Ebony *f.*

The name of an intensely black wood which symbolises blackness, Ebony began to be used by Afro-American parents in the 1970s. It reached a peak of popularity in the 1980s after the song *Ebony and Ivory* by Paul McCartney and Stevie Wonder, but then began to fade. Its other spellings include **Ebbony**, **Eboney**, **Eboni**, **Ebonie** and **Ebonnee**.

Ed, Eddie *see* Edgar, Edmund, Edward

Edan, Edana *see* Aidan, Edna

Edgar *m.*

From the Old English meaning 'fortunate spear'. Owing to the popularity of King Edgar, King Alfred's grandson, the name continued in use after the Norman Conquest, but it faded out at the end of the 13th century. It was then used by Shakespeare in *King Lear*, and revived with other Old English names by 18th-century writers of fiction. Its popularity in the 19th century probably stems from its use for the hero of Scott's novel *The Bride of Lammermoor*. It is shortened to **Ed** or **Eddie**.

Edina *see* **Edna**

Edith *f.*

From the Old English name Eadgyth, meaning 'fortunate war'. There were at least two English saints of that name in the 10th century. The name survived the Norman Conquest and was probably adopted by the Normans and used to replace several English names. Edith was in use throughout the Middle Ages, after which it became rather rare, but it returned to favour in the 19th and early 20th centuries. Often shortened to **Edie**, it has a rare form, **Editha**.

Edmund *m.*

From the Old English Eadmund, meaning 'happy protection'. It was the name of two kings of England and of two saints. **Edmond** is a French form which was used from the late Middle Ages. **Eamon(n)** is the Irish form. It was well used in the 19th century, then went rather out of fashion but is now steadily coming back into use. Shortened forms are **Ed**, **Eddie**, **Ted** and **Teddy**.

Edna *f.*

One source of this name may be **Edana**, a feminine form of the Irish name **Edan**, meaning 'fire' (see **AIDAN**). It has also been connected with a shortened form of **Edwina** (see **EDWIN**), via **Edina**.

In addition the name occurs twice in the Apocrypha and its Hebrew meaning is probably 'rejuvenation'. The modern use of it may stem from the popularity of the novelist Edna Lyall in the late 19th century.

Edward *m.*

From the Old English meaning 'fortunate guardian'. Edward the Confessor established its popularity in England and ensured its survival after the Norman Conquest. It was further strengthened by the accession of Edward I in 1272, after which there was an Edward on the English throne for over a hundred years. It has remained in use ever since. The short forms **Ned** and **Ted**, together with **Neddy** or **Teddy**, have been used since the 14th century, but **Ed** and **Eddie** are the more common abbreviated forms found today.

Edwin *m.*, Edwina *f.*

From the Old English meaning 'fortunate friend'. Edwin was the first Christian king of Northumbria, in the 7th century. The name survived the Norman Conquest and became popular in the 18th century. Edwina is a 19th-century female form.

Effie *see* Euphemia

Egbert *m.*

From the Old English meaning 'bright sword'. This was the name of the first king of a united

England and of a 7th-century Northumbrian saint. It enjoyed some degree of popularity in the 19th century, but is now rarely found.

Eibhlin *see* Evelyn

Eileen *f.*

An Irish development of EVELYN. Like other Irish names it spread throughout Britain at the beginning of the 20th century. **Eily** is a short form. It is not uncommon to find it spelt **Aileen**.

Eilis, Ailis *f.*

In theory Eilis, sometimes spelt **Eil(l)ish** to reflect its pronunciation, is an Irish form of ELIZABETH, and Ailis (**Ailish**) an Irish form of ALICE, but in practice many users do not distinguish between the two.

Eithne *f.*

A name prominent in Irish legend and history, being used by a goddess, a number of queens and no less than nine saints. It means 'kernel' which in old Irish poetry is a term of praise. Modern variants include **Ethne**, **Ethna** and the phonetic **Enya**.

Ekata *f.*

An Indian name from the Sanskrit meaning 'unity'.

Elaine *f.*

An Old French form of HELEN, which occurs in

medieval literature. It came into general use through the popularity of Tennyson's *Idylls of the King* (1859), which is based on Malory's *Morte d'Arthur* and which includes the story of *Lancelot and Elaine*. There is also a Welsh name **Elain**, meaning 'fawn'.

Eleanor *f.*

Eleanor and **Elinor** are French forms of HELEN which have been used in this country since the Middle Ages. **Eleanora**, the Italian form which gives us LEONORA, is also found, as is **Elena**. Eleanor is shortened to **Ellie** (currently very popular as a given name), ELLA, ELLEN, NELL and NORA.

Elfrida *see* Alfred

Eli *m.*

From the Hebrew meaning 'elevated'. It was the name of the high priest in the Old Testament who looked after the prophet Samuel when he was given to the Temple as a baby. It was used as a first name in the 17th century. Eli is also a shortened form of ELIAS, **Eliza** (see ELIZABETH) and **Elihu**, which means 'God is the Lord'.

Elias, Elijah *m.*

From the Hebrew meaning 'Jehovah is God'. Both forms were very common in the Middle Ages, along with the pet forms **Ellis** and **Eliot(t)** or **Elliot** which became surnames, and are now used as first names. **Elisha**, 'god is', is often thought of as a variant of this name.

Eliot(t) *see* Elias

Elissa *m.*

A name by which Dido, Queen of Carthage, was known, but in modern use it is probably a pet form of **ELIZABETH**. The Austrian-Italian film actress Elissa Landi (whose full name was Elizabeth Zanardi-Landi), was well known in the 1930s.

Elizabeth, Elisabeth *f.*

From the Hebrew *Elisheba*, meaning 'oath of God' or 'God has sworn'. The present form developed from the Greek **Elisabet** through the Latin **Elisabetha** to Elizabeth. In Britain the 'z' form is usual, on the Continent the 's' is used, for in the Authorised Version of the New Testament, the name is spelt **Elisabeth**. It was first used by members of the Eastern Church, then found its way across Europe to France, where it developed the form **ISABEL(LE)**. This was also the usual medieval form in England. Elizabeth became common about the end of the 15th century, and its later popularity in England stemmed from the long reign of Elizabeth I. Among the many pet forms are: **Bess(ie)**, **Betsy**, **Betty**, **Beth** (with **Bethan** in Wales, see **BETHANY**), **Buffy**, **Eliza**, **Lizzy**, **Liz**, **Liza**, **Libby** and the Scottish **Elspeth**, **Elspie** and **Elsie**, which are now used independently. The German **ELSA**, **ELISSA** (see also **ALICE**), **Lisa**, **Liese** or **Liesel**, the Italian **Bettina**, and the French **Elise**, **Lisette** and **Babette**, are also used in Britain.

Elke *f.*

A German pet form of the name **ALICE**. It is found in a slightly different form used by the singer **Elkie** Brooks.

Ella *f.*

A name used by the Normans probably derived from the Old German **Alia**, meaning 'all'. It can also be a pet form of **Isabella** (see **ISABEL**), **ELLEN** or **ELEANOR** and is currently an increasingly popular choice for parents (see also **LUELLA**). The real name of the Australian model **Elle** Macpherson, who has brought this form of the name to popular attention, is Eleanor.

Ellen *f.*

An older English form of **HELEN**, now used independently, and also a short form of **ELEANOR**. In the past it has been especially popular in Scotland and Ireland and is now showing signs of wider popularity.

Ellie *see* **Eleanor**

Elliot(t), Ellis *see* Elias

Elmer *m.*

This is a surname which comes from both the Old English Ethelmer, 'noble and famous' and Ethelward, 'noble guard'. It became a first name in the USA in honour of two brothers with the surname Elmer who were prominent in the American War of Independence. **Aylmer** is another form of the name. While **Elma** is actually a short form of **Wilhelmina**, a German feminine of **WILLIAM**, it can also be used as a female form of Elmer.

Eloise *f.*

Currently, the more popular version of the name known to history as **Heloise**. Abelard and Heloise were two famous and tragic 12th-century lovers, and Heloise was renowned for her beauty, intellect and faithfulness in love. The name can be spelt **Heloïse** or **Eloïse** and sometimes occurs as **Eloisa**. Experts do not agree on its origins: some say it is an Old German name perhaps meaning 'helmet power'; others say it comes from the same source as **LEWIS** by way of an old southern French name **Aloys** or **Aloyse** (see **ALOYSIUS**).

Elsa, Elsie *f.*

One source of Elsa is the Old German for 'noble one', but both names are also used as abbreviations of **ELIZABETH**, and Elsie is sometimes a short form of **ALISON**. Elsie was originally Scottish and is the more common form in Britain. Elsa is the heroine in Wagner's opera *Lohengrin*, which made the name popular in the 19th century.

Elspeth, Elspie *see* Elizabeth

Elton *m.*

A surname, probably meaning 'Ella's settlement', used as a first name. The singer, Elton John, effectively began its first-name use.

Eluned *see* Lynette

Elvira *f.*

A Spanish name, probably introduced by the conquering Visigoths in the Dark Ages. Its meaning is not clear. It has been used occasionally since the beginning of the 19th century. It is perhaps best known as the name of the ghost in Noël Coward's play, *Blithe Spirit* and from the 1967 film *Elvira Madigan*.

Elvis *m.*

A name that was almost unknown until given world fame by Elvis Presley. It is probably a version of the name of the Irish saint **Alby** or **Ailbhe** (a name which in Irish can be used for either sex, and which is pronounced 'alva') which is found in Wales in the

form St Elvis. Although Presley was not the first
member of his family to bear the name, modern
uses come from him.

Emanuel *m.*

From the Hebrew meaning 'God with us'. It was
the name given to the promised Messiah by the
prophet Isaiah in the Old Testament. It was
introduced as a first name by the Greeks in the
form **Manuel**. This is also the Spanish form.
Manny is used as a pet form, and there is a
feminine, **Em(m)anuelle**.

Emer *f.*

Emer (pronounced with a long 'ee' at the
beginning) is currently one of the more popular
Celtic names in Ireland. In legend it was the name
of the woman loved by Cuchulainn, the great hero
of the Ulster cycle of legends. She is described as
having the following six desirable gifts: those of
beauty, voice, sweet speech, skill with the needle,
wisdom and chastity. It is occasionally found as **Emir**.

Emerald *see* Esmeralda

Emily *f.*

From the Latin Aemilius, the name of a Roman
family. Boccaccio, the 14th-century Italian writer,
used **Emilia**, popularizing this form in the Middle
Ages, and Chaucer borrowed it in the form Emelye.

The name has been used since then. In the 19th century it was sometimes shortened to EMMA. Nowadays, these two names are among the most popular girls' names. **Milly** is a pet form. **Emmeline** is an old French pet form, and **Emil(e)** can be used for boys.

Emir *see* Emer

Emlyn *m.*

A common Welsh name, possibly derived from the Latin Aemilius, also the source of EMILY, but which is more likely to be from a Welsh place-name.

Emma *f.*

A shortened form of Old German compound names beginning *ermen* meaning 'universal', as in the name **Ermyntrude**, 'universal strength'. It was introduced to England by Emma, daughter of Richard I, Duke of Normandy. The English form was Em(m), and this was used until the mid 18th century, when the original form was revived. Jane Austen's novel *Emma* (1816) has also been influential. Today, Emma is one of the commonest girls' names. **Emmy** is a pet form, and Emma is also used as a short form of EMILY.

Emmeline *see* Emily

Emrys *see* Ambrose

Ena *f.*

This name can come from a number of sources. It can be a short form of any name ending with '-ina' or '-ena', or an English form of **EITHNE**, but its popularity in the last century came from affection for Queen Victoria's daughter, Princess Ena, who became Queen of Spain. Her name came from neither of these sources, but was due to a misreading of her intended name 'Eva' at her christening, when the priest read the handwritten 'v' as an 'n'.

Enid *f.*

This is a Welsh name, meaning 'life, soul', that came into use in England in the 19th century through Tennyson's Arthurian poem, *Geraint and Enid* in *Idylls of the King* (1859).

Enoch *m.*

From the Hebrew, meaning 'trained, skilled' or 'dedicated'. It was the name of an Old Testament patriarch and was adopted in the 17th century by the Puritans. It is now rare, although a well-known modern example is the politician, Enoch Powell (1912–98).

Enya *see* **Eithne**

Eoan, Eoghan *see* **Eugene, Evan**

Eoin *see* **Eugene, John**

Ephraim *m.*

From the Hebrew meaning 'fruitful', an Old
Testament name that was revived in the 17th century
by the Puritans. It is seldom used in England, but is
still found in North America. **Eph** is a short form.

Eppie *see* Euphemia

Eric *m.,* Erica *f.*

From Scandinavia; the second syllable means 'ruler',
the first is doubtful but may mean 'ever'. The name
was brought to Britain by the Danes about the 9th
century. Possibly Dean Farrar's book *Eric or Little
by Little* was responsible for its popularity with
19th-century parents. Erica, the feminine form, is
now sometimes identified with the Latin botanical
name for heather. Both forms are sometimes spelt
with a 'k' instead of 'c'. Short forms are **Rick**,
Rickie or **Ricky**.

Erin *f.*

From the Gaelic *Eireann*, a poetical name for
Ireland. It is a modern name, particularly popular in
the USA and Australia.

Erle *see* Earl

Ermyntrude *see* Emma

Ernest *m.*

From the Old German, meaning 'vigour' or
'earnestness'. It is sometimes spelt **Earnest**. It was

introduced by the Hanoverians in the late 18th century and was common in the 19th century. Oscar Wilde's play, *The Importance of Being Earnest* (1899) increased its popularity. Neither **Ernestine**, the female form, nor Ernest, is popular today. Shortened forms are **Ern** and **Ernie**.

Errol *m.*

Probably a surname used as a first name, although it is not certain whether the surname is a development of Eral, a medieval form of **HAROLD**, or whether it is a variant of **EARL**.

Ertha, Erthel *see* Eartha

Esmé *f. and m.*

Probably from the French for 'esteemed', this is now usually treated as a form of the French **Aimée**, meaning 'beloved' (see **AMY**). It passed from France to Scotland in the 16th century, and then much later to England. It is now more often used as a girl's name, in which case it can also take the forms **Esmée** and **Esma**.

Esmeralda *f.*

The Spanish for 'emerald'. The 19th-century French writer Victor Hugo introduced it when he used it for the heroine in his novel *The Hunchback of Notre Dame*. The English form **Emerald** is also found, as is the form **Esmeraldah**.

Esmond _m._

From the Old English _east_ and _mund_, meaning 'grace' and 'protection'. This name was never common and fell out of use in the 14th century. Its modern use probably dates from Thackeray's novel _The History of Henry Esmond_ (1852). It is nowadays rather rare.

Ess, Essie, Essy _see_ Esther

Essylt _see_ Isolda

Estella _see_ Stella

Esther _f._

In the Old Testament, this name is the Persian equivalent of a Hebrew word meaning 'myrtle'. It was frequently used in the form **Hester** and appears in England in the 17th century, adopted by the Puritans. It can also be spelt **Ester**. Shortened forms include **Essy**, **Essie** and **Ess**, with Hester becoming **Hetty**.

Etain _f._

In Irish legend, _The Wooing of Etain_ is the story of the love of the fairy Princess Etain of the Fair Hair for a mortal man. This tale was retold in an opera called _The Immortal Hour_ first performed in 1914. The opera was a great success at the time, and led to a use of the name outside Ireland. In Ireland the name is usually **Etan** or **Eadan** and pronounced 'ad-an'.

Ethan *m.*

This is a Hebrew name meaning 'firmness', which occurs several times in the Old Testament. It has recently become a popular choice for boys.

Ethel *f.*

Not originally an independent name, but developed in the 19th century as a shortening of various Anglo-Saxon names beginning with the root 'Ethel-', from *aethel*, meaning 'noble' (see **AUDREY**).

Ethelbert *see* **Albert**

Etheldreda *see* **Audrey**

Ethna, Ethne *see* **Eithne**

Etta, Ettie *see* **Henrietta**

Euan *see* **Eugene**

Eufemia *see* **Euphemia**

Eugene *m.*, Eugenie *f.*

From the Greek meaning 'well-born'. In North America the masculine form is usually abbreviated to **Gene**. The Celtic names **Eoghan** (pronounced 'eoh-un') or **Eoan** ('ohn'), and their Scots form **Ewan**, **Ewen** or **Euan** have traditionally been interpreted as forms of Eugene, although sometimes confused with **Eoin**, a form of **JOHN**. However, some would claim that they are a native Celtic name meaning 'born of the yew'. **Eugenie**, the French feminine form, came into use from the French Empress Eugénie (1826–1920) who spent the last 50 years of her life in England. **Eugenia** is also used for girls.

Eunice *f.*

From the Greek, meaning 'happy victory'.
The name is mentioned in the New Testament and was adopted by the Puritans in the 17th century. In Greek it is pronounced as three syllables, with a hard 'c' and the final 'e' sounded, but modern users soften the 'c' if they use the three-syllable pronunciation or more often use the pronunciation indicated by the phonetic spelling **Unice**.

Euphemia *f.*

From the Greek, meaning 'fair speech' or, by implication, 'silence'. It occurs as **Eufemia** and **Euphemie** from the 12th century. Later it became confined to Scotland, where it is still found, usually abbreviated to **Effie** (very popular at the beginning of the 20th century), **Eppie** or, occasionally, **Fay** or **Phoebe**.

Eustace *m.*

From the Greek meaning 'rich in corn' and hence 'fruitful' generally. Because of the two saints

Eustachius, this name was in use in Britain before the Norman Conquest and was popular from the 12th to the 16th centuries. **Eustacia**, the female form, was used in the 18th and 19th centuries but is now rare. A short form, **STACEY** (or **Stacy**), is now a name in its own right.

Eva *see* Eve

Evaline *see* Evelyn

Evan *m.*

This is a Welsh form of **JOHN**, the anglicised form of the Welsh spelt variously **Iefan**, **Ifan** or **Ieuan**. In Scotland it is also an anglicised form of the Irish **Eoghan** (see **EUGENE**).

Evangeline *f.*

From the Greek meaning 'bringer of good news', the same word that gives us 'evangelist'. It was first introduced by Longfellow for his poem *Evangeline* (1847), and still tends to have a rather literary flavour. **Evangelina** is also found.

Eve *f.*

From the Hebrew meaning 'life', and in the Old Testament this is the name of the first woman. **Eva** is the Latin form, Eve the English. It was in use in Britain in the Middle Ages, when Old Testament names were not generally popular. In Ireland it was used as a substitute for the earlier Gaelic **Aoife** (pronounced 'ee-fa'), meaning 'radiant', currently a very popular name. The pet form of Eve is **Evie** and **Evita** is a Spanish pet form (see also ZOE).

Evelyn *f. and m.*

When the Normans conquered Ireland they brought with them a girl's name **Aveline**, meaning 'wished for (child)'. It was adopted by the Irish in the form **Eibhlin** (pronounced either with the 'bh' as a 'v', or silent, giving EILEEN), which in turn was anglicised **Eveline** or **Eveleen** and later developed forms such as **Evaline**, **Evelena** and **Evelina**. It was also adopted as a surname, usually spelt Evelyn, and around the 17th century the surname started to be used for boys. The boy's form is usually spelt Evelyn; all spellings are used for girls.

Everard *m.*

From the Old German for 'brave boar'. The name was brought to Britain by the Normans and was fairly common in England in the 12th and 13th centuries and has been used occasionally ever since. In Scotland, it became **Ewart**. The surname **Everett** comes from Everard, and is also used as a first name.

Everild, Everilda *see* Averil

Evie, Evita *see* Eve

Ewan, Ewen *see* **Eugene**

Ewart *see* **Everard**

Ezekiel *m.*

From the Hebrew meaning 'may God strengthen'.
It is the name of an Old Testament prophet,
and was used from the 17th century in Britain.
It is still current in North America and is beginning
to re-appear here. **Zeke** is the usual short form.

Ezra *m.*

From the Hebrew meaning 'help', Ezra is the
name of the author of one of the books of the Old
Testament. It was adopted as a first name by the
Puritans in the 17th century. The name is no longer
common, but a well-known example from the 20th
century is the American poet, Ezra Pound.

Fabian *m.*

From the Latin family name Fabianus, possibly meaning 'bean-grower'. There was a pope of this name and a St Fabian in the 3rd century, and there is a record of the name's use by a 13th-century sub-prior of St Albans. There is little other evidence of it until the 16th century, but its use as a surname shows that it was known previously. The Roman general **Fabius**, known as the 'delayer' for his tactics of awaiting the right moment to achieve his ends, was the inspiration for the socialist Fabian Society, founded in 1884. A female form, **Fabienne**, comes from the French **Fabien**. Spanish forms are **Fabio**, and **Fabiola** for girls.

Fahimah *f.*

A Muslim name from the Arabic for 'discerning' or 'intelligent'.

Faisal *see* Faysal

Faith *f.*

One of the Christian virtues used as names after the Reformation. It was formerly used for both sexes, but is now a girl's name. **Fay(e)** or **Fae** is a short form.

Fallon *f.*

This is an English form of the Irish surname 'O Fallamhain', or 'leader'. It was made known as a first name by a character in the TV series *Dynasty* and came into limited use in the USA and Britain as a result.

Fanny *see* **Frances, Myfanwy**

Farah *f.*

From the Arabic meaning 'joy, cheerfulness'. **Farrah** is also found. American actress Farrah Fawcett claimed that her parents were unaware that Farah existed when they invented her first name. **Farhanah** is from the Arabic for 'joyful'.

Farall, Farrell *see* **Fergal**

Fatima *f.*

This is an Arabic name which means either 'chaste' or 'motherly'. It was the name of the Prophet Muhammad's favourite daughter, the only one of his children to have children of her own. It has been popular in the USA with Black Muslims. It is also occasionally used in a Christian context in honour of Our Lady of Fatima.

Faustine *f.*

Fausta and **Faustus** were names given to his twin children by the ancient Roman dictator, Sulla. The names mean 'fortunate' and Sulla had always considered himself particularly blessed with good luck, taking the nickname **FELIX**. **Faustine** is the French form of the name. Although the two girls' names are sometimes used, the legend of Dr Faustus, who sells his soul to the Devil, has made it difficult to use the boy's name.

Fawn *f.*

The word for a young deer used as a first name.

Fay *f.*

A short form of both **FAITH** and **EUPHEMIA**, and also an old form of the word 'faith'. In addition it is an old version of the French word for 'fairy' found in the name of the Arthurian enchantress Morgana le Fay. It was in use by 1872, at least in fiction. It is also spelt **Faye**.

Faysal *m.*

This Arabic name indicates one who decides between right and wrong, a decision-maker or a judge. This has been a royal name in modern times, borne by kings of Iraq and Saudi Arabia. The name is also found as **Faisal** and **Feisal**.

Feargus *see* Fergus

Fedelm, Feidhelm *see* Fidelma

Feisal *see* Faysal

Felice, Felicia *see* Felix

Felicity *f.*

From the Latin *felicitas*, meaning 'happiness'. It was the name of two saints and was used by the Puritans in the 17th century.

Felix *m.*, Felicia *f.*

From the Latin meaning 'happy, lucky'. Felix was widely used in the Middle Ages and had a fairly strong hold in Ireland, where it was used to replace the Irish **Phelim**. It is currently enjoying a revival in popularity. The female form, Felicia, has a long history of use and was also very popular in the Middle Ages. **Felice** was a variant form.

Fenella *f.*

A Gaelic name meaning 'white-shouldered'. The name became known in Britain in the 19th century as a result of Sir Walter Scott's novel *Peveril of the Peak*. The Irish form of the name is **Finola** or **Fionnuala** (pronounced 'Fin noola'), which can be shortened to **Nola** or **Nuala**, a popular choice in Ireland.

Ferdinand *m.*

From the Old German for 'brave journey'. Never a popular name in Germany, it was common in Spain, especially in the forms **Fernando** and **Hernando**. Short forms are **Ferd**, **Ferdie** and occasionally **Nandy**. At the moment the name is being used slightly more often than before.

Fergal *m.*

This is an Irish name meaning 'valorous'. The surnames **Farrell** and **Farall**, which come from it, reflect the Irish pronunciation.

Fergus *m.*

Fergus or **Feargus** come from the Irish words for 'man' and 'strength'. It is a fairly common first name in Scotland and Ireland and is also used in the North of England. **Fergie** is a short form.

Fern *f.*

The plant name used as a first name.

Ffion *f.*

Ffion is the Welsh word for the foxglove flower, and a word used in poetry to describe the cheek of a beautiful girl.

Fi *see* **Fiona**

Fidelma *f.*

The more usual form of the Irish name **Fedelm** or **Feidhelm** (in modern Irish, pronounced 'fed-elm'). Its meaning is not clear, but several of the early women who bore the name were famous for their beauty.

Fifi *see* **Josephine**

Finbar, Finnbar, Fionnbharr *see* **Barry**

Finch *see* Raven

Fingal *m.*

This is the name given to the Scottish legendary hero (the equivalent of the Irish **FINN**), who figures in the 18th-century Ossianic poetry. He was a mighty warrior, a defender of the underdog and righter of wrongs. Fingal's Cave is named after him. The name means 'blond stranger' and was a term used of the Vikings.

Finlay *m.*

This is a Scottish name meaning 'fair hero'. It is also found as **Finley** and **Findlay**.

Finn *m.*

Finn, **Fynn** or **Fionn** is an Irish name meaning 'white, fair' or can also be used as a pet form of **Finbar** (see **BARRY**). Finn Mac Coul (Finn mac Cumaill) is a great hero of Irish mythology and folklore. He was chosen to lead the Fenians (an elite armed troop) because of his truthfulness, wisdom and generosity, but he was also of great physical strength. However, all these qualities were not enough to prevent Finn's fiancée **GRAINNE** from running away with his companion, **DERMOT**. **Finnian** or **Finian** comes from the same root, and was the name of a 6th-century British saint; **Fintan** means either 'white ancient one' or 'white fire'.

Finola *see* **Fenella**

Fintan *see* **Finn**

Fiona *f.*

From Gaelic, meaning 'fair, white'. It was first used in the 19th century by William Sharp as a pen name (Fiona Macleod). He modelled it on the Irish man's name **Fionn** or **FINN**. It was long thought of as a particularly Scottish name, but is now used throughout the English-speaking world. **Fi** is the short form.

Fionn *see* **Finn**

Fionnuala *see* **Fenella**

Flann *m.*

This is an Irish name meaning 'red' that would have started life as a nickname. **Flannan** started as a pet form of this.

Flavia *f.*

A Roman family name, which probably meant something like 'golden or tawny-haired'. **Fulvia** has much the same meaning.

Fleur *f.*

The French word for 'flower'. It was first used as a name in the 20th century, in John Galsworthy's series of novels, *The Forsyte Saga*. The English equivalents **Flower** and **Blossom** are also found. (See also **FLORA**).

Flip *see* **Philip**

Flo, Floy *see* **Florence**

Flora *f.*

From the Latin meaning 'flower'. Flora was the Roman goddess of flowers and the spring. The male equivalent names **Florent** and **Florian** are now little used in Britain but are found on the Continent.

Florence *f.*

From the Latin name Florentius, derived from the word meaning 'blooming'. In the Middle Ages, Florence was used as often for men as for women. Florence Nightingale was named after the town in Italy where she was born, and her fame popularised the name in the 19th century. Abbreviated forms are **Florrie**, **Flossie**, **Floy** and **Flo**.

Florent, Florian *see* **Flora**

Flower *see* **Fleur**

Floyd *see* **Lloyd**

Forbes *m.*

Forbes is a Scottish surname now used as a first name. It comes from a place near Aberdeen, meaning 'field, district'.

Forrest *m.*

This is the word 'forest' in its surname form. It was originally used as a first name in the southern US in the late 19th century, when it was fashionable to name boys after Confederate generals – in this case, General Nathan Bedford Forrest. The name continues to be used sporadically in Britain as well as the USA. It is sometimes found as **Forest**.

Frances *f.*

This name derives from **Francesca**, the feminine form of the Italian *Francesco* (see **FRANCIS**). It was first used in Italy in the 13th century, about the same time as the French form **Françoise** began to appear. **Francine** is another French form. Frances was not used in Britain until the 15th century, and it became popular with the English aristocracy at the time of the Tudors. The short forms are **Fanny**, **Fran**, **Francie** and **Frankie**.

Francis *m.*

From the Latin meaning 'little Frenchman'. The name became popular in Europe in the 13th century because of St Francis of Assisi. The Italian word *Francesco* was the saint's nickname, his Christian name being Giovanni, the Italian form of **JOHN**. It was given to him in his worldly youth because of his love of fashionable French things. It was first used in Britain in the 15th century. **Fran** is a short form along with **Frank** and **Frankie**. Frank can be used as an independent name.

Françoise see **Frances**

Frank, Frankie see **Frances, Francis**

Franklin m.

From a medieval English word meaning 'free'.
A franklin was a man who owned land in his own
right, but was not a noble. The name came into use in
America in honour of Benjamin Franklin (1706–90),
statesman, writer and inventor. A famous holder of
the name was Franklin D. Roosevelt (1882–1945),
32nd US President.

Fraser, Frazer m.

A Scottish surname of unknown meaning, used as a
first name. **Frasier** is another form of the name.

Frea see **Freya**

Fred, Freddie, Freddy see **Alfred, Frederick**

Freda see **Frederick, Winifred**

Frederick m., Frederica f.

From the Old German, meaning 'peaceful ruler'.
It is also found with such spellings as **Frederic** and
Frederik. Common abbreviations are **Fred**, **Freddie**
and **Freddy**, also used as independent names.
The female form is **Frederica**, the origin of the
names **Freda**, **Frida** or **Frieda** (the last two
influenced by the German form, **Friede**).

Freya *f.*

The name of the ancient Norse goddess of beauty, love and fertility. It can also be found as **Frea** or spelt the Swedish way **Freja**. The name became better known through the indomitable travel writer Freya Stark (1893–1993).

Frida, Frieda *see* **Frederick**

Fulvia *see* **Flavia**

Gabriel *m.*, Gabrielle *f.*

From Hebrew, containing the elements 'God', 'man' and 'strength', and possibly implying the phrase 'strong man of God' or 'God is my strength'. In St Luke's Gospel, Gabriel is the Archangel who announces to Mary that she is to bear the baby Jesus. Use as a first name used to be restricted to Ireland, where it can be shortened to **Gay**, but it is now increasingly fashionable elsewhere. **Gabrielle**, a French form, or the Italian **Gabriella**, the female forms, are much more common. A short form is **Gaby**.

Gaenor *see* Jennifer

Gaia *f.*

In Greek myth **Gaea** or Gaia is the earth goddess, the universal mother, probably once the most important divinity. Her name is occasionally found used as a first name, usually with 'green' or feminist overtones.

Gail *f.*

Originally a pet form of **Abigail**, now widely used as a name in its own right. The spellings **Gale** and **Gayle** are also found.

Gaius *see* **Caius**

Galal, Galil, Galila *see* **Jalal**

Ganesh *m.*

A title of the Hindu god **Shiva**, and the name of his elder son, derived from the Sanskrit for 'lord of the hosts'. It is customary to appease Ganesh at the beginning of Hindu ceremonies.

Gareth *m.*

From the Welsh meaning 'gentle'. This name was used for one of King Arthur's knights by the 15th-century writer Malory in his *Morte d'Arthur*, and later by Alfred Tennyson, the 19th-century poet, in his version of Malory's story, *Gareth and Lynnette*. It was due to the latter that the name was revived in the 20th century. **Garth** and **Gary** or **Garry** can be used as short forms.

Garfield *m.*

A surname meaning 'spearfield' in Old English, used as a first name, probably after J.A. Garfield (1831–81), 20th president of the USA. The cricketer Sir Garfield (Gary) Sobers is a well-known holder of the name, and also shows its short form.

Garret, Garrett *see* **Gerard**

Garth, Garry *see* **Gareth**

Gary *m.*

While this can be used as a short form of both **GARETH** and **GARFIELD**, its use as an independent name owes much to the film star Gary Cooper (1901–61). He was born Frank James Cooper, and chose his stage name from the American town of Gary. **Garry** is also found, reflecting the usual pronunciation, although Gary Cooper pronounced his name to rhyme with 'airy'.

Gaspar, Gaspard *see* Jasper

Gaston *m.*

A French name, originally spelt Gascon and meaning a man from the region of Gascony. It is a common French first name which has been used occasionally in Britain.

Gauri *f.*

This name is from the Sanskrit for 'white', and was applied to the wife of the Hindu god **SHIVA** when she had acquired a fair complexion after meditating in the snows of the Himalayas.

Gavin *m.*

The name of Sir **Gawain**, King Arthur's famous nephew, was Gauvin in Old French, and from France was adopted in Scotland as Gavin. Originally confined to Scotland, the name is now found throughout the English-speaking world.

Gay(e) *f.*

This name is simply the adjective meaning happy and lively, and its use dates from the 20th century. Since the adoption of the word 'gay' by the homosexual community, few parents have used the name. In Ireland Gay is a short form of the boy's name **GABRIEL**.

Gayle *see* **Gail**

Gaynor *see* **Jennifer**

Geena *see* **Gina**

Geeta *see* **Gita**

Gemma *f.*

The Italian word for 'gem'. Its modern use is probably due in part to the Italian saint Gemma Galgani (1875–1903), canonised in 1940. Rare before the 1980s it then became one of the most popular names in the country. It is also spelt **Jemma**.

Gene *see* **Eugene**

Genevieve *f.*

A French name possibly meaning 'lady of the people'. It is found in Latin records as **Genovera** and **Genoveva**. St Genevieve is the patron saint of Paris; she saved the city from the Huns in the 5th century by cool thinking, courage and prayer.

The name has been used in Britain since the 19th century. French pet forms are **GINA**, **Ginette** and **Veva**.

Geoffrey, Jeffrey *m.*

From the Old German *Gaufrid* the second half of which means 'peace', but the meaning of the first half is unclear. Geoffrey or Jeffrey was popular between the 12th and 15th centuries in England resulting in many surnames e.g. Jeffries, Jeeves, Jepson. It fell from favour from the 15th until the 19th century, when it was revived. **Geoff** and **Jeff** are common abbreviations.

George *m.*

From the Greek for 'farmer'. The famous St George is said to have been a Roman soldier who was martyred in Palestine in AD 303. In early Christian art many saints were represented as trampling on dragons, as a symbol of good conquering evil. This may be an explanation of how the legend of St George and the dragon originated. In the Middle Ages, St George was closely associated with knighthood and chivalry, and after 1349, when Edward III of England founded the Order of the Garter and put it under St George's protection, he became the patron saint of England. Despite this, the name was not much used until the Hanoverian succession in 1714 brought a line of four Georges

to the throne. It is currently popular with parents.
Geordie is a Scottish and North Country pet form
which is used as a nickname for Tynesiders;
Georgie is more common elsewhere.

Georgina *f.*

Georgina and **Georgia**, the most common female
forms of **GEORGE**, are both a popular choice at the
moment. They were first used in Britain in the
18th century, when George became popular. The
commonest form then was **Georgiana**, which is still
sometimes used. Other feminine forms of George
are **Georgette** and **Georgine**.

Ger, Gerry *see* Gerald, Gerard

Geraint *m.*

This is a very old Welsh name, a variant form of the
Latin Gerontius, which is in turn derived from a
Greek word meaning 'old'. The 19th-century poet
Alfred Tennyson used the old Welsh story of
Geraint and Enid in his *Idylls of the King*, and it
was from this that the name's modern use has
stemmed. The real-life hero on which the fictional
character is based died in battle about AD 530.

Gerald *m.*

From the Old German, meaning 'spear rule'.
It was used in England from the 11th to the 12th
century and was probably introduced by the

Normans. The name flourished in Ireland due to the influence of the Fitzgerald ('Sons of Gerald') family, the powerful rulers of Kildare. It was probably from Ireland that the name returned to England in the late 19th century. Shortened forms are **Ger**, **Gerry** and **Jerry**.

Geraldine *f.*

Geraldine started life as a poetic nickname used by the 16th-century Earl of Surrey, in a poem praising the beauty of Lady Elizabeth Fitzgerald. Geraldine therefore means 'one of the Fitzgeralds'. It shares short forms with **GERALD**.

Gerard *m.*

From the Old German, meaning 'spear-brave'. It was brought to Britain by Norman settlers and was very common in the Middle Ages. The surnames **Gerrard** and **Garret(t)** are derived from it, and these were the most common medieval pronunciations of the name, although it is not always possible to distinguish between forms of Gerard and **GERALD**. **Ger**, **Gerry** and **Jerry** are its short forms.

Germaine *f.*

Several early saints bore this name, which probably indicated someone who came from Germany, in the way that **FRANCIS** indicated a Frenchman. Germaine is little used in English-speaking countries, but has been made well known by the writer and academic Germaine Greer. **Jermain(e)** is a form of the French **Germain**, which is quite popular in the USA, and is also found as **Jermyn**.

Gerry *see* Gerald, Geraldine, Gerard

Gertrude *f.*

From the Old German for 'strong spear'. The name came to Britain in the Middle Ages from the Netherlands, where a saint of that name was popular. It was much used in the 19th and earlier 20th centuries, but is not often chosen by parents now. Pet forms are **Gert** or **Gertie**, and **Trudi**, **Trudie** or **Trudy** come from a German pet form of the name.

Gervais, Gervase *m.*

From the Old German meaning 'spear vassal' or 'armour bearer'. The name was first used among English churchmen of the 12th-century in honour of the 1st-century martyr St Gervase. It spread to the general public, giving rise to the surname **Jarvis**. Gervais is the French spelling.

Geunor *see* Jennifer

Ghislaine *f.*

This is an Old French name, related to **GISELLE** and meaning 'pledge, hostage'. It has only come to be used in Britain comparatively recently. It is also found in the forms **Ghislane** and **Ghislain**, although in France this last form is used for boys. It is pronounced with a hard 'g' and the 's' is silent.

Gianna *f.*

A short form of the Italian name **Giovanna**, feminine of **Giovanni**, or **JOHN**. Use of Gianna is currently increasing in the USA. Other short forms of Giovanna include **Gina**, **Giannina** and **Vanna**.

Gib *see* **Gilbert**

Gideon *m.*

From the Hebrew, now generally thought to mean 'having a stump for a hand', although the traditional translation was 'a hewer'. It is the name of an Old Testament Israelite leader who put the forces of the Midianites to flight. The name was adopted at the Reformation and was a favourite among the Puritans who took it to North America where it is still in use.

Gigi *f.*

This name became well known in 1958, when the novel *Gigi* by the French writer Colette was made into a successful musical film. In the book Gigi is the pet form of **Gilberte**, the French feminine form of **GILBERT**.

Gilbert *m.*

From the Old German meaning 'bright hostage'. The Normans brought the name to England and it was common in medieval times, when St Gilbert of Sempringham (died 1189) was much admired. Shortened forms are **Gib**, **Gilly**, **BERT** and **Bertie**.

Giles *m.*

According to legend, St Giles was an Athenian who took his name, Aegidius, from the goatskin that he wore. He left Greece in order to escape the fame that his miracles had brought him, and became a hermit in France. There the name became Gilles. The name is first recorded in England in the 12th century, but it was not popular. It has been suggested that this may be because of St Giles's association with beggars and cripples, of whom he is the patron saint. However, recent years have seen an increase in its popularity. It is sometimes spelt **Gyles**.

Gillian *f.*

This name, which is an English rendering of the Latin name **JULIANA**, was so common in the Middle Ages that its short form, **Gill**, was used as a general term for a girl, as Jack was for a man. It was revived in the 20th century and once again became very popular. A variant form is **Jillian**, and **Jill**, the abbreviated form, is now given as an independent name. **Jilly** is also found.

Gilly *see* **Gilbert**

Gina *f.*

A short form of such names as **GEORGINA** and **Regina** (see **QUEENIE**), now used as an independent name. In France, Gina and **Ginette** are pet forms of **GENEVIEVE** and it is also a short form of the Italian **GIANNA**. **Geena** is also found.

Ginette *see* **Genevieve, Gina**

Gini, Ginny *see* **Virginia**

Giovanna, Giovanni *see* **Gianna**

Giselle *f.*

From the Old German meaning a 'pledge' or 'hostage'. **Gisèle** has for a long time been a common French name, and the English form Giselle and the latinised **Gisela** have been used in Britain (see also **GHISLAINE**).

Gita *f.*

An Indian name from the Sanskrit meaning 'song'. **Geeta** is a popular alternative spelling.

Giulia, Giulietta *see* **Julia**

Gladys *f.*

This is the anglicised form of **Gwladys**, which means 'ruler'. It is recorded in Wales as early as the 5th century, but only moved into the mainstream of names in the 19th century. In the earlier part of the 20th century it was very popular, but in recent decades it has become less fashionable. It is often shortened to **Glad**.

Glen(n), Glyn(n) *f. and m.*

These are both forms of Celtic words for 'a valley'. In the last forty years they have become popular names throughout the English-speaking world. **Glenna** and **Glenne** are also found for girls.

Glenda *f.*

This is a Welsh name meaning 'holy and good'.

Glenys *f.*

From the Welsh meaning 'holy'. It is spelt in a variety of ways, including **Glen(n)is**, **Glennys** and **Glenice** (see also GLYNIS).

Gloria *f.*

This is Latin for 'glory' or 'fame'. The name seems to have been coined by George Bernard Shaw (1889) in his play *You Never Can Tell*. It was very common in the first half of the 20th century.

Glyn(n) *see* Glen

Glynis *f.*

From the Welsh for 'a little valley', and thus related to GLEN and Glyn. It can be spelt **Glinys**, and is often confused with GLENYS.

Gobind *see* Govind

Godfrey *m.*

From the Old German meaning 'God's peace'.
It was brought to Britain by the Normans.

Gopal *m.*

This Indian name can be taken to mean 'a devotee
of Krishna'. It derives from the Sanskrit words
meaning 'cow-protector', indicating a cowherd,
but the name was applied to Krishna in medieval
devotional texts. In southern India the name is
sometimes given as **Gopalkrishna**.

Gordon *m.*

Originally a Scottish place name from which the
local lords took their name, it then became the
name of a large and famous clan. It was rarely used
as a first name until 1885, when the dramatic death
of General Gordon at Khartoum gave the name
immense popularity.

Govind *m.,* Govindi *f.*

This Indian name is similar to **Gopal**, deriving
from the Sanskrit words which mean 'cow-finding',
a reference to a cowherd, but the 12th-century
Song of Govind associated the name firmly with
Krishna. Sikhs often make use of the form **Gobind**
for boys.

Grace *f.*

The vocabulary word, originally used in its religious sense. This name existed as **Gracia**, the Latin form, in the Middle Ages but did not become common until the Puritans adopted Grace along with other Christian qualities as a name. The pet form **Gracie** is sometimes given as a separate name, and forms from other languages, such as **Gracia**, **Graciela**, **Gratia** and **Grazia** are also found.

Graham *m.*

Like **GORDON**, this was originally a place name which developed into a family name, particularly on the Scottish/English border. At first restricted to this area, it gradually came into general use as a first name. **Graeme** and **Grahame** are also found.

Grainne, Grania *f.*

In Irish and Scottish legend, Grainne was a princess betrothed to **FINN**, the famous chieftain. However Grainne preferred **DERMOT** and eloped with him. The story of Finn's pursuit of the couple and Grainne's suicide after Finn brought about Dermot's death is an important subject in Irish literature. Grania is the anglicised form of the name, reflecting the pronunciation 'grahn-ya'.

Grant *m.*

A surname from the French for 'tall, large' used as a first name. It seems to have come to this country from the USA, where its use may have been connected with the popularity of General Ulysses Grant (1822–85), the 18th President. But as it is a common Scots surname there is no reason why the name would not have developed independently in the UK.

Gregory *m.*

From the Greek meaning 'watchman'. The name first came to Britain through St Gregory the Great, the pope who sent St Augustine to England. It was in common use from the Norman Conquest, when most Latin names were introduced, until the Reformation when, because of its association with the papacy, it fell out of favour. Gregour was the usual medieval form, which is still found as **Gregor** in Scotland, and hence the surname MacGregor. The most common shortened form is **Greg**.

Greta *f.*

A Swedish abbreviation of **MARGARET**. It was rare in England until the 20th century, when the fame of the film actress Greta Garbo led to some parents using it. **Gretel** and **Gretchen** are the German forms.

Griffith *m.*

From the Welsh name **Gruffud** or **Gruffydd**, meaning 'lord' or 'strong warrior'. It has always been fairly popular in Wales, and was the name of several Welsh princes. **Griff** is a pet form.

Griselda *f.*

The meaning of this old Germanic name is disputed, but it may mean 'grey battle-maiden'. Chaucer told the story of *Patient Griselda* in the *Canterbury Tales*, which encouraged its use by parents who wanted meek and virtuous daughters. **Grizel** is an old Scots form which is little used nowadays, and **Zelda** started as a short form.

Guendolen *see* Gwendolyn

Guenevere, Guinevere *see* Jennifer

Gulab *f.*

A Hindu flower name, from the Sanskrit for 'rose'.

Gus, Gussie *see* Augusta

Guy *m.*

From the Old German Wido, the meaning of which is uncertain, possibly 'wide' or 'wood'. Wido became Guido in Latin records and Guy was the French form introduced to Britain by the Normans. Medieval clergy identified the name with the Latin **Vitus** meaning 'lively', hence the disease St Vitus' Dance is known in France as *la danse de Saint Guy*. St Vitus was a Sicilian martyr who was invoked for the cure of nervous ailments. Guy fell out of use after Guy Fawkes' gunpowder plot of 1605. It was revived in the 19th century with the help of Walter Scott's novel, *Guy Mannering*.

Gwen *f.*

The pet form of several names, such as
GWENDOLYN, which come from the Welsh word
meaning 'white'. Gwen and **Gwenda** (a pet form,
which can also mean 'fair and good') are now used
as separate names and have spread to the rest of
Britain.

Gwendolyn, Gwendolen, Guendolen *f.*

From the Welsh meaning 'white circle', probably a
reference to the ancient moon-goddess. The name
occurs frequently in Welsh legend. Its wide range of
spellings also include **Gwendoline** and
Gwendolyne. It was a popular name at the
beginning of the century, but is not much used now.

Gwenfrewi *see* Winifred

Gwenhwyfar *see* Jennifer

Gwill, Gwilym *see* William

Gwladys *see* Gladys

Gwyn *m.*

From the Welsh meaning 'white' or 'blessed'.
This name has been anglicised as **Wyn** or **Wynne**.
Its use is mainly confined to the Welsh. **Gwynfor** or
Wynfor is Gwyn with the word for 'great' added to
the end.

Gwyneth *f.*

From the Welsh meaning either 'fair maiden' or 'happiness'. **Gwyn** is the pet form.

Gyles *see* Giles

Hadrian see **Adrian**

Hal see **Henry**

Haley see **Hayley**

Ham see **Abraham**

Hamish *m.*

The anglicised form of **Seumas** (see **SEAMAS**), the Gaelic form of **JAMES**. This name became popular in the second half of the 19th century and is still used, mostly in Scotland.

Hamzah *m.*

The name of the Prophet Muhammad's uncle, probably from the Arabic for 'lion'. It is also spelt **Hamza**.

Hana *f.,* Hani *m.*

Hana is from the Arabic for 'bliss' or 'happiness'. **Hani** (*m*) and **Haniyya** (*f*), meaning 'joyful, delighted', and **Hanan** (*f*), 'tenderness, affection', come from the same root.

Hank see **Henry**

Hannah *f.*

From the Hebrew meaning 'God has favoured me'. In the Old Testament it was the name of Samuel's mother. The Greek form of this, **Anna** (see ANNE), was used at first. Hannah was not adopted in England until after the Reformation. It is currently one of the most popular girls' names.

Hari *m.*

This Indian name occurs frequently in classic Hindu texts and is often applied to Vishnu or Krishna. It derives from a Sanskrit word which indicates a yellowy-brown colour.

Harley *f. and m.*

Harley (sometimes **Harleigh**, **Harli(e)** or **Harlee**, particularly for girls) is an English aristocratic surname, but its use as a first name probably owes much to the glamour of the Harley Davidson motorbike. Use of the similar-sounding **Harlan**, although found in the 19th century, was encouraged by respect for Judge John Marshall Harlan (1899–1971).

Harmony *see* **Melody**

Harold *m.*

From the Old Norse, meaning 'army-power'; **Harald** is the original Scandinavian form. It was used in the Middle Ages, but went out of fashion until it became popular again in the 18th century. It is not much used at the moment. It shares the abbreviation **Harry** with the name **Henry**.

Haroun *see* **Aaron**

Harriet *f.*

A female form of **Henry**, derived from **Harry**, which was the usual form of the name Henry in the Middle Ages. The name was very popular in the 18th and 19th centuries and again in the 20th century. Short forms are **Hattie** or **Hatty**.

Harrison *see* **Henry**

Harry *see* **Harold, Henry**

Harsha *f.*

A Hindu name derived from the Sanskrit for 'happiness'.

Harun *see* **Aaron**

Harvey *m.*

From the French meaning 'battle-worthy'. It was common until the 14th century, and had a slight revival in the 19th. Its modern use as a first name may be due in part to its widespread use as a surname.

Hasan *m.*

One of the most popular Muslim names, derived from the Arabic for 'handsome' or 'good'. Al-Hasan was the Prophet's grandson. Similar names derived from the same Arabic word are **Hasin**, **Hassan**, **Husayn**, **Husni**, **Hussain** and **Hussein**.

Hattie, Hatty *see* Harriet

Hayden *m. and f.*

This appears to be a form of **Haydn**, a name used in honour of the Austrian composer Franz Josef Haydn. As a first name, it is also spelt **Haydon**. The surname Haydn in its turn derives from the Old German word for 'heathen'. Once restricted to boys and used mainly in Wales, it has been well used in the USA for some years, and its popularity is spreading.

Hayley *f.*

From a surname meaning 'hay field'. This name came into use in the 1960s, after the success of the film actress, Hayley Mills, and has since become very popular. It is spelt in many different ways including **Hailee**, **Haley** and **Haylie** and is occasionally used for boys.

Hazel *f.*

One of the plant names adopted as a girl's name in the 19th century.

Heather *f.*

This is one of several plant names first used in the 19th century. Since heather is a feature of northern Britain, the name became especially popular in Scotland and is now popular in the USA. **Heath**, another name for the same plant, is also used for both sexes.

Hector *m.*

From the Greek meaning 'hold fast'. It was the name of the Trojan hero who was killed by the Greek Achilles and took quite a strong hold in Scotland, where it was used as an equivalent for the quite unconnected Gaelic name **Eachan**, which means 'a horseman'.

Heena *see* Hina

Heidi *f.*

This name is a pet form of the German version of **ADELAIDE**. It has come into use in the English-speaking world thanks to the popularity of Johanna Spyri's *Heidi* stories.

Helen *f.*

From the Greek meaning 'the bright one'. The popularity of this name in Britain was due originally to the 4th-century St **Helena**. She was the mother of Constantine the Great and was supposed to have been the daughter of the ruler of Colchester, the

Old King Cole of nursery rhyme. When she was over eighty she made a pilgrimage to the Holy Land where she was believed to have found the true cross of Christ. The name is first found as **Elena** and then **ELAINE** and **ELLEN**. The 'H' was not used until the Renaissance, when the study of classical literature brought Homer's story of the Trojan war and the beautiful Greek queen Helen to public notice. **Lena** is a contraction and **NELL** is a pet form. **Ilona** is a Hungarian form.

Helga *f.*

From the Norse, meaning 'holy'. It has occasionally been used in Britain but is more common in North America, where it was introduced by Scandinavian immigrants (see also **OLGA**).

Heloïse, Heloïse *see* Eloise

Hema *f.*

An Indian name which derives from the Sanskrit for 'golden'.

Henrietta *f.*

The female form of **HENRY**. It was introduced into England in the 17th century by Henriette Marie, Charles I's French wife. The full form gave way to the abbreviated **HARRIET**, but was revived in the 19th century. Abbreviations are **Etta**, **Ettie** and **Hetty**.

Henry *m.*

From the Old German, meaning 'home ruler'.
The Latin Henricus became **Henri** in France.
Harry, reflecting the French pronunciation, was the
original English form of Henri, used until the 17th
century and often abbreviated to **Hal**. Today, Harry
is used as the pet form of Henry and increasingly as
a name in its own right. **Hank** is a pet form more
common in the United States. **Harrison**, 'son of
Harry' has become well known through the actor
Harrison Ford. Its use as a first name is influenced
by the fact that it was the surname of two US
Presidents, William (1773–1841) and his grandson
Benjamin Harrison (1833–1901).

Herbert *m.*

From the Old German for 'bright army'. It seldom
appears before the Norman Conquest, after which
it became quite common. It was revived at the start
of the 19th century and became quite popular again
towards the century's end, due in part to the fashion
for using aristocratic surnames as first names. **Herb**,
Herbie and **BERT** or **Bertie** are short forms.

Herman *m.*

A Germanic name meaning 'soldier'. The French
form of the name is **Armand**, and the old English
form **Armin** or **Arminel**, which along with
Arminelle can also be used as a feminine name.

Hermione *f.*

Hermione (pronounced with four syllables) has recently come to public attention as the name of a major character in J.K. Rowling's *Harry Potter* books. It comes from the Greek meaning 'daughter of Hermes'. In Greek mythology Hermione was the daughter of Menelaus and **HELEN**. Shakespeare's use of the name in *A Winter's Tale* gave rise to its use in modern times. He used another form, **Hermia**, in *A Midsummer Night's Dream*, and this has also been found occasionally.

Hernando *see* Ferdinand

Hester *see* Esther

Hetty *see* Esther, Henrietta

Hew *see* Hugh

Hilary, Hillary *f. and m.*

From the Latin meaning 'cheerful'. The original Latin forms **Hilaria** and **Hilarius** are very occasionally found, and the writer **Hilaire** Belloc used the French form. It was once quite usual as a boy's name, but is now rarely used except for girls. Hillary is the usual spelling in the USA.

Hilda *f.*

From the Old English word for 'battle'. There was an Anglo-Saxon St Hilda, a woman of outstanding ability who founded an abbey at Whitby in the 7th century. When the names of Anglo-Saxon saints were revived in the 19th century Hilda became popular but is now often felt to be rather old-fashioned.

Hina *f.*

A Hindu name meaning 'henna', the dye used to colour the hair and fingernails. It is also found as **Heena** and **Henna**.

Hiram *m.*

From the Hebrew, meaning 'brother of the high one', and the name of an Old Testament king of Tyre. It was a favourite 17th-century name and was taken at that time to North America where it still flourishes.

Holly *f.*

A plant name used as a first name, currently popular on both sides of the Atlantic.

Honoria *f.*

From the Latin meaning 'reputation' or 'honour'. The Latin forms **Honora**, Honoria and **An(n)ora** were predominant until the Reformation, when the Puritans adopted the abstract virtue names and used **Honour** and **Honor**. They were then used both as masculine and feminine names. In the 19th century the Latin forms were revived (see also **NORA**).

Hope *f.*

This Christian virtue was adopted as a first name in the 17th century, in the same way as FAITH and CHARITY. It was especially popular among Puritans at this time, who used it for both sexes. It is now only used for girls.

Horace, Horatio *m.*

From the Roman clan named Horatius borne by the Latin poet Horace. Horatio seems to have come from Italy to England in the 16th century, and has been kept alive by the fame of Nelson, although Horace is the form more likely to be found today. **Horatia** is a rare feminine form.

Howard *m.*

Like other aristocratic family names, this was adopted as a first name by the general public in the 19th century. The origin of the surname is disputed. It may be from the Old German meaning 'heart-protection' or the French for 'worker with a hoe', or even from the medieval official, the 'hogwarden', who superintended the pigs of a district. **Howie** can be used as a short form.

Hubert *m.*

From the Old German meaning 'bright mind'. This name was popular in the Middle Ages, probably as a result of the fame of St Hubert of

Liège, the patron saint of huntsmen. It was not much used from the 16th to the 18th centuries, after which it was revived to some extent, but it has since gone out of fashion again. **BERT** is the short form.

Hugh, Hugo *m.*

From the Old German meaning 'heart' or 'soul'. It appears frequently in the Domesday Book. It was further strengthened by the popularity of St Hugh, Bishop of Lincoln in the 14th century. Hugo is the Latin form. **Hew** and **Huw** are Welsh forms of the name; **Hughie** and **Huey** are used as pet forms.

Humayra *f.*

This name was given by the Prophet Muhammad to his wife **AISHA**. Its meaning is unclear.

Humphrey *m.*

From the Old German meaning 'peace'. This name was originally spelt with an 'f', the 'ph' coming in when it was equated with the name of the obscure Egyptian saint, Onuphrios, in order to Christianise it.

Hunter *m. and f.*

The Old English vocabulary word used as a first name, this is another surname that has come to be used as a boy's name. Its increasing use as a girl's name in the USA may be inspired by the actress Hunter Tylo, who appears in *The Bold and the Beautiful* soap opera.

Husayn, Husni, Hussain, Hussein *see* **Hasan**

Huw *see* **Hugh**

Hywel *m.*

A Welsh name meaning 'eminent'. It has become well known through the actor Hywel Bennett.

Iain, Ian *see* John

Ianthe *f.*

This is an ancient Greek name meaning 'violet flower'. It has a strong literary flavour, having been used by a number of poets including Byron and Shelley. It is still quietly but steadily used.

Ibrahim *m.*

The Arabic form of **ABRAHAM**.

Ida *f.*

From the Old German, meaning 'hard work'. The name was introduced by the Normans, and lasted until about the middle of the 14th century. In the late 19th century it was revived by Tennyson for the name of the heroine of his poem *The Princess*, which Gilbert and Sullivan subsequently took as a basis for the operetta *Princess Ida*. These uses led to a revival of the name at the end of the 19th century.

Idris *m.*

This is a Welsh name meaning 'fiery lord'. In Welsh legend, Idris the Giant was an astronomer and magician, who had his observatory on Cader Idris.

Ieasha, Ieesha, Iesha *see* **Aisha**

Iefan, Ieuan, Ifan *see* **Evan**

Ifor *see* **Ivor**

Ignatius *m.*

Ignatius or **Inigo** is a Latin name, derived originally from a Greek name of obscure origin, possibly meaning 'fiery'. It took root mainly in Russia and Spain and was carried further afield by the Jesuits whose founder was Inigo Lopez de Recalde, better known as St Ignatius of Loyola.

Ike *see* **Isaac**

Ilona *see* **Helen**

Iman, Imana, Imani *see* **Amir**

Imelda *f.*

Imelda is probably the Italian form of the Germanic name **Irmhilde** 'universal battle'. It is the name of a rather obscure saint, and had a certain popularity in Ireland in the middle of the 20th century.

Imogen *f.*

First appearing in Shakespeare's *Cymbeline*, this name is thought to be a misprint of the name Innogen which appears in Shakespeare's source for the story. It may be derived from the Greek meaning 'beloved child'. It is a popular choice at the moment.

Ina *f.*

This name can come from three different sources.
It is an Irish form of **AGNES**, a form of the name
ENA, and can also be a pet form of first names
ending '-ina', such as **Christina** and **GEORGINA**.

Inderjit *m.*

An Indian name from the Sanskrit meaning
'conqueror of the god Indra'. The spelling **Indrajeet**
is also used.

India *f.*

This was the name of a character in *Gone with the
Wind*, but its popularity is more likely to be due to
the interest, particularly since the 1970s, in Indian
culture and religion and the model India Hicks,
given the name as the grand-daughter of Lord
Mountbatten, last viceroy of India.

Indira *f*

An Indian name associated with the goddess
Lakshmi, wife of Vishnu. It is usually derived from
a Sanskrit word meaning 'beauty', but is possibly
connected with **Indra**, the name of the god of the
sky and rain in Hindu tradition. The meaning of the
name is uncertain, but may be connected with the
Sanskrit for 'raindrop'.

Indrajeet *see* **Inderjit**

Inés, Inez *see* **Agnes**

Ingrid *f.*

From the Old Norse, meaning 'Ing's ride'. In Norse mythology Ing was the god of fertility and crops who rode a golden-bristled boar. It is a common name in Scandinavia and was made famous in this country by the Swedish film star, Ingrid Bergman (1915–82). **Ingeborg** ('Ing's fortress') and **Inga**, the short form of these two names, are also found occasionally.

Inigo *see* Ignatius

Iola *f.*

The Latin form of a Greek name meaning 'dawn cloud'. In Greek mythology Hercules fell in love with a princess **Iole**. The name is rare in Britain.

Iolanthe *see* Yolanda

Iona *f.*

This is the name of the Scottish island used as a first name. The island seems originally to have been called Ioua, 'yew-tree island', but at some point the 'u' was misread as 'n' and so the island got its present name. The name's popularity has been increasing in recent years. **Ione** ('eye-oh-nee') is not the same name, but a Greek name connected with the word 'violet'.

Ior *see* Ivor

Ira *m.*

A name from the Old Testament meaning
'watchful'. The name was used by the Puritans, who
took it over to America where it is now much more
common than in Britain. The song-writer Ira
Gershwin was a famous bearer of the name.

Irene *f.*

The name of the goddess of peace and also of one
of the seasons in ancient Greece. Although the
name was used earlier in other parts of Europe,
it did not appear in England until the late 19th
century. The abbreviation **Renie** is sometimes used
and it can also be found in the form **Irena**. Irene is
pronounced in two different ways: in the Greek way
with three syllables and the final 'e' pronounced,
and the usual modern way with only two syllables.

Iris *f.*

Although this name is usually associated with the
flower, it comes from the Greek word for 'rainbow',
after which the flower was named because of its
bright colours. In Greek mythology Iris carried
messages from the gods to men, across the rainbow
which was her bridge. It was not used in England
before the 19th century.

Irma *f.*

This was originally a German name meaning
'universal'.

Irving *m.*

Irving or **Irvine** are Scottish place names which were used first as surnames and then as first names.

Isa *see* **Isabel**

Isaac *m.*

From the Hebrew meaning 'laughter'. It was the name given by SARAH, wife of ABRAHAM, to the son born in her old age, traditionally because she laughed when she was told that she would conceive. The name appears in Britain in the Middle Ages and came to be regarded as a specifically Jewish name. It came into general use in the 16th and 17th centuries, when it was spelt with a 'z' as in **Izaak** Walton, the author of *The Compleat Angler*. In the mid-17th century the 's' spelling came into fashion, as in Sir Isaac Newton, the great scientist. **Zak** or **Ike** are used as pet forms.

Isabel(le), Isobel *f.*

These are forms of ELIZABETH which developed in medieval France. Elizabeth became Ilsabeth and then Isabeau, and finally **Isabelle**. Up to at least the end of the 17th century, the derivatives Isabel(le) in England, Isobel in Scotland and the Gaelic **Iseabail**, sometimes spelt phonetically as **Ishbel**, were interchangeable with Elizabeth. **Isa** and **Bel** or **Belle** were the common short forms. The Latin **Isabella** and **Bella** were used from the 18th century.

Isaiah m.

From the Hebrew meaning 'Jehovah is salvation', and the name of the great Old Testament prophet. It was first used by the 17th-century Puritans. It is currently well used in the USA and increasingly frequent in the UK.

Iseabail see **Isabel**

Iseult see **Isolda**

Isha see **Aisha**

Ishbel see **Isabel**

Ishmael see **Ismail**

Isidore m., *Isidora* f.

From the Greek, possibly meaning 'gift of Isis'. There were two Spanish saints of this name. The scandal caused by the private life and dancing style of **Isadora** Duncan (1878–1927) made the feminine form of the name well known.

Isla f.

A Scots island name, used as a girl's name in Scotland since the 1950s. It has now spread to other parts of Britain. The 's' is silent, as in 'island'.

Isleen see **Aisling**

Ismail *m.*

This is the Arabic form of **Ishmael**. Arabs are sometimes known as Ismailites, 'descendants of Ismail'.

Isobel *see* Isabel

Isolda *f.*

From Old Welsh **Essylt** meaning 'fair one'. It was a common name in medieval times because of its place in the tragic legend of **Tristan** and Isolda. **Iseult** was the Norman form which became Isolda in Latin, Isot(t) in Middle English. Isolda or **Isolde** had a brief revival in the 19th century owing to the popularity of Wagner's opera *Tristan and Isolde*. It is also spelt **Yseult(e)** and **Ysolde**.

Israel *f.*

From Hebrew, although its meaning is disputed; the most likely translation is 'may God prevail'. In the Old Testament Jacob was named Israel after his struggle with the angel of God. The name was first adopted by Christians after the Reformation.

Ivan *m.*

The Russian form of **John**, found occasionally in Britain.

Ivo *m.*

From the Old German meaning 'yew'. It was common in Brittany in the form **Yves**, and was brought to Britain at the time of the Norman Conquest. It has been used occasionally since.

Ivor, Ifor *m.*

Ifor is a Welsh name which means 'lord', and Ivor is the anglicised spelling. It was originally **Ior**, but was probably influenced by **Yves** (see Ivo).

Ivy *f.*

This is a plant name which came into use in the 19th century. Because ivy clings so firmly, the name may have been used to indicate faithfulness.

Izaak *see* **Isaac**

Jacey, Jacie *see* Jay

Jack *m.*

Originally the pet form of **JOHN**, this is now a very popular name in its own right. In the Middle Ages **Jan** evolved from John, and then developed the pet form Jankin, later shortened to Jack. **Jock** is a traditionally Scottish form. Jack shares the pet form **Jake**, now a name in its own right, with **JACOB**. **Jackson**, a surname meaning 'son of Jack', is also found as a first name.

Jacob *m.*

The meaning of this Hebrew name is uncertain. In the Old Testament, it was the name of Isaac's younger son, who tricked his brother Esau out of his inheritance. This explains the popular interpretation of the name as 'he supplanted'. There were two Latin forms, Jacobus and Jacomus. Jacob came from the former and **JAMES** from the latter. Jacob has survived as a first name because translators of the Bible kept this form for the Old Testament Patriarch, although they called the two New Testament apostles James. **Jacoba**, **Jacobine** and **Jacobina** are rare feminine forms. **Jake** is an abbreviation shared with **JACK** and now a popular choice as a name in its own right.

Jacqueline *f.*

Jacqueline and **Jacquetta** are French feminines of **Jacques**, the French equivalent of **JAMES** and **JACOB**. Both were introduced into this country in the 13th century, and have been in use ever since. Jacqueline, with its pet forms **Jacky**, **Jacki(e)** or **Jacqui**, is found in a very wide range of spellings which include **Jackalyn**, **Jacaline**, **Jacquelyn** and **Jaqueline**.

Jade *f.*

The name of the precious stone used as a first name. Although the names of precious stones have been in use as girls' names since the last century, this one seems only to have come into use in the 1970s and has been popular again recently. **Jada** (**Jayda**) and **Jaden** can be seen as developments of either Jade or **JAY**.

Jaelin, Jai *see* Jay

Jaimal *see* Jamila

Jake *see* Jack, Jacob

Jalal *m.,* Jalila *f.*

An Arabic name which means 'glory' or 'greatness'. A similar name is **Jalil**, meaning 'honoured' or 'revered'. Jalila is the feminine form of both. The names are also found as **Galal**, **Galil** and **Galila**.

Jaleesa *f.*

Also spelt **Jalisa**, this is a popular and apparently newly formed name, blending the 'Ja-' of names like **JANE**, **JANET** and **JACQUELINE** with the sound of **Lisa**. It was introduced in 1988 through a character in the TV comedy show *A Different World*. Afro-American parents immediately responded to the name with great enthusiasm.

Jalil *see* Jalal

Jalisa *see* Jaleesa

Jamal *see* Jamila

James *m.*

This name has the same root as **JACOB**. It became established in Britain in the 12th century when pilgrims started to visit the shrine of St James at Compostella in Spain. At that time the name was more common in Scotland. With the accession of James VI as the first king of both Scotland and England in 1603, the name became more popular in England. It was unfashionable in the 19th century, but is now probably the most used boy's name. The pet forms are **Jim**, **Jimmy** and **JAMIE**. The Irish form is **SEAMAS** and the Scots **HAMISH**.

Jamie *f. and m.*

This was originally a Scottish pet form of **JAMES** but it has since spread throughout the English-speaking world and become popular in its own right. Since at least the 1950s it has also been used as a girl's name, particularly in the United States.

Jamila *f.,* Ja(i)mal *m.*

An Arabic name meaning 'beautiful'. The name is popular in the male and female forms in the Arab world and with Black Muslims in the USA, where it is also spelt **Jamil** and **Jamel**. It is also used in France, where it can be found as **Djamila**.

Jan *see* Janet, Jack

Jane *f.*

This is now the commonest female form of **JOHN**. It comes from the Old French form Jehane. It was very rare before the 16th century, the medieval female forms of John being **JOAN** and **JOANNA**. An early example was Jane Seymour, third wife of King Henry VIII of England and mother of Edward V. Since Tudor times the name has been in and out of fashion. At the moment it is freely used as a second name, but rarely as a first unless in some combination like Sarah Jane. It can also be spelt **Jayne**. The commonest pet forms are **Jenny** and **Janey** or **Janie** (see also **JANET**). **Jancis** seems to be a combination of Jane with **FRANCES** or **Cicely**.

Other elaborations include **Janice** or **Janis**; **Jana**, a form found in a variety of other languages; **Janae** and **Janelle** (see also **SHEENA**, **SIAN**).

Janet *f.*

This was originally derived from **Jeanette**, the French pet form of **JEAN**. It was first used in Scotland. **Janette** and **Janetta** are also found, and **Net**, **Nettie**, **Netta** and **Jan** are pet names. A Scottish pet form is **Jessie** (see also **SHEENA**).

Janey, Janice, Janie, Janis *see* Jane

Janine *f.*

Like **JANET**, this name comes from a pet form of **Jeanne**, the French form of **JEAN**. It is also spelt **Jannine** and **Janene**, and the latinised **Janina** is also used.

Jaqueline *see* Jacqueline

Jared *m.*

A biblical name meaning 'to descend' and connected with **JORDAN**. It was used in the past by the Puritans but had become very rare until the mid-1960s when it became popular in the United States and Australia. It is also found in the forms **Jarred**, **Jarod** and **Jarrod**, although some of these forms may be influenced by similar surnames. **Jaron** is also used.

Jarvis *see* Gervais

Jasmine *f.*

A flower name also found in its normal botanical form, **Jasmin**. The word comes from Persian, and the name is also used in the Persian form **Yasmin**, with variants such as **Yasmine** and **Yasmina**. It is currently popular.

Jason *m.*

This name was adopted in the 17th century when biblical names became popular, because it is the traditional name for the author of Ecclesiasticus. It has been a popular name in recent years, when parents probably associated it more with the Greek hero Jason, who won the Golden Fleece. A short form, **Jace**, is sometimes used.

Jasper *m.*

Gaspar or **Caspar** (**Kaspar**) is the traditional name of one of the three kings or wise men of the Christmas story. It may mean 'keeper' or 'bringer of treasure'. **Gaspard** is the French form which became Jasper in English.

Jawahir *f.*

An Arabic name which means 'jewels'.

Jay *f. and m.*

As an Indian name for boys, Jay comes from a Sanskrit word for 'victory' and can also be spelt **Jai**.

Otherwise it comes from a short form of any name beginning with a 'J', or from a surname, originally a nickname for someone who chattered like the bird. It is sometimes spelt **Jaye**. There are a number of elaborations such as **Jaelyn** or **Jaylin** (*f*); **Jac(e)y** (*m* and *f*) and its variants; **Jayla** (*f*); **Jaden** or **Jayden** (*f* and *m*).

Jayne *see* Jane

Jean *f.*

This name started as a Scottish form of **JANE** or **JOAN** derived from the Old French Jehane. The diminutive **Jeanette** is also found (see **JANET**). The commonest pet forms are **Jeanie** and **Jenny**.

Jed *m.*

A short form of the biblical name **Jedidiah**, which means 'beloved of the Lord'. It is more common in the United States than in the UK.

Jeff, Jeffrey *see* Geoffrey

Jem *see* Jeremy

Jemima *f.*

From the Hebrew meaning 'dove' or 'handsome as the day', and the name of one of Job's daughters in the Old Testament. First used in the 17th century by Puritans, it was very popular in the 19th century and is used steadily today. **Mima** is a pet form.

Jemma see **Gemma**

Jennifer f.

An old Cornish form of **Guenevere**, from the Welsh meaning 'white ghost', and the name of King Arthur's wife. It was practically obsolete until its 20th-century revival. It spread rapidly, and was very popular in the 1950s and 60s. **Jenny** or **Jenni** is the pet form, shared with **JANE** and **JEAN**. **Gaenor**, **Geunor** and **Gaynor** are other forms of Guenevere, which is also spelt **Guinevere** and in Wales, **Gwenhwyfar**. **Jenna**, another Cornish version, has recently become popular.

Jenny see **Jane, Jean, Jennifer**

Jeremy m.

From the Hebrew, meaning 'may Jehovah exalt'. **Jeremiah** was the Old Testament prophet who wrote the Book of Lamentations. The traditional English form is Jeremy, which appears from the 13th century onwards, although in the 17th century, the two forms **Jeremias** and Jeremiah were more common. **Jerry** is a short form, which is shared with **GERALD**, and **Jem** and **Jez** are also used. **Jer(r)ell** is a recent variant.

Jermain(e), Jermyn see **Germaine**

Jerome m.

From the Greek Hieronymos, meaning 'holy name'.

This name is pre-Christian in origin, but soon became popular with the early Church. St Jerome translated the Bible into Latin in the 4th century, and was an important religious influence in the Middle Ages. The name appears in England in the 12th century as Geronimus, which gradually gave way to the French form Jerome.

Jerry *see* **Gerald, Geraldine, Gerard, Jeremy**

Jesse *m.*

From the Hebrew meaning 'God exists', and in the Old Testament, the name of King David's father. It was adopted in the 17th century by the Puritans who took it to America where it has been commoner than in the UK. Jesse James, the outlaw, and the politician Jesse Jackson are probably the best known examples. **Jess** is a short form. The name is sometimes spelt **Jessie**.

Jessica *f.*

The source of this name is much debated, but it was probably invented by Shakespeare for his play *The Merchant of Venice* in which Shylock's daughter is called Jessica. It is shortened to **Jess** or **Jessie** (also a Scottish pet form of **JANET**), which is sometimes spelt **Jessye**. It is very popular at the moment.

Jesus *see* **Joshua**

Jethro *m.*

From the Hebrew meaning 'abundance' or 'excellence'. In the Bible it is the name of **MOSES'** father-in-law. It has been used as a first name since the Reformation.

Jez *see* Jeremy

Jill, Jillian, Jilly *see* Gillian, Juliana

Jim, Jimmy *see* James

Jinny *see* Virginia

Jo *see* Joseph, Josephine

Joan, Joanna *f.*

This is the oldest female form of **JOHN** and is a contraction of **Johanna**, the Latin feminine form of Johannes. The name came over from France as Jhone and Johan in the second half of the 12th century, but by the 14th century Joan was the established form. By the mid 16th century it was so common that it became unfashionable, and **JANE** superseded it. It was revived at the beginning of the 20th century. **Joni** is the pet form. **Joanne** was a later development of the name. **Juanita** is the Spanish pet form, which can be shortened to **Nita**.

Job *m.*

From the Hebrew meaning 'hated' or 'persecuted'. **Jobey**, **Jobie** or **Joby** are pet forms of the name.

Jocelyn, Jo(s)celin *f. and m.*

These names seem to be derived from several different names which have come together over a period of time to form one name. The most important source is probably from the Latin meaning 'cheerful, sportive'. There is also a possibility that it is derived from an Old German name meaning 'little Goth'. A further derivation has been traced from the name **Josse**, 'champion', a form of **Jodoc**, the name of an early Breton saint which also gave us **JOYCE**. Jocelyn is the usual form for boys, although the name is now rarely masculine.

Jock *see* Jack

Jodi(e), Jody *see* Judith

Joe *see* Joseph, Josephine

Joel *m.*

From the Hebrew, meaning 'Jehovah is God' and the name of one of the minor Old Testament prophets. It was adopted by the Puritans, like many other biblical names, after the Reformation. **Joelle** is a form of the name for girls.

John *m.*

From the Hebrew, meaning 'the Lord is gracious'. Its earliest form in Europe was the Latin Johannes, which was shortened to **Johan** and **Jon** before becoming John. However, in France the name became Jean, and both forms of the name were introduced into the British Isles, which resulted in two groups of names developing. Thus the Johannes-form, where the 'J' was pronounced as an 'I', gives us the Gaelic **Ian** and **Iain**, **Ieuan** and **EVAN** in Welsh, and Eoin ('oh-n') in Irish, while the Jean-form gives **SEAN** or **Shane** in Irish and **Sion** in Welsh. Since the 16th century, John has been one of the commonest boys' names in Britain (see also **IVAN**, **JACK**).

Jolyon *see* Julian

Jon *see* John, Jonathan

Jonah, Jonas *m.*

From the Hebrew meaning 'dove'. The Old Testament story of Jonah and the whale was very popular in the Middle Ages and because of this the name was common. It continued to be used occasionally until the 19th century, when it became rare probably because of the association of the name with bad luck. Jonas is the Greek form of the name and is now the more common of the two.

Jonathan *m.*

A Hebrew name meaning 'the Lord has given'. In the Old Testament, Jonathan was the son of King Saul and it was his great friendship with David that gave rise to the expression 'David and Jonathan' to describe two close friends. The name came into use at the time of the Reformation, and it is popular today. The short form, **Jon**, is often used as a separate name and the name is sometimes spelt **Jonathon**.

Joni see **Joan**

Jordan f. and m.

Jordan was quite a popular name in the Middle Ages when it was given to children baptised with water from the River Jordan brought back by pilgrims to the Holy Land. It has recently been revived as a first name and is currently a popular choice. The name of the river means 'to descend, flow' and comes from the same word that gives us the name **JARED**.

Jos see **Joseph, Josiah**

Joscelin see **Jocelyn**

Joseph m.

From the Hebrew meaning 'the Lord added' (i.e. to the family). In the Old Testament it was the name of Jacob and Rachel's elder son who was sold into slavery in Egypt. In the New Testament, there are Joseph, the husband of Mary, and Joseph of Arimathea, who is believed to have buried Jesus and whom legend connects with Glastonbury and the Holy Grail. The name was not often used until the 17th century, when Old Testament names were adopted by the Puritans, and Joseph became a favourite. **Joe** and **Jo** are common abbreviations and well used as names in their own right, and **Jos** is also found.

Josephine *f.*

Josephine is the French female form of **JOSEPH**. It was Napoleon's first wife, the Empress Josephine, who started the fashion for the name in Britain and France. **Josepha** and **Josephina** are less common forms of the name. Pet forms are **Jo(e)** and **Josie**, and in France Josephine has the pet form **Fifi**.

Joshua *m.*

From the Hebrew meaning 'the Lord saves'. In the Old Testament Joshua succeeded Moses and finally led the Israelites to the Promised Land. The name was not used in England before the Reformation. **Josh** is a short form. **Jesus** is the Greek form of the name, popular as a first name with Spanish speakers.

Josiah *m.*

From the Hebrew meaning 'may the Lord heal'. The 18th-century potter, Josiah Wedgwood, in whose family the name is still used, is possibly the best known British bearer of the name. **Josias** is an alternative form of the name, and **Jos** a short form.

Josie *see* Josephine

Josse *see* Jocelyn, Joyce

Joy *f.*

This is the vocabulary word used as a first name. It occurs as early as the 12th century but then disappears, to be revived in the 19th century.

Joyce *f. and m.*

In the Middle Ages when this name was most common it usually had the form **Josse**. A 7th-century saint from Brittany, who also gave us the name **JOCELYN**, was the cause of the name's popularity. One of its French variants was Joisse, and it was from this that the name's final form was derived. Joyce was little used after the Middle Ages until the general revival of medieval names in the 19th century. It is now very rare as a man's name.

Juanita *see* Joan

Jude *m.*

The Hebrew form of this name is **Yehudi**, which was rendered as **Judah** in the Authorised Version of the Old Testament. **Judas** Iscariot bore the Greek

form, and because of him Jude was not used by
Christians until the Reformation. The name was
brought back to public attention by Thomas
Hardy's novel *Jude the Obscure* and the Beatles'
song *Hey Jude*. The actor Jude Law is a well-known
current user. It means 'praise'.

Judith *f.*

From the Hebrew meaning 'a Jewess', and in
the Apocryphal Book of Judith the name of the
resourceful woman who saves the Israelites by
letting the enemy general think he was seducing her,
and then cutting off his head with his own sword.
The short form **Judy** is often given independently,
while the pet forms **Jody** and **Jodi(e)** are now the
most common form of the name.

Jules *see* Julian

Julia, Juliet *f.*

Julia is the feminine form of **Julius**, which came to
England from Italy as **Giulia** in the 16th century.
It did not become common in Britain until the 18th
and 19th centuries. **Julie** is the French form. Julia
was popular in the middle of the 20th century, then
fell out of favour, but is now coming back into use.
Shakespeare's heroine in *Romeo and Juliet* gets her
name from the Italian pet form **Giulietta**, which is
Juliette in French. **Julissa** is a modern elaboration.

Julian *m.*

Julianus was a Roman family name which meant 'connected with the family of **Julius**'. Julius probably comes from the same root that gives the Latin word for 'god', but in Roman times the family believed that it referred to the soft growth of hair that forms a boy's first sign of a beard, as this was the state of development that a founding member of the clan had reached when he first distinguished himself in battle. The most famous of numerous saints of this name was St Julian the Hospitaller, who devoted himself to helping poor travellers. The name came to Britain in the Latin form, which was anglicised as **Julyan**, and in the North of England as **Jolyon**. **Jules**, the French form of Julius, is also used as a short form of Julian.

Juliana *f.*

This is the feminine form of **JULIAN**. It was a popular name in the Middle Ages, when the name normally took the form Julian, still occasionally used for girls. The variant forms **GILLIAN** and **JILL** were among the commonest girls' names from the 12th to the 15th centuries. The name subsequently dropped out of use but was revived in the 18th century. The short form **Julie** is shared with **Julia** (see also **LIANNE**) and **Julianne** is a common variant.

Junayd *m.*

An Arabic name meaning 'warrior'. It also occurs as **Junaid**.

June *f.*

This is simply the name of the month which, like **APRIL**, has been used as a girl's name in the 20th century.

Juno *see* **Una**

Justin *m.,* Justine *f.*

From the Latin meaning 'just'. These were uncommon names until the later 20th century when they came back into fashion. **Justina** is an old feminine form and **Justice** has recently started appearing as a given name for both sexes.

Kacey *see* **Casey**

Kadie, Kady *see* **Kay**

Kai *see* **Kay, Caius**

Kaitlyn *see* **Caitlin**

Kalli(e), Kally *see* **Callie**

Kamal *m.*, Kamala *f.*

In India this name derives from the Sanskrit, where it means 'pale red' but it is specifically associated with the lotus flower. Kamala, the feminine form, is one of the goddess Lakshmi's names in classical Hindu texts, where it is also a name of **SHIVA**'s wife. In the Arab world Kamal is from an Arabic word which means 'perfection'.

Kamil *m.*, Kamila(h) *f.*

From the Arabic meaning 'complete' or 'perfect'.

Kanisha *f.*

A modern variation of **TANISHA**, much used in the early 1990s by Afro-American parents, with whom names beginning with a 'k' sound have recently been fashionable. It is sometimes spelt **Quanisha**.

Kanta *f.*

An Indian name, from the Sanskrit for 'beautiful, desired'.

Kara, Karena, Karissa *see* Cara

Karel *see* Carol

Karen *f.*

A Scandinavian form of **KATHARINE** which was only introduced into the UK in the 1930s. Variants include **Karan** and **Karin**, **Karyn**, **Caryn**, **Caron** and **Karyna**, although some of these could be analysed as belonging to **CARA** (see also **KEREN**).

Karenza *see* Kerensa

Karina *see* Cara

Karl, Karla *see* Carl

Kashif *m.*

An Arabic name which means 'discoverer'.

Kasia *see* Kezia(h)

Kaspar *see* Jasper

Katelyn *see* Caitlin

Katharine, Katherine, Catharine, Catherine *f.*

A name of unknown meaning, but from an early date associated with the Greek *katharos* meaning 'pure'. The name came to the UK in the early 12th century when crusaders brought back the legend of St Katharine of Alexandria. She was an Egyptian princess who was tortured and put to death in the early 4th century for her learned defence of Christianity. There are a number of further spellings for the name, of which **Kathryn** is one of the most frequent. The most common short forms are **Kate**, **Kitty**, **Katie**, **Cathy** and **Kay**, all of which are used as independent names. The Irish forms, **Kathleen** and **Cathleen**, are now used throughout Britain, while **Caitlin** is an older Irish form which has recently become popular. **Kathlyn** is a variant of Kathleen. Russian **Katarina**, **Katia** or **Katya** and **Katinka** are occasionally found (see also **Catriona**, **Karen**).

Katrina, Katrine see **Catriona**

Kay *f. and m.*

A pet form of names beginning with a 'K', such as **Katharine**. It has been used as a first name for over a century and can also be spelt **Kai** and **Kaye** (see also **Caius**). Blends such as **Kaylyn** (**Kaylin**, **Kaylan**, but see **Keely**), **Kaya** (**Kia**) and **Kady** (perhaps a form of Katie) are also found.

Kayla *f.*

This name has been immensely popular in the USA since 1990. It may have started as a pet form of

Michaela (see **MICHAEL**), particularly as this often takes the form **Makayla** in the USA, or be a variant of **KAYLEIGH**, especially in the relaxed pronunciation of rural western states such as Montana, where use of Kayla seems to have begun in the 1970s.

Kayleigh *f.*

This name was brought to the public attention as the title of a 1985 hit song by the group Marillion. The song's writer, Derek Dick ('Fish'), wrote it about his former girlfriend whose first two names were Kay and Lee. The fact that both **LEE** and similar-sounding names such as **KYLIE** and **KELLY** were popular at the time probably helped its rapid spread. Spellings such as **Kayley** and **Kaylee** are common.

Keanu *m.*

The actor Keanu Reeves has made this Hawaiian name, meaning 'cool breeze over the mountains', widely known. **Kean(n)a** can be seen as a feminine form, or as a part of the **KIARA** group.

Keely *f.*

This increasingly popular name comes from an Irish word meaning 'slender, graceful'. In the case of one early populariser of the name, the American singer Keely Smith (b. 1932), it was originally her surname. The name is also spelt **Keeley**. **Keelin** comes from the same root, and may be a source of **Kaylan** (see **KAY**), as well as of **Keelan** for boys.

Keenan *m.*

Kean, whose name means 'ancient', was a leader of the victorious Irish troops against the Vikings in the great battle of Clontarf in 1014. **Kean**, also found as **Cian**, **Kian** and **Keane**, developed the pet form Keenan (**Keenen**, **Keenon**), well known as a surname, and now increasingly used once more as a first name.

Keiran *see* **Kieran**

Keisha *f.*

Another of the names beginning with a 'K' sound which proved so popular with Afro-Americans in the 1980s and 90s (see also **LAKEISHA**). Keisha is probably a similar adaptation of **AISHA**, or **Iesha** as it is frequently spelt by Black American Muslims.

Keith *m.*

This is a first name from Scotland which has spread throughout the rest of Britain. It was originally a surname which was taken from the Scottish place name, probably from the Gaelic meaning 'wood' or 'windy place'.

Kelly *f. and m.*

A modern first name which has rapidly become very

popular. It is an Irish surname which means 'warlike' used as a first name. At first mainly a boy's name, it is now more usual for girls. **Kelley** is also found (see also KAYLEIGH, KYLIE).

Kelsey *f. and m.*

The surname, which in turn comes from an Old English name meaning 'ship-victory', used as a first name. Despite the success of the American actor Kelsey Grammer, it is more common for girls than boys.

Kelvin *m.*

This is the name of the river which flows through Glasgow, used as a first name. The river's name possibly means 'narrow water'.

Kendall *f. and m.*

The surname, which can have various sources, used as a first name. Another surname, the similar-sounding **Kendrick**, is also used for boys, and from it a feminine form, **Kendra**, has evolved.

Kennedy *f. and m.*

Use of this Irish surname is spreading from the USA to the rest of the English-speaking world. Its choice no doubt owes much to the respect and glamour surrounding the assassinated president, John F. Kennedy (1917–63).

Kenneth *m.*

This is the English form of the Gaelic **Coinneach**, meaning 'handsome', and equivalent to modern Welsh **Cenydd**. It is basically a Scottish name which became popular when Kenneth MacAlpine became first King of Scotland in the 9th century, uniting the Picts and the Scots. From there it gradually spread over Britain. It is often shortened to **Ken** or **Kenny**.

Kent *m.*

This is the surname taken from the English county used as a first name. It first became popular in the United States. The county name is an ancient one, meaning 'border' from its position on the coast. The similar-sounding **Kenton** is from a different surname, a common place name meaning 'royal manor', and now used as a first name.

Kentigern *see* **Mungo**

Kenya *f.*

The name of this African country has attracted parents wishing to identify with their African roots. The form **Kenia** is also used.

Kenzie *see* **Mackenzie**

Kera *see* **Kyra**

Keren *f.*

Although some modern uses of this may be as a

form of **KAREN**, this is an ancient name, a short
form of the Old Testament **Kerenhappuch**, one of
the beautiful daughters of **JOB**. The name means
'horn (container) of kohl'. It has also been found in
the form **Kerena** and **Ker(r)yn**.

Kerensa, Kerenza *f.*

A Cornish name meaning 'affection, love'. It is also
found as **Karenza**.

Keri *see* Ceri

Kerr *m.*

An ancient Scottish aristocratic surname, now
sometimes used as a first name, and pronounced
as in 'care'. The surname originally referred to
someone who lived in wet scrubland, although it
is traditionally associated with a Gaelic term for
'left-handed'.

Kerry *f. and m.*

The Irish county name used as a given name. It is a
modern name, apparently first used in Australia
usually for boys, but it is now in general use, mainly
for girls. It is also found as **Kerri**. Its spread may
have been helped by the Welsh name **CERI**,
pronounced in the same way.

Keshia *see* Kezia

Kester *see* Christopher

Ketan *m.*, Ketana *f.*

A Hindu name meaning 'home'.

Kevin *m.*

From the Irish meaning 'handsome birth'.
The name was very popular in Ireland on account
of St Kevin, a 6th-century hermit and abbot of
Glendalough. It is now widely used across the
English-speaking world.

Keyanna *see* Kiara

Kezia(h) *f.*

The Hebrew word for the spice cassia, and the
name of one of **JOB**'s beautiful daughters in the
Bible. The form **Keshia** also occurs, with short
forms **Kezie**, **Kizzie** and **Kissie** or **Kissy**. **Cassia** and
Kasia have also been recorded, with the latter also a
Polish pet form of **KATHARINE**.

Khadija *f.*

A Muslim name from the Arabic meaning
'premature child'. Khadiya bint-Khuwaylid, the first
wife of the Prophet Muhammad, was the mother of
all his children. The name is also spelt **Khadeeja**,
Khadeejah and **Khadijah**.

Kiara *f.*

A name which is currently popular among African-
Americans. It probably adapts the word **Tiara**, also

used as a first name, making use of the fashionable
'K' sound. **Tiana** and **Kiana** (also found in forms
such as **Kean(n)a**, **Keyanna** and even **Quiana**) are
similar coinages; while **Kia** and **Kaya** hover
somewhere between this group and **KAY**.

Kiefer *m.*

The American actor Donald Sutherland named his
son Kiefer after the writer-director Warren Kiefer,
who had been instrumental in furthering his career.
The success of Kiefer Sutherland as an actor in his
turn brought the name into use.

Kieran *m.*, Kiera *f.*

This is a form of the Irish name **Ciaran**, meaning
'dark-haired'. It was the name of 26 Irish saints and
in the last two or three decades it has become
increasingly popular. It is sometimes spelt **Cieran**,
Keiran or **Kieron**, **Ciara** (but see also **SIERRA**),
Ciera, **KIARA** and Kiera are used for girls.

Kim *f. and m.*

Probably from Old English *cynebeald*, meaning
'royally bold', developing through the surname
Kimball. Rudyard Kipling's hero in the novel *Kim*
(1901) used a shortened form of his true name,
Kimball O'Hara, showing the use of the surname as
a first name. More recently the name has been
commoner for girls. **Kym** is also found.

Kimberl(e)y *f.*

Another possible source of the name **KIM**. Kimberley is a diamond-mining town in South Africa, and the association with jewels seems to have encouraged its use. It spread rapidly after its first use in the 1940s. There was also a brief fashion for Kimberley as a boy's name at about 1900, no doubt commemorating events of the Boer War.

Kira *see* Kyra

Kiran *m.*

An Indian name deriving from the Sanskrit for 'ray of light, sunbeam'.

Kirk *m.*

A Scandinavian name for 'church', brought to prominence as a first name by the actor, Kirk Douglas. It would originally have been the surname of someone who was connected with the church, or lived near one.

Kirsty, Kirsten *f.*

Both these are forms of the name **CHRISTINE**. Kirsty was originally a Scottish pet form, while Kirsten comes from Scandinavia. **Kiersten** or **Kirstin** are also found.

Kishan, Kishen *see* Krishna

Kissie, Kissy *see* Kezia(h)

Kistna *see* **Krishna**

Kit *see* **Christopher**

Kitty *see* **Katharine**

Kizzie *see* **Kezia(h)**

Klaus *see* **Nicholas**

Kodey, Kody *see* **Cody**

Kori, Korey, Korrie, Kory *see* **Corey**

Krishna *m.*

The name of a popular Hindu god, a partial incarnation of Vishnu, and deriving from a Sanskrit word for 'black'. In northern India it occurs as **Kishen**; other regional forms include **Kishan**, **Krishan** and **Kistna**.

Krista, Kristin, Kristina, Kryssa, Krystyna *see* **Christine**

Kumar *m.*, **Kumari** *f.*

The boy's name derives from the Sanskrit for 'boy', but it is usually taken to mean 'prince'. The feminine form means 'girl' or 'daughter'.

Kurt *see* **Conrad**

Kushal *m.*

An Indian name meaning 'clever'.

Kyle *f. and m.*

This is a Scottish place and surname meaning 'a strip of land'. It is more usual as a name for boys than girls, for whom **Kyla** is also used.

Kylie *f.*

Originally an Australian Aboriginal word for a 'curled stick' or 'boomerang', it was this name's pleasant sound, at a time when similar-sounding names were popular, rather than its meaning which appealed to parents. It first became familiar to white Australians through the novelist Kathleen Tennant (b. 1912), whose nickname and pen name were both Kylie. Its use spread from Australia throughout the English-speaking world, particularly after being given publicity by the actress and singer, Kylie Minogue. **Kylee** and **Kyleigh** are also found.

Kym *see* Kim

Kyra *f.*

While this name can be interpreted as a feminine form of **KIERAN** or **CYRUS**, its popularity is more likely to come from the attractive character of **Kira** Neris in the *Star Trek* sequel *Deep Space Nine*. It is also found as **Kera**.

Lacey f.

Although this is on the surface the surname, which comes from a French place name used as a first name, its recent popularity in the USA probably owes much to its associations with 'lace'.

Lachlan m.

From Gaelic **Lachlann** or **Lochlann**. Primarily a Highland name, it was introduced as a term for Viking settlers there, but was taken by Scots emigrants to Australia and Canada where it flourished. Short forms are **Lachie** and **Lochie** and there is an occasional feminine form **Lachina**.

Laeta, Laetitia see Letitia

Laila see Leila

Lakeisha f.

An adaptation of the name **KEISHA** used by Afro-American parents. The prefix 'La-' became fashionable in the early 1970s in names such as **LATASHA** and **LATOYA**, and was popular until the 90s when it began to be replaced by 'Sha-' although this, too, has largely gone out of fashion now. Other frequently used names with this prefix include **Laquisha**, **Lashay**, **Lashonda**, **Latisha**, **Latrice** and **Latonya**.

Lakshmi *f.*

The name of the Hindu goddess of wealth and good fortune. Lakshmi derives from the Sanskrit for 'mark', referring to a lucky birthmark.

Lal *m.,* Lalita *f.*

An Indian name and endearment. As a Hindi term of address the male form, Lal, means 'darling boy', though it derives from a Sanskrit word meaning 'caress'. Lalita, the feminine form, means 'playful' or 'charming'. The name has been in use since the Middle Ages.

Lalage *f.*

From the Latin for 'one who prattles'. Short forms are **Lal** and **Lally**.

Lana *see* Alan

Lancelot *m.*

A name of disputed meaning, possibly from the Old French for 'servant'. It can also be spelt **Launcelot**, and was used in Britain from the 13th century due to the popularity of Sir Lancelot, the knight without equal, in stories of King Arthur. The short form **Lance** is more common today.

Laquisha *see* **Lakeisha**

Lara *f.*

A short form of the Russian name **Larissa**, the meaning of which is uncertain, although it may well be used by some parents as a variation of **LAURA**. Lara came into general use in the 1960s after the success of the film of Pasternak's *Dr Zhivago*, with its tragic heroine of this name.

Laraine *see* **Lorraine**

Larissa *see* **Lara**

Lark *see* **Raven**

Larrie, Larry *see* **Laurence**

Lashay, Lashonda *see* **Lakeisha**

Latasha *f.*

There is a strong tradition of name-creating among certain sections of American society, which goes back to at least the 19th century. This name and **LATOYA** are among the commonest of a large group of names which have grown up in the American Black community over the last forty years. They are mostly blends, or combinations of syllables taken from different names, which work because they sound right at the time, echoing the sounds from other popular names. Many of them start with 'La' and particularly 'Lat'. Since names such as **Laverne** (with the option of **Leverne** for boys) were popular with an earlier generation, it may be that the French influence found in place and surnames in the southern USA is the source, although it could just as well come from the many girls' names which begin with these letters. (See also Latisha at **LETITIA**).

Latrice, Latonya *see* **Lakeisha**

Latoya *f.*

A name introduced to Afro-Americans by the well-known singer LaToya Jackson. Her mother invented the name, making use of the fashionable prefix 'La-'. **LaToy** and **Toya(h)** are also used.

Launcelot *see* **Lancelot**

Laura, Lauren *f.*

Laura comes from the Latin for 'laurel', a symbol in the classical world of victory and poetic genius. **Lauretta** is the diminutive form. Together with **Laurencia** and **Lora** these names were common from the 12th century. Lauren or **Loren** (see also **LAURENCE**) and **Lori** and **Lauryn** are popular variants. Other diminutives which are sometimes used are **Laureen**, **Laurene**, and **Laurissa**, **Loretta** and **Lolly**. **Laurel**, the plant name, sometimes spelt **Lorel**, is also found (see also **LARA**, **LORRAINE**).

Lauraine *see* **Lorraine**

Laurence, Lawrence *m.*

From the Latin meaning 'of Laurentium', a town which took its name from the laurel plant, symbol of victory. It became common in the 12th century. St Laurence, the 3rd-century Archdeacon of Rome, was a favourite medieval saint. The name was popular in Ireland because of St Laurence O'Toole, a 12th-century Archbishop of Dublin, whose real name was **Lorcan** (Irish for 'fierce'). **Larrie** or **Larry** is the usual abbreviation in England, while **Laurie** or **Lawrie** is used in Scotland. **Loren** is a form of the name used for both boys and girls.

Laverne *see* Latasha

Lavinia *f.*

The meaning of this name is unknown, but in classical legend it was the name of Aeneas' wife, for whose hand in marriage he fought and defeated a rival suitor. The town of Lavinium, originally called Latium, was renamed after her. The name was very popular for a while during the Renaissance, but then faded out, only returning to fashion in the 18th century. **Lavina** is probably a variant.

Lawrence, Lawrie *see* Laurence

Layla *see* Leila

Lea *see* Leah, Lee, Leo

Leah *f.*

A Hebrew name, probably meaning 'cow'. In the Bible, Leah was the sister of Rachel and the first wife of Jacob. **Lea** and **Lia**, the Italian form of the name, are sometimes used, although they can also be a short form of a number of names ending in the sound.

Leanne *see* Lianne

Leanora, Leanore *see* Leonora

Lee, Leigh, Lea *f. and m.*

From the various forms of the surname meaning 'meadow'. It may have spread from the southern US, and probably owes its popularity there to the Confederate general, Robert E. Lee (1807–70). See also **KAYLEIGH**.

Leena *f.*

An Indian name which means 'devoted'. In some cases it may be a form of the Arabic name **LINA**.

Leigh Ann *see* Lianne

Leila *f.*

A Persian name meaning 'night', probably indicating 'dark-haired'. Byron started the fashion for it in the 19th century by using it in a poem with an oriental setting called *The Giaour*. The name also appears in the Persian romantic legend of **Leilah** and Mejnoun, the Persian equivalent of the Greek story of Cupid and Psyche. **Laila** is also used, but the commonest variant is **Layla**, the form used by Eric Clapton in his song that managed the remarkable feat of being a hit in 1972, 1982 and 1992.

Len *see* Leonard

Lena *see* Helen

Lennie, Lenny, Lennard *see* Leonard

Lenore *see* Leonora

Leo *m.,* Leonie *f.*

From the Latin for 'lion'. Six emperors of Constantinople and thirteen popes were named Leo. **Leon** is the French form, from which the feminine **Leonie** comes. Other versions used for girls include **Lea**, **Leola**, **Leona** and **Leontine**.

Leon *see* Leo, Lionel

Leonard *m.*

From the Old German meaning 'brave as a lion'. The 6th-century St Leonhard was a Frankish nobleman who was converted to Christianity. He became a hermit and devoted his life to helping prisoners, of whom he is the patron saint. His popularity made the name common in medieval England and France and it was revived in the 19th century. The usual shortened forms are **Len**, **Lennie** and **Lenny**. It is sometimes spelt **Lennard**.

Leonie *see* Leo

Leonora, Lenore, Leonore *f.*

These names are European forms of **ELEANOR**, all of which have been used from time to time in Britain, although none of them appeared there before the 19th century and their introduction was probably due to contemporary literary and musical influences. The spellings **Leanore** and **Leanora** are also found. A short form which all these names share is **NORA**.

Leontine *see* Leo

Leopold *m.*

From the Old German words meaning 'people' and 'bold'. This name came to Britain through Queen Victoria's uncle, King Leopold of Belgium, after whom she named her fourth son. It has not been used much in the 20th century.

Leroy *m.*

A surname from the Old French meaning 'the king' which was probably given to royal servants. It has been very popular as a first name in the US, particularly among Black Americans in recent years.

Leslie, Lesley *m. and f.*

These were respectively the usual masculine and feminine spellings of the name, although they are both now used for girls. It is a Scottish surname, perhaps meaning 'garden of hollies', used originally by the Lords of Leslie in Aberdeenshire. It was taken into general use as a first name in the late 19th century.

Letitia *f.*

From the Latin meaning 'gladness'. **Lettice** was the usual form of this name from the 12th to the 17th centuries, during which time it was very popular. In the 18th century the Latin **Laetitia** superseded it, now more frequently spelt Letitia. The phonetic form **Leticia** has recently become quite popular in the USA, giving a short form **Tiesha**, used independently and, most importantly, developing into **Latisha**, one of the most popular of the La-names (see further **LATASHA**). **Laeta** is also found. The short forms of **Lettice**, **Lettie** and **Letty** are sometimes used independently.

Leverne *see* Latasha

Levi *m.*

This is a Hebrew name, meaning 'associated', which has recently become more popular in the USA, possibly due to familiarity with the word as a brand name. It is occasionally given to girls, and has been elaborated into **Levon**.

Lewis, Louis *m.*

Old German Chlodowig, meaning 'famous warrior', was latinised into Ludovicus (source of **Ludovic**).

This became **Clovis** in Old French which was the name of the founder of the French monarchy. His name later became Louis, the name of eighteen other French kings. The Normans brought the name to England where it became Lewis. Use in the UK of the French form, Louis, is comparatively recent, with Robert Louis Stevenson an early example; this form is quite common in the Scottish lowlands and the more usual form in the USA. Short forms are **Lou** and **Louie**, **Lew** and **Lewie**.

Lex *see* Alexander

Lexi(e), Lexus *see* Alexis

Lia *see* Leah

Liam *see* William

Lianne, Leanne *f.*

A pet form of the name **JULIANA**, via the French Julianne, which has become popular as an independent name. It can also be spelt **Liane** and occurs in such forms as **Leigh Ann**.

Libby, Liese, Liesel *see* Elizabeth

Lilian, Lily *f.*

Originally these names may have been pet forms of **ELIZABETH**. **Lillian** is found in Shakespeare's time but the name was probably associated with the lily flower even then. In the 19th century Lily was definitely given as the name of the flower, which is a Christian symbol of purity. **Lil** is the usual abbreviation. Other forms of the name include **Lillah** or **Lila**, and, **Lil(l)ian(n)a** and, in Scotland, **Lillias**.

Lilith *f.*

From the Hebrew meaning either 'serpent' or 'belonging to the night'. In mythology Lilith was an evil spirit who haunted the night and who had been Adam's rejected wife before Eve. It has been used very rarely.

Lin *see* **Linda, Lyn**

Lina *f.*

A short form of names ending in '-lina', such as **Angelina** and **Carolina**, used as an independent name. It can also be used as a pet form of these names. In the Arab world it derives from a word meaning 'tender'. Some Arabic experts refer the name to a type of palm tree.

Linda *f.*

This was a common ending for girls' names in Old German, and comes from the word for a snake, an animal which was held in great reverence by primitive German tribes. It represented wisdom and suppleness, and the names derived from it were therefore complimentary. In Spanish *linda* means pretty, and this may also have had some effect on the use of Linda as an English first name, which dates only from the 19th century. It is also used as a contraction of **BELINDA**. Linda is also spelt **Lynda**, while **Lindy**, **Lindi(e)**, **Lin** and **LYN** are pet forms.

Lindsey *f. and m.*

From the Scottish surname meaning 'pool island'. Together with its other forms, **Lindsay**, **Linsey** and **Linsay**, this name is used for both boys and girls. The form Lindsay tends to be the more usual one for boys. At the moment all forms of the name are used much more frequently for girls than for boys and can then take the form **Linzi**.

Linet, Linette, Linnet *see* Lynette

Lionel *m.*

This name means 'young lion'. A French diminutive of **Leon**, it thus derives from the same root as **LEO**. It was the name of one of King Arthur's knights and was given by Edward III of England to his third son, later Duke of **CLARENCE**. The name was very popular in the Middle Ages and survived into more recent times, particularly in the north of England, where it has come back into general, though infrequent, use.

Lisa, Lisette, Liz, Liza, Lizzy *see* Elizabeth

Llewellyn *see* Lyn

Lloyd *m.*

A Welsh name meaning 'grey'. **Floyd** is a variant form which has arisen due to the difficulty of pronouncing the Welsh 'll', and which appears to come from the USA.

Lo *see* Dolores

Lochie, Lochlann *see* Lachlan

Logan *f. and m.*

This Scottish place name, meaning 'little hollow', became a surname, which led in turn to its use in Scotland as a first name. Since 1990 the name has become one of the top fifty names for boys in the USA and is spreading to other English-speaking countries.

Lois *f.*

In the New Testament Lois was the grandmother of **TIMOTHY**. As the rest of the family had Greek names, Lois is probably Greek also, but its meaning is not known. Like many obscure biblical names, it was adopted in the 17th century by Puritans. It fell out of use but was revived at the beginning of the 20th century.

Lola *f.*

This was originally a diminutive of the Spanish **DOLORES** and of **Carlotta** (see **CHARLOTTE**).

The pet form, **Lolita**, became well known in the 20th century through Vladimir Nabokov's novel of that name.

Lolly, Lora, Lorel, Loren, Loretta *see* Laura

Lorcan *see* Laurence

Loren *see* Laura, Laurence

Lori *see* Laura, Lorraine

Lorna *f.*

This name was created by R.D. Blackmore for the heroine of his novel *Lorna Doone*, published in 1869. In the book she was the lost daughter of the Marquis of **Lorne**, an ancient Scottish first name sometimes used for boys.

Lorraine *f.*

This is the French district, whose name derives from the Old German place name Lotharingen, meaning '**Lothar's** place'. Lothar was an Old German warrior name meaning 'famous army'. Lorraine is the form used in France. In Britain and North America it sometimes takes forms such as **Loraine**, **Laraine** or **Lauraine** and it is not always possible to distinguish between variants of this name and forms of **LAUREN**. **Lori** is a pet form.

Lottie, Lotty *see* Charlotte

Lou, Louie *see* **Lewis, Louisa**

Louis *see* **Lewis**

Louisa, Louise *f.*

Louise is the French, and Louisa the Latin female form of **Louis** (see **LEWIS**). Though common much earlier in France, Louise did not come to Britain until the 17th century when Louise de Keroual became Charles II's mistress. It was popular for about a century until Louisa replaced it but nowadays Louise is once more the popular form. Pet forms are **Lulu**, **Lou** and **Louie** (see also **LUELLA**).

Lourdes *f.*

In 1850 St Bernadette of Lourdes, in south-west France, had numerous visions of the Virgin Mary at a grotto near her home town. It has since become one of the major pilgrimage sites in Europe. When the singer Madonna (see **DONNA**) had a daughter she chose a name linked with her own, which has since come into more general use.

Lowena *f.*

Lowena is an old Cornish name meaning 'joy', which can also be spelt **Lowenna**. Its popularity has been growing rapidly in Cornwall, and it is beginning to spread to other areas. The name **Lowenek**, 'joyful', can also be used. Both names are stressed on the second syllable.

Lucas *see* **Luke**

Lucasta, Lucette, Lucia *see* **Lucy**

Lucille *f.,* **Lucius** *m.*

From the Latin word *lux*, meaning 'light' (see **Lucy**). **Lucilla** retains the Latin form, and Lucille is French. The male form Lucius and its variants **Lucien** and **Lucian** are much less common than the feminine names.

Lucina *see* **Lucy**

Lucinda *f.*

Originally a poetic form of **Lucy**, this name is now given independently, and has recently become quite popular. The short forms **Cindy**, **Cindi** or **Cindie** are sometimes used as names in their own right.

Lucy *f.*

Lucy is the usual English form of the Latin **Lucia** from *lux*, 'light'. In Roman times the name was often used for a child born at dawn; the goddess **Lucina** was the patroness of childbirth, bringing children into the light of day. St Lucy was a Sicilian martyr who was much beloved in the Middle Ages, and the name became well established after the Norman Conquest. Other forms are **Lucette**, **Lucinda**, **Lucasta** and **Lulu**.

Ludovic *see* Lewis

Luke *m.*

A Greek name, latinised as **Lucas**, meaning 'a man of Lucania' in southern Italy. St Luke the Evangelist is the patron saint of doctors and also of painters, and the name was often given by a craftsman to his son. The name appeared in the 12th century as Lucas but a century later it was well established in the English form, Luke.

Lulu *see* Louisa, Lucy

Luned *see* Lynette

Luther *m.*

From the Old German, meaning 'people's warrior'. The modern use of Luther as a first name is entirely due to Martin Luther, the German leader of the Reformation, and to the American civil rights campaigner Martin Luther King, named after him.

Lydia *f.*

From the Greek meaning 'a Lydian girl'. Lydia was a district of Asia Minor where the people were famous merchants, and were said to have invented coinage. In the Acts of the Apostles, Lydia was a widow of Philippi who was converted by St Paul when he stayed at her house. The name was not used in this country before the 17th century.

Lyn *f. and m.*

A short form of such names as **LINDA**, **LYNETTE** and **Carolyn** (see **CAROLINE**) when used for girls. It can also take the form **Lin**, **Linne**, **Linn**, **Lynn** and **Lynne**. As a boy's name it can take the form **Lyn** or **Lynn** and is derived either from a surname or from a short form of the Welsh name **Llewellyn**, a name of uncertain meaning.

Lynda *see* **Linda**

Lynette *f.*

From the Welsh name **Eluned**, which probably comes from a word for 'idol', via its short form, **Luned**. The form Lynette was introduced by the poet Tennyson in the story of 'Gareth and Lynette' in his *Idylls of the King*. It is also spelt **Linet**, **Linnet** (although this can also be from a bird's name), **Linette** and **Lynnette**, and **LYN** is used as a short form.

Lynn, Lynne *see* **Lyn**

Lyric *see* **Melody**

Mabel *f.*

Mabel is a shortening of **AMABEL**, with **Mabella** as the Latin form. Both were current from the 12th to the 15th century, but were rare thereafter until Mabel was revived in the 19th century and became very common. It then suffered another fall from favour. The pet form often used is **MAY**. **Maybelle** and **Maybelline** are developments of the name.

Macauley *f. and m.*

Made famous by the actor Macauley Culkin, this Scottish surname is now used for children of both sexes, although more frequently for boys. It can be spelt starting with a Mc-, and the final syllable is sometimes -lee or -leigh. The similar-sounding **Mackinley**, originally meaning 'son of **FINLAY**', is also found.

Mackenzie *f. and m.*

As a Scottish surname, this refers to a 'son of Coinneach', a Gaelic name which usually takes the anglicised form **KENNETH**. It was popularised as a girl's name by the actress Mackenzie Phillips who appeared in a 1970s American TV series. In the

USA the short form **Kenzie** is also used. The similar
Mckenna, originally from a Scots surname meaning
'ardent love', is also found, but more rarely.

Macsen *see* **Maximilian**

Macy *f.*

This name, famous in the USA from Macy's
department stores, has been popular with American
parents for some years. The surname was originally
French, from a place name meaning 'Marcius'
estate'. It is also found as **Macey** and **Maci**.

Madel(e)ine *f.*

Magdalene, the original form of the name, is
Hebrew and means 'woman of Magdala', a town
on the Sea of Galilee which was the birthplace of
St Mary Magdalene. From about the 12th century
the name was used in England in the French form
Madeline, often abbreviated to Maudlin and Madlin.
Magdalen, the biblical form, was adopted after the
Reformation. It was usually pronounced Maudlin,
but because the meaning of this word developed the
sense of 'weak and sentimental', this form was
replaced by the current pronunciation. It shares the
short form **Madge** with **MARGARET**. **Maddie** or
Maddy is also used. A Continental short form is
Magda (shortened from **Ma(g)dalena**) which has also
been given as an independent name. It now sometimes
takes the form **Madelyn** (**Madlyn**, **Madilyn**).

Madge see **Madeline, Margaret**

Madison *f.*

Use of Madison as a first name derives ultimately from the surname, which means 'son of **MAUD** or **MADELEINE**'. The name was used by a character in the 1984 film *Splash,* sparking its real-life use as soon as the film was released. It continues to grow in popularity and now takes forms such as **Madisen, Madisyn, Maddison, Madyson**.

Madoc, Madog *m.*

A Welsh name meaning 'fortunate'. It is rarely used outside Wales (see also **MARMADUKE**).

Madonna see **Donna**

Mae see **May**

Maegan see **Margaret**

Maeve *f.*

The more usual phonetic form of the Irish name **Meadhbh**, meaning 'she who makes drunk'. It was the name of a famous queen in Irish legend. A diminutive is **Meaveen**, and the name is occasionally spelt **Meave** or **Mave**.

Magda, Magdalen(e) see **Madeline**

Maggie see **Margaret**

Magnus *m.*

This is a Latin adjective meaning 'great'. The spread of this name was due to the Emperor Charlemagne, Carolus Magnus in Latin. Some of his admirers took Magnus for a personal name, and among those who christened their sons after him was St Olaf of Norway. The name spread from Scandinavia to Shetland and Ireland. From Shetland the name became well established in Scotland. In Ireland it became **Manus**, hence the common Irish surname McManus.

Mahomed, Mahommed *see* Mohammed

Mai *see* May

Maia *see* Maya

Mair, Maire *see* Mary, Moira

Mairead *see* Margaret

Mairi *see* Mary

Mairin *see* Maureen

Maisie *see* Margaret

Makayla *see* Michael

Malcolm *m.*

From the Gaelic *mael Colum*, 'follower of St Columba'.

This was a very popular Scottish name, borne by four kings of Scotland. It was used very occasionally in medieval England, but only became common in the 20th century. Short forms are **Mal** and **Col(u)m** (see **CALLUM**).

Malik *m.*

From the Arabic for 'king'. The black activist and leader of the Nation of Islam, otherwise known as Malcolm X, took the name El-Hajj Malik El-Shabazz, which has led to the use of this name in the USA.

Mallory *f.*

This name has a pleasant sound, but a less pleasant meaning: as a surname it derives from the French and means 'ill-omened' or 'unfortunate'. It was nevertheless well used by American parents in the 1990s, having been launched in its first-name role by a character in the TV series *Family Ties*

Malvina *f.*

A name invented by the Scottish poet, James Macpherson (1736–96). He may have taken it from the Gaelic meaning 'smooth brow'. The form **Melvina** is also found.

Manish *m.,* Manisha *f.*

An Indian name which refers to the Sanskrit for 'intellect' or 'intelligence'.

Manju *f.*

An Indian name derived from the Sanskrit for 'beautiful'. Similar names are **Manjubala** and **Manjulika**, both meaning 'beautiful girl'.

Mamie *see* **Mary**

Mandy *see* **Amanda**

Manny *see* **Emanuel**

Manon *see* **Mary**

Manuel *see* **Emanuel**

Manus *see* **Magnus**

Maol Mhuire *see* **Miles**

Marc, Marcel *see* **Marcus**

Marcia *f.*

The feminine form of the Latin Marcius, a Roman clan name which probably was derived from Mars, the god of war. St Marcia was an early Christian martyr. The name can be pronounced with either three syllables, or with two, reflected in the alternative spelling **Marsha**. **Marcy** is used as a short form. **Marcella**, **Marcelle**, **Marcelline** and **Marcine** are all developments of the name.

Marcus *see* **Mark**

Marcy see **Marcia**

Maredudd see **Meredith**

Margaret f.

From the Latin *margarita*, derived from the Greek word meaning 'a pearl'. However, the ultimate origin is said to be Persian for 'child of light', the ancients believing that pearls were formed when oysters rose from their beds at night to look at the moon, and trapped a drop of dew in their shells which was then transformed into a pearl by the moonbeams. The name first appears in Scotland in the 11th century, thanks to St Margaret, wife of Malcolm III. She was born in Hungary where the name had spread through respect for St Margaret of Antioch, a 3rd-century martyr. The name became very common in medieval England and, after a decline, regained popularity in the 19th century. The most common pet forms are **Maggie**, **Madge**, **Meg** and **Peg(gy)**. **Maisie** was a particularly Scottish variant, and **MEGAN**, Welsh. The Irish form is **Mairead** ('mar-ed'). Other diminutives sometimes used are the Swedish **GRETA**, French **Margot** (now also spelt **Margaux**) and **Marguerite**, and **RITA**, from **Margarita**, which is also the source of the Scandinavian pet form **Meta**. Other forms include **Marghanita**, **Margaretta** and **Margoletta** (see also **DAISY**, **MARGERY**, **MAY**, **PEARL**).

Margery, Marjorie *f.*

Margerie was originally a pet form of the French **Marguerite** (see **Margaret**), but it became established in England as early as the 12th century. Marjorie is the spelling in Scotland, where the name was popular from the late 13th century after Robert the Bruce gave it to his daughter, founder of the **Stewart** or STUART dynasty through her marriage to Walter the Steward. **Marge** and **Margie** are pet forms.

Marghanita, Margot, Margoletta, Marguerite *see* Margaret, Margery

Mari, Maria(h) *see* Mary

Mariam, Mariamne *see* Miriam

Marian *f.*

Marian or **Marion** was originally a pet form of the French **Marie** (see MARY), which was early established as an independent name and was common on both sides of the Channel in medieval times. Marian was later extended to **Marianne**, giving rise to the double name **Mary Anne** in the 18th century. **Marianna** is the Spanish equivalent, which is sometimes given in England. In the USA **Marion** is occasionally found as a boy's name, as in the case of Marion Morrison, the real name of actor John Wayne (1907–79). In such cases it uses the surname Marion as a first name, possibly influenced by Francis Marion who played an important part in the American War of Independence.

Marie, Mariel(la), Marielle, Marietta, Mariette *see* Mary

Marigold *f.*

This name, borrowed from the flower, was adopted with others in the late 19th century, but has never been common.

Marilyn *f.*

This diminutive of **MARY** is now used independently. Its popularity was heightened by the film actress, Marilyn Monroe (1926–62).

Marina *f.*

From the Latin *marinus*, meaning 'of the sea'. The name has been used occasionally from at least the 14th century, probably on account of St Marina of Alexandria, a martyr of the Greek church. The name became more popular in Britain in 1934, when Prince George married Princess Marina of Greece, who later became Duchess of Kent.

Marisa, Marise, Marisol, Marissa *see* Mary

Marius *m.*

From a Roman family name which was adopted as a first name during the Renaissance. It has never been common in this country, although the Spanish and

Italian form **Mario** is well used on the Continent and in the USA. The name is probably derived from Mars, the Roman god of war and so related to **MARK**.

Marjorie *see* **Margery**

Mark, Marcus *m.*

These names are probably derived from Mars, the Roman god of war, and were used as Roman family and personal names. Although it occurs from the Middle Ages in Britain, Mark, the modern form of the name, has only become common since the 1950s. The French forms **Marc** and **Marcel**, the latter derived from the Latin diminutive of the name, Marcellus, are also used in Britain today.

Marlene *f.*

This is a German shortening of Mary Magdalene (see **MADELEINE**). It was introduced to English speakers by the song *Lili Marlene* and by the actress Marlene Dietrich (1901–92). **Marlena** is a form which reflects the German pronunciation of the name, but a two syllable pronunciation, the second half of the name sounded as in the word 'lean' as opposed to the German 'lane', is common in this country (see also **ARLENE**). A shortening, **Marlee** (**Marley**) is also used.

Marlon *f. and m.*

A name of unknown origin, brought into use

through the fame of the actor, Marlon Brando (b. 1924). **Marlin** and **Marlo** have also been used for both sexes in the United States, while **Marlen** for girls seems to be half way between this and MARLENE.

Marmaduke *m.*

From the Irish *mael Maedoc*, meaning 'servant of MADOC'. The name is mainly confined to Yorkshire, where Celtic civilisation lingered after the Norse invasions of northern England. **Duke** is sometimes used as an abbreviation, but in America its use usually derives from the title.

Marsha *see* Marcia

Martha *f.*

From the Aramaic, meaning 'lady'. In the New Testament Martha was the sister of Mary and Lazarus. The name was common in France in the Middle Ages where there was a legend that Martha had come to France after the Crucifixion. It was not adopted in Britain until after the Reformation. Variants include **Marta** and **Martella**. **Martie** is the commonest pet form.

Martin *m.*, Martina *f.*

From the Latin Martinus, a diminutive of Martius meaning 'of Mars', the Roman god of war. According to popular legend, St Martin was a 4th-century soldier who cut his cloak in half to share it with a beggar one winter's night; he later became Bishop of Tours in France. Martin has been used more or less without a break since the 12th century. **Martyn** is the Welsh spelling, and **Marty** a short form. **Martina** and **Martita** are the female forms of the name. **Martinella** and the French feminine **Martine** are also found for girls.

Marvin *see* Mervyn

Mary *f.*

A biblical name, traditionally meaning 'dew of the sea', but possibly going back to an ancient Egyptian name. The earliest form of the name was MIRIAM which later translations of the Bible changed to **Mariam** and **Maria** (now also spelt **Mariah** and pronounced with a long 'i' sound), and finally Mary. Out of respect for the Virgin Mary, the name was held to be too sacred for general use until about the 12th century when the French form, **Marie**, and the diminutive, MARIAN, were common. The Scots kept the French Marie and used the Gaelic **Mairi** and **Mhairi** or **Mhari**. **Maire** is the Irish form, and **Mair** or **Mari** the Welsh. The latinised Maria was adopted in the 18th century, giving a pet form of **Ria**. **Marise** and **Maris(s)a** are Continental forms of the name. Other elaborations are **Mariel(le)**, **Marietta**, **Mariette**, and **Mariella**. Pet forms of Mary are **Molly**, currently a popular choice, **Polly**, **Mimi**,

Mamie and **MAY**, with **Manon** a French pet form (see also **MARIAN**, **MARILYN**, **MAUREEN**, **MAYA**, **MIA**, **MIRIAM**, **MOIRA**). A recent trend has been to adopt the Continental habit of linking Marie with another name, to produce names such as **Marie-Rose** and **Marie-Louise**. One such combination **Marisol**, combining Mary with the Spanish name **Sol**, 'sun', is particularly popular with Spanish speakers.

Maryann, Maryanne, Mary Anne *see* Marian

Mason *m.*

The surname, which comes from the occupation, used as a first name.

Matilda *f.*

From the Old German meaning 'mighty in battle'. This name was particularly popular in medieval court circles, introduced by William the Conqueror's wife who bore the name. Later, their granddaughter, sometimes known as **MAUD**, fought her cousin Stephen for the throne. The name fell into disuse but returned to favour in the 18th century. **Matty**, **Tilda** and **Tilly** are pet forms. Although by no means common, there has been a recent increase in the use of this name.

Matthew *m.*

From the Hebrew meaning 'gift of God', and the name of one of the Evangelists. The name was particularly popular from the 12th to the 14th centuries. After the Reformation the Greek form, **Matthias**, was adopted. In the Bible it is used for the name of the apostle chosen to succeed Judas Iscariot. Today the English form is popular, and the usual short form is **Matt**.

Matty *see* Matilda

Maud *f.*

The Old French form of the name **MATILDA**. This name was popular in Britain after the Norman Conquest, but fell out of use about the 15th century. It was revived in the 19th century by Tennyson's well-known poem *Maud* (1855). It is also spelt **Maude**, and **Maudie** is sometimes used as a pet form.

Maura *see* Moira

Maureen *f.*

A phonetic form of the Irish **Mairin**, meaning 'little **MARY**'. The variant forms in Britain are **Moreen** and **MOIRA**. The Irish also have a name **Mor** meaning 'tall', with a pet form **Moirin**, which can be anglicised as **Moreen**.

Maurice, Morris *m.*

From the Latin *Mauritius*, meaning 'a Moor'. The spread of the name was due to St Maurice, a 3rd-century martyr in Switzerland, after whom the town of St Moritz was named. The Normans brought the name to England as Meurisse, which was soon anglicised to Morris. The more modern French form, Maurice, has now to a large extent replaced the English form, although it is usually pronounced the same way in the UK: in the USA it is often pronounced in the French manner. There is a Welsh equivalent, **Meurig**, which occurs from the 5th century. Short forms are **Morrie** and **Maurie**.

Mave *see* Maeve

Mavis *f.*

From the old word for song thrush. It was first used by Marie Corelli in her novel *The Sorrows of Satan* (1895).

Max *see* Maximilian, Maxwell

Maximilian *m.*

Maximus in Latin means 'greatest'. Two 3rd-century saints bore its derivative, Maximilian, yet it is popularly thought to have been invented by German Emperor Frederick III, combining the last names of Quintus Fabius Maximus and Scipio Aemilianus, two Roman generals. His son, later Emperor Maximilian I, was a huntsman and fighter, and the name became very popular in German-speaking countries. It has recently become more popular in this country, particularly in its short form, **Max**. **Macsen** is the Welsh form of Maximus. **Maxime** is used in France for both sexes, but in Britain this, or **Maxine**, tends to be used for girls, keeping **Maxim**, also a Russian form of the name, for boys. Max can also be a short form of **Maxwell**, from a Scottish surname and place name meaning 'Mac's well'.

May *f.*

This was originally a pet form of **MABEL**, **MARGARET** or **MARY** but it has more recently been associated with the month, and it is now a separate name. Variants are **Mae**, as in the actress Mae West (1892–1980), and **Mai** (see also **AVRIL/JUNE**). Forms such as **Mayra** fall somewhere between May and Maria (see **MARY**).

Maya *f.*

In India this name derives from a Sanskrit word meaning 'illusion', an important word in Hindu philosophy. In America the author Maya Angelou has made the name famous. In her case it is a nickname, derived from her brother's way of pronouncing 'my sister'. The name can also be interpreted as a pet form of Maria (see **MARY**). It is also found as **Maia**.

Maybelle, Maybelline *see* Mabel

Mckenzie, Mckenna *see* Mackenzie

Meadhbh, Meave, Meaveen *see* Maeve

Meena *f.*

From the Sanskrit for 'fish, Pisces', this is the name of a Hindu goddess.

Meera *f.*

A Hindi name which means 'saintly woman'.

Megan *f.*

Megan started life as a Welsh pet form of **Meg**, itself a pet form of **MARGARET**. It is currently very popular throughout the English-speaking world. In Australia, Canada and the USA it is quite often spelt as **Meghan**, as if it were an Irish name, and Americans also use forms such as **Maegan** and **Maygen**.

Mehul *f.*

This Hindi name refers to 'rain-clouds'. It is also found as **Mehal**.

Mel *see* Melvin

Melanie *f.*

From the Greek for 'black' or 'dark-skinned'. Melania is an ancient name used by both the Greeks and the Romans. It came to England from France in the mid-17th century in its French form, Melanie, which also became **Melony** or **Mel(l)oney** and **Melany** in Britain. It is shortened to **Mel**.

Melicent, Melisenda, Melisande, Melisent *see* Millicent

Melissa *f.*

From the Greek meaning 'a bee' and the name of a nymph in Greek mythology. It was used occasionally in the 18th century, and has been quite popular in recent years. Other names with the sense of 'bee' or 'honey' that are used are **Melinda,** sometimes shortened to **Mindy,** and **Melita.**

Melloney, Meloney, Melony *see* Melanie

Melody *f.*

This vocabulary word has come into first-name use in recent years. Other names with musical associations that are sometimes used are **Harmony** and **Lyric.**

Melvin, Melvyn *m.*

Various theories have been put forward as the source of this name. It seems likely that it comes from a surname, which can come from a variety of sources, several of them Scottish. **Mel** is the short form.

Melvina *see* Malvina

Mercedes *see* Dolores

Mercy *f.*

This is the virtue used as a first name, in the same way as **HOPE**. The pet form is **Merry**, which is also used as an independent name.

Meredith *f. and m.*

From the surname from the ancient Welsh **Maredudd** or **Meredydd**, 'great chief'. It can be spelt **Meridith** and shares **Merry** as a short form with **MERCY**. Use of the name for girls was a 20th-century innovation.

Meriel *see* Muriel

Merle *f. and m.*

This is the French for 'blackbird' originally derived from Latin. It was adopted as a first name in the 19th century. It became well known as the name of the film actress, Merle Oberon (1911–79). As a boy's name its use is mainly restricted to the USA.

Merlene, Merlin, Merlyn *see* Mervyn

Merrill *see* Muriel

Merry *see* Mercy, Meredith

Mervyn *m.*

From the Welsh name **Myrddin** ('sea fort'), which is the true form of **Merlin**, the name of King Arthur's legendary magician. It is also spelt **Mervin**. Merlin has recently come to be used for girls, sometimes in the forms **Merlene** or **Merlyn**. **Marvin**, also a common surname, is probably a form of Mervyn, although some would dispute this.

Meryl *see* Muriel

Meta *see* Margaret

Meurig *see* Maurice

Mhairi, Mhari *see* Mary

Mia *f.*

A Scandinavian pet form of **MARY**, although some associate it with the Italian and Spanish word for 'my'. The actress Mia Farrow brought the name into more general use. **Mya(h)** is also found.

Michael *m.*, Michelle *f.*

From the Hebrew meaning 'who is like the Lord?' In the Bible Michael was one of the seven archangels and their leader in battle, and he therefore became the patron saint of soldiers. The variant form **Micah**, the name of a minor prophet in the Old Testament, was used in the 17th century among Puritans and can now be found used for both sexes, sometimes as **Mica** or **Myka**. Michael has pet forms **Mike**, **Mick** or **Micky**. The surname **Mitchell**, derived from Michael, is also used as a boy's name, with the short form **Mitch**. **Michelle** is the French female form of the name, also found as **Michele**, which can be shortened to **SHELLEY**. **Michaela** is another feminine form of the name currently popular in the USA, where it can take numerous exotic forms such as **Makayla** or **Mykala** (see also **KAYLA**). **Misha** or **Mischa** is in Russia a pet form of Michael, but because of the 'a' ending is sometimes thought of as a girl's name. Spanish forms are **Miguel** and **Miguela**.

Milan *m.*

In Europe this name usually derives from the Czech for 'grace'. As an Indian name the derivation is from a word meaning 'union'.

Mildred *f.*

The 7th-century King Merowald of the Old English kingdom of Mercia had three daughters: Milburga ('gentle defence'), Mildgyth ('gentle gift'), and Mildthryth ('gentle strength'). It was from the last of these that Mildred developed and the popularity of the three sisters, all of whom became saints, led to the name becoming common in the Middle Ages. It was revived in the 19th century.

Miles *m.*

An old name of unknown meaning. The Normans brought to Britain the forms Miles and **Milo**. It has also been used to transliterate the Irish **Maol Mhuire** ('devotee of Mary') and its Gaelic form **Mael Moire**. A variant spelling is **Myles**.

Millicent *f.*

From the Old German meaning 'strong worker'. This name was common in France about a thousand years ago, when it had the form **Melisenda**, now also **Melisande**. The French brought it to England in the late 12th century in the form **Melisent**, and it survived with minor changes of spelling such as **Melicent** well into the 17th century. In the 19th it was revived. **Millie** or **Milly** is a common abbreviation.

Millie, Milly *see* **Amelia, Camilla, Emily, Millicent**

Milo *see* **Miles**

Milton *m.*

From the Old English surname derived from a place name meaning 'mill-enclosure'. Initial use as a first name may have been due to the poet, John Milton (1608–74). It has been particularly popular in the US.

Mima *see* **Jemima**

Mimi *see* **Mary**

Mindy *see* **Melissa**

Minerva *see* **Athene**

Minna, Minnie *see* **William**

Minta, Minty *see* **Araminta**

Mira *see* **Myra**

Miranda *f.*

From the Latin meaning 'deserving admiration'. This name was coined by Shakespeare for the heroine of *The Tempest* (1612), a young woman blessed with many admirable qualities. Like other Shakespearian names it came into use in the 20th century. **Mirabel** (**Mirabelle**, **Mirabella**) from Latin 'admirable, wonderful' is related.

Miriam *f.*

This is the old form of **MARY**, and in the book of Exodus in the Old Testament it was the name of the sister of **MOSES** and **AARON**. It is traditionally interpreted as meaning 'dew of the sea', but possibly, like Miriam's brothers' names, goes back to ancient Egyptian sources. It first became common in Britain in the 17th century. **Mariam** and **Mariamne** are variant forms which have recently gained popularity. **Mitzi** can be a short form of Miriam or **Maria**.

Mischa, Misha, Mitch, Mitchell *see* **Michael**

Mitzi *see* **Miriam**

Mohammed *m.*

The name of the Prophet of Islam, which comes from the word 'praise'. It is probably the most popular Islamic name, the only one to enter the top 50 boy's names in the UK, and is spelt in various ways, **Muham(m)ad**, **Mahom(m)ed** and **Moham(m)ad** being the common variants.

Mohan *m.*, Mohana *f.*

In early times a name of **KRISHNA'S**; from the Sanskrit for 'attractive', bewitching.

Moira, Moyra *f.*

Moira or **Maura** is an English phonetic spelling of **Maire**, the Irish form of **MARY**. **MAUREEN** has the same origin, but has developed as a separate name, though Moira is occasionally used as its short form.

Moirin *see* Maureen

Molly *see* Mary

Mona *f.*

This name is derived from a diminutive of the Irish **Muadhnait** ('mooa-nid'), meaning 'noble, good'. It came into use in the late 19th century along with other Irish names which spread throughout Britain at that time, during a general revival of interest in Celtic culture. It can also be a short form of **MONICA**.

Monica *f.*

The etymology of this name is uncertain, but it could be connected with Greek *monos* meaning

'alone' or Latin *monere* meaning 'to advise'.
St Monica was the mother of St Augustine and was
a paragon of motherly virtues. **MONA** is sometimes
used as a short form, and there are French and
Scandinavian forms, **Monique** and **Monika**.

Montagu(e), Montgomery *m.*

Founder of the ancient noble family of Montague
was Drogo de Montacute, William the Conqueror's
companion who received estates in Somerset.
He took his name from Mont Aigu, a 'pointed hill'
in Normandy. Montagu(e)'s first-name use dates
from the 19th century, when many aristocratic
surnames, e.g. **CECIL**, **HOWARD**, **DUDLEY**,
MORTIMER, **PERCY**, were adopted by the public.
It shares **Monty** as a short form with **Montgomery**,
from the Old French meaning 'mountain of the
powerful one'.

Montserrat *see* Dolores

Montana *f.*

The name of the mountainous American state is
starting to appear as a first name, sometimes spelt
Montanna.

Moosa *see* Moses

Morag *f.*

A Scottish name from the Gaelic and Irish name
Mor meaning 'great' or 'tall'. (see also **MAUREEN**).

Moray *see* **Murray**

Moreen *see* **Maureen**

Morgan *f. and m.*

In its earliest form, **Morcant**, this name meant 'sea-bright' (see **MURIEL**), but it later absorbed another name, **Morien**, meaning 'sea-born'. Its earliest celebrated male bearer was the first recorded British heretic, who was known as Pelagius, a Greek translation of the name. It was almost always a male name until the 20th century, but now is more common for girls. The most famous female precedent for the name was Morgan(a) le Fay, King Arthur's wicked half-sister.

Morna, Myrna *f.*

Both these names come from the Gaelic name **Muirne**, which means either 'gentle', the traditional interpretation, or possibly 'high-spirited'.

Morrie, Morris *see* **Maurice**

Mortimer *m.*

An aristocratic surname adopted as a first name in the 19th century. The surname was derived from a French place name meaning 'dead sea'. The Mortimer family connect it with the Dead Sea in Palestine, where their ancestors fought in crusading times. The pet form **Morty** was also used

independently in Ireland as a form of the Irish
name **Murtaugh** or **Murty** ('skilled sailor').
The short form **Mort** is also used.

Morwenna *f.*

Morwenna comes from Welsh and probably means
'maiden'. There was a 5th-century saint of this name
about whom little is known, and the name used to
be confined to Wales and Cornwall but now seems
to be spreading. It is also found as **Morwen**.

Moses *m.*

The meaning of this name is uncertain and it is
possibly Egyptian rather than Hebrew. It became
common among Jews after their return from
captivity in Babylon. In Britain it first appears in the
Domesday Book as Moyses, which became Moyse
or **Moss** in general use. The present form, Moses,
which was not used until the Reformation, is the
form used in the Authorised Version of the Bible.
Moosa or **Musa** is the Arabic form of the name.

Moyra *see* **Moira**

Muadhnait *see* **Mona**

Muhammad *see* **Mohammed**

Muhsin *m.,* Muhsina *f.*

A popular name in the Arab world, derived from an
Arabic word meaning 'charitable' or 'benevolent'.

Muirne *see* **Morna**

Muneer *see* **Munir**

Mungo *m.*

This name was originally a term of affection given to St **Kentigern** by his followers, and in Gaelic means 'beloved'. Kentigern was a 6th-century Bishop of Glasgow and is generally known as St Mungo. The name is confined to Scotland and the most famous bearer was Mungo Park, the 18th-century explorer of the River Niger.

Munir *m.*, Munira *f.*

From the Arabic for 'brilliant' or 'illuminating'. The name has the alternative male form **Muneer**.

Murali *f.*

From the Sanskrit word for 'flute'. The reference is to the young Krishna, who played the flute to attract female cowherds to his side.

Murdo, Murdoch *m.*

This Scottish name is derived from the Gaelic meaning 'seaman', and is equivalent to the Irish **Murtaugh** (see **MORTIMER**).

Muriel, Meriel *f.*

A Celtic name meaning 'sea-bright'. It came to England at the time of the Norman Conquest, via the many Celts who had settled in Brittany and Normandy in earlier centuries. Both forms were in common use until the mid-14th century. Muriel was revived in the 19th century and Meriel came back into use at the beginning of the 20th century. Other forms such as **Meryl** and **Merrill** have appeared more recently.

Murray *m.*

From the Gaelic meaning 'sea'. The Scottish clan of Murray, or Moray, probably took its name from the Moray Firth in the northeast of Scotland. James Stewart, Earl of Moray, was half-brother of Mary, Queen of Scots, and he acted as Regent when she was imprisoned in Lochleven Castle. His fame gave rise to the use of **Moray** as a first name in Scotland, but today the form Murray is more common, with **Murry** a variant.

Murtaugh, Murty *see* Mortimer

Musa *see* Moses

Mustafa *m.*

From the Arabic meaning 'chosen'. It is one of the names used to describe the Prophet Muhammad.

Mya(h) *see* Mia

Myca, Mykala *see* Michael

Myfanwy *f.*

A well-known Welsh name meaning 'my fine one'. The commonest short forms in Wales are **Fanny** and **Myfi**.

Myles *see* **Miles**

Myra *f.*

This name appears to have been invented in the 16th century by Fulke Greville, Lord Brooke, for the heroine of his love poems, and until the 19th century it was used exclusively by poets and novelists. He may have wanted to echo the sound of 'admired'. The variant form **Mira** is found but this can also be a short form of **Mirabel**, 'admirable', or **MIRANDA**.

Myrddin *see* **Mervyn**

Myrna *see* **Morna**

Myron *m.*

The Greek word for 'fragrant'. It was the name of a famous sculptor in the 5th-century BC.

Myrtle *f.*

One of the flower names which has been used as a name since the 19th century. The name is Greek, and in Ancient Greece the myrtle was a symbol of victory, while in the last century, myrtle was a traditional element in a bride's bouquet. The variant form **Myrtill(a)** is also found occasionally.

Nadim *m.*

This Arabic name refers to a 'drinking companion' or 'friend'. It is also spelt **Nadeem**.

Nadine *f.*

A French name, derived from the Russian for 'hope'. Variants are **Nada** and **Nadia**.

Nafisa(h) *f.*, Nafis *m.*

From the Arabic for 'precious, delicate'. It is more commonly used for girls and has other spellings, such as **Nafeesa**.

Naim *m.*, Naima *f.*

From the Arabic word meaning 'comfortable', 'contented' or 'tranquil'. Some families prefer to spell the names **Naeem** and **Naeema**.

Nan *see* **Anne**

Nancy *f.*

This was originally a pet form of **ANNE**, but has long been established as a name in its own right. **Nancie** is occasionally found, and **Nanette** and **Nana** are French forms.

Nandy *see* **Ferdinand**

Nanette, Nanny *see* **Anne, Nancy**

Naomi *f.*

From the Hebrew meaning 'pleasant'. In the Old Testament Naomi was the mother-in-law of Ruth, and loved her daughter-in-law so much that when their menfolk died, she left her home to travel back to Israel with Ruth. The name was adopted by the Puritans in the 17th century and has recently increased in popularity.

Nastasia *see* **Anastasia**

Nat *see* **Nathan, Nathaniel**

Natalie, Natasha *f.*

These names come from the Latin *natale domini*, meaning 'the birthday of the Lord', and were originally restricted to children born around Christmas. Natalie comes from Russia where it is spelt **Natalya**, and has the pet form Natasha, both popular choices in recent years. Natasha is sometimes spelt **Natacha** or **Natasja**, and can have the short form **Tasha**. **Natalia** or Natalie can be shortened to **Talia**, **Talya** or **Tally**.

Nathan, Nathaniel *m.*

Nathan comes from the Hebrew meaning 'gift'. It was the name of the prophet in the Old Testament who condemned King David for killing Uriah by putting him in the front line of battle, so that David could marry his widow, **BATHSHEBA**. The name shares the short form **Nat** with **Nathaniel**, meaning 'gift of God'. It was the name of the apostle who was better known by his second name, **BARTHOLOMEW**. Both names are increasingly popular.

Nayan *m.,* Nayana *f.*

An Indian name derived from the Sanskrit for 'eye'. The feminine form refers to a girl with lovely eyes.

Neal, Neil *see* Nigel

Neelofar *see* Niloufer

Ned, Neddy *see* Edward

Neha *f.*

This Indian name comes from the Sanskrit for 'rain'.

Neirin *see* Aneurin

Nell, Nelly *f.*

These are pet forms of **HELEN** and **ELEANOR**. They were already in use in Britain in the Middle Ages. A famous holder of the name was Nell (Eleanor) Gwyn, the mistress of Charles II.

Nelson *see* Nigel

Nerissa *f.*

This is one of the less common names taken from
Shakespeare, in this case **PORTIA**'s witty maid
from *The Merchant of Venice*. It is not clear what
Shakespeare meant by the name, but he may have
taken it from *nereis*, the Greek word for a sea-nymph.

Nerys *f.*

An unusual Welsh name, meaning 'lady', which has
become widely known through the actress, Nerys
Hughes.

Nessa, Nessie, Nest, Nesta *see* Agnes

Net, Netta, Nettie *see* Anthony, Janet

Neville *m.*

From the French surname Neuville, meaning 'new
town'. It was introduced into England at the time
of the Norman Conquest, when the Neville family,
which came over with William the Conqueror, was
very powerful. Their influence continued, but the
name was not adopted as a first name until the 17th
century. **Nevil** is a variant spelling.

Nia *see* Niamh

Niall *see* Nigel

Niamh *f.*

This name, pronounced 'nee-av' or 'neev', is currently

very popular in Ireland. It means 'radiance, brightness' and was originally the name of a pagan goddess. In Irish legend Niamh was a fairy woman who fell in love with **OSSIAN** and carried him off to the magical Land of Promise. **Nia** is a pet form, but when used by Black Americans can also represent a Swahili word meaning 'intention, purpose'.

Nic *see* Dominic

Nicholas *m.*

From the Greek meaning 'victory of the people'. The name was common in the Middle Ages as a result of the popularity of St Nicholas, the patron saint of children and sailors. The usual form then was **Nicol**. In Latin the name is Nicholaus and the use of **Claus** in 'Santa Claus' is taken from **Klaus**, the modern German development of the Latin. **Nick(o)** and **Nicky** are the pet forms. (See also COLIN, NICOLA.)

Nicola, Nicole *f.*

Nicola is one of the Italian forms of **NICHOLAS**, others being Nocolo and Niccolo. The feminine Italian form is **Nicoletta**, but in Britain Nicola has wrongly been assumed to be feminine because of the '-a' ending. American and Australian parents have always used **Nicole**, the French feminine form of Nicholas. The names are also spelt **Nichola** and **Nichole**, and **Nicolette** is also used. **Nickie, Nikki** and **Nicci** are short forms shared with Nicholas (see also **COLETTE**).

Nigel, Niall, Neal, Neil *m.*

The origin of these names goes back to an Irish name, the meaning of which could be 'champion', 'cloud' or 'passionate'. Niall is the Irish spelling of the name, but it early on developed different spellings. When medieval scribes wanted to write the name in Latin documents they gave it the form *Nigellus*, as if it were a name which came from the Latin *niger* meaning 'black'; and when interest was strong in all things medieval in the 19th century, this Latin form was adopted as Nigel. Nigel has rare girls' forms, **Nigella** and **Nigelia**. **Nelson** is an old surname meaning 'Neal's son'.

Nikhil *m.*

An Indian name derived from the Sanskrit for 'entire', 'complete'.

Nikita *f. and m.*

Nikita was originally a Russian, masculine name, from the Greek meaning 'unconquered' and adopted by Russians in honour of a 2nd-century pope. However, in many languages it looks like a feminine name, and after its use for a woman in the successful 1990 French film *La Femme Nikita* and the subsequent American television series based on it, it has come to be used as a girl's name. Nikita or **Nikhita** is also an Indian name used for both sexes, from the Sanskrit for 'the earth'.

Nikki, Nicci, Nickie *see* Nicola

Niloufer *f.*

An Indian name which means 'celestial being'. It occurs in various spellings, such as **Neelofar**.

Nina *f.*

A pet form of various Russian names ending '-nina', which is now established in this country as a name in its own right.

Ninian *m.*

The name of a 5th-century saint who converted the Picts in the south of Scotland to Christianity. It is mainly found in Scotland.

Nisha *f.*

A Sanskrit name meaning 'night'. **Nishant** means 'dawn', the end of the night.

Nita *see* Joan

Noah *m.*

Despite the wide fame of Noah and his Ark, this Hebrew name meaning 'rest' has been rare in the past, but its use is now increasing.

Noel *f. and m.*

This is an old French name derived from the Latin *dies natalis*, meaning 'birthday'. The name refers to Christmas Day and was often given to children born then. **Nowell** is an English spelling which is also used and **Noelle** is an alternative girl's form. **Christmas** is also found occasionally as a first name. (See also **NATALIE**).

Nola *see* **Fenella**

Nona *see* **Anne**

Nora(h) *f.*

An Irish abbreviation of **HONORIA**, now used as a separate name. It is also found as a short form for **ELEANOR** and **LEONORA**. In Ireland the pet forms **Noreen** and **Nonie** are used.

Norma *f.*

Possibly from the Latin meaning 'rule' or 'precept'. The great success of Bellini's opera *Norma* (1831) brought the name into popular favour. It has been used as a feminine counterpart of **NORMAN**.

Norman *m.*

From the Old English for 'Northman', used first of all for the Vikings, and then for the descendants of the Viking settlers in France who were known as 'Normans'. It was popular in Scotland, and for a while was considered a purely Scottish name, being used as a substitute for the Gaelic **Tormod** ('protected by Thor'), itself originally a Viking name. **Norm** and **Norrie** are short forms.

Nuala *see* **Fenella**

Nye *see* **Aneurin**

Oberon see **Aubrey**

Octavia f., **Octavius** m.

A Roman family name derived from the Latin meaning 'eighth'. It was also used as a given name for an eighth child in the 19th century, but now that such large families are rare it is used without regard to its original sense. **Octavian** is an alternative masculine form. The short forms **Tavia**, **Tavian** and **Tavius** are sometimes used independently.

Odette, Odile see **Ottilie**

Odysseus see **Ulysses**

Oengus see **Angus**

Oisin see **Ossian**

Olaf see **Oliver**

Olga f.

From the Norse word *helga*, meaning 'holy'. The founder of the Russian monarchy is supposed to have been a Scandinavian traveller, and it was in

Russia that Olga evolved from the Scandinavian form, HELGA. St Olga was the wife of the Duke of Kiev in the 10th century, and she helped spread Christianity in Russia.

Oliver *m.*

In Old French legend Oliver was one of Charlemagne's greatest knights. Since these knights were of Frankish origin – that is to say of Germanic ancestry – their names are likely to be from Old German. Thus it is thought that this name goes back to the same source as the Scandinavian **Olaf** ('heir of his ancestors'). However, users probably associate it with the more obvious source of the olive tree, symbol of peace. Oliver was popular until the parliamentary revolt led by Oliver Cromwell in the 17th century, after which the name fell out of favour. It was revived in the 19th century and is now very popular. **Ol** and **Ollie** are short forms.

Olivia *f.*

The female form of **OLIVER**, but even more strongly associated with the Latin *oliva*, meaning 'olive'. St **Oliva** was venerated as the protectress of the olive crops in Italy. Olivia was first found in England in the early 13th century, was used by Shakespeare in *Twelfth Night*, and is currently very popular. **Olive** is a rarer form, although well known as the name of the cartoon character Olive Oyl, Popeye's girlfriend.

Olwen, Olwyn *f.*

From the Welsh, meaning 'white foot-print'.
The name first occurs in an old Welsh legend in
which Olwen, a giant's daughter, is wooed by a
prince, who has to get help from King Arthur to do
the tasks that are set him. She was named Olwen
because white clover sprang up wherever she trod.
The name became very popular in Wales and
spread to England in 1849 when a new translation
of the story was published.

Omar *m.*

A popular Muslim name from the Arabic for
'flourishing, long life'. It was the name of the
Prophet Muhammad's lifetime companion and
supporter. Another form of the name is **Umar**.
Omari, the Kiswahili form, is sometimes used by
Black American parents.

Oona, Oonagh *see* Una

Ophelia *f.*

From the Greek meaning 'help'. Its use is due to
Shakespeare's *Hamlet* (1601). In the play, Ophelia
is Hamlet's lover but goes mad after he murders her
father and abandons her, and is finally drowned.

Oprah *f.*

This name is well known through the talk show host
Oprah Winfrey, but perhaps because of this close

association with one person, it has not yet come into general use in either the USA or Britain. Oprah Winfrey has explained that her parents intended to call her **Orpah**, a biblical place name which possibly means 'gazelle'. The registrar misspelt the name as Oprah, which her parents then preferred.

Oriel, Oriole *see* Aurelia

Orla *f.*

An Irish name meaning 'golden princess'. It also occurs as **Orlagh** and in the Old Irish spelling **Orlaith**, and is currently popular in Ireland.

Orlando *m.*

This is the Italian form of **ROLAND**. Italian names were fashionable in the 16th century and Shakespeare used this one in his play *As You Like It* (1600). It has become rather more common recently.

Orville *m.*

A name invented by the 18th-century novelist, Fanny Burney, for the hero of her novel *Evelina*. It is fairly rare in Britain. A famous American example was Orville Wright, aviation pioneer and brother of **WILBUR**.

Osbert *m.*

From the Old English, meaning 'bright god'. It shares **Oz** and **Ozzy** as pet forms with **OSWALD**.

Oscar *m.*

In the 1760s James Macpherson gave this name to **OSSIAN**'s warrior son in his poems on the legendary past of Scotland, and Napoleon's enthusiasm for the Ossianic legend caused him to give the name Oscar to his godson, later King of Sweden. It became widespread on the Continent, and was regularly used in England and Ireland. The trial of Oscar Wilde in 1895 for homosexuality caused an abrupt fall in the name's popularity in Britain for many years, but it remained in use in the US, where it is found as **Oskar**, the Scandinavian spelling.
It probably means 'deer-lover'.

Osman *see* **Uthman**

Ossian *m.*

In legend Ossian ('little deer') is the son of **FINN** and father of **OSCAR**. It is spelt **Oisin** in Irish, while **Osheen** reflects the Irish pronunciation, although it is usually pronounced as it is spelt in England.
A female form **Ossia** also exists.

Oswald *m.*

From the Old English meaning 'god power'. Oswald, King of Northumbria in the 7th century, was killed fighting the Welsh at Oswestry. He was later canonised, and the place is said to take its name from him. A second St Oswald helped St **DUNSTAN** with his church reforms in the 10th century. Because of these two saints, the name was popular in the Middle Ages and has never entirely died out. **Oz** and **Ozzy** (**Ozzie**) are pet forms shared with **OSBERT**.

Ottilie *f.*

This is a modern form of **Ottilia**, which comes from the Old German meaning 'prosperity'. St Ottilie is the patron saint of Alsace. **Ottoline** is another form of the name, and the French **Odette** and **Odile** have also been used in Britain. The Continental male form, **Otto**, is less common in this country.

Owen, Owain *m.*

This is one of the most popular of all Welsh names, but its origin is uncertain. It may well have come from the Greek name **EUGENE** meaning 'well-born', or from Welsh *oen*, meaning 'lamb'. There are many bearers of the name in Welsh history and legend, but the best known is Owen Glendower, who fought for Welsh independence in the 15th century. The name has spread to the rest of Britain and to North America.

Oz, Ozzie, Ozzy *see* Osbert, Oswald

Paayal *see* **Payal**

Padma *f. and m.*

This Indian name, usually identified with the goddess Sri or Lakshmi, derives from a Sanskrit word meaning 'lotus'. Other forms are **Padmal**, **Padmini** and **Padmavati**. In some parts of India **Padma** and **Padman** are used as boys' names.

Paddy, Padraig *see* **Patrick**

Paige *f.*

The surname, originally given to someone who acted as a page, used as a first name. It has been popular for some time in the USA, and has recently become well used in the UK, probably because of the name's prominent use in several imported television series.

Paloma *f.*

This means 'dove', the symbol of peace. Its use by the artist, Pablo Picasso, for his daughter made the name more widely known.

Pamela *f.*

From the Greek meaning 'all honey'. This name dates from the late 16th century when it was coined by Sir Philip Sydney for his romance *Arcadia*. It did not come into general use until the publication of Samuel Richardson's novel *Pamela* (1740). It has been most used in the 20th century, and **Pam(mie)** is the usual pet form.

Pandora *f.*

In Greek legend Pandora ('all-giving') is a beautiful but foolish woman created by the gods to plague mankind. She opened the box that contained all the ills that afflict us. After their escape, only hope, which had been sealed up with them, was left to help mankind.

Paris *f. and m.*

This has been an increasingly popular choice in the USA for some years and is beginning to make headway in the UK. It is difficult to tell if parents choose it for the glamorous associations of the French capital, or for the Trojan prince who had to choose between three goddesses and was given the beautiful Helen of Troy as his reward, although the former seems the more likely.

Parvati *f.*

An Indian name, from the Sanskrit meaning 'of the mountain', a reference to the wife of **SHIVA**.

Pascal *m.*, Pascale *f.*

A French name meaning 'Easter', which has come into general use since the 1960s.

Patience *f.*

This name was fashionable in the 17th century when girls were named after abstract virtues and Sir Thomas Carew could call his four daughters Patience, Temperance, Silence and **PRUDENCE**.

Patricia *f.*

The feminine of Latin *patricius*, meaning 'nobleman'. It was originally only used in Latin records to distinguish a female bearer of the name **PATRICK** then used for both sexes, but it was used independently from the 18th century. It has become common only in the last hundred years, possibly encouraged by the popularity of Queen Victoria's granddaughter Princess Patricia of Connaught. Current abbreviations are **Pat**, **Patsy**, **Patti(e)**, **Patty** and **Tricia**.

Patrick *m.*

From the Latin *patricius*, meaning 'nobleman'. St Patrick adopted this name at his ordination. He was born in Britain in the late 4th century, captured by pirates when still a boy and sold as a slave in Ireland. Although he escaped, he wished to convert the Irish to Christianity, so after training as a missionary in France, he returned to devote his life to this cause. **Pat** and **Paddy** are short forms, and **Padraig** the Irish form.

Paul *m.*

From the Latin *paulus*, meaning 'small'. The New Testament tells how SAUL of Tarsus adopted this name after his conversion to Christianity. The name was not common until the 17th century. It was often coupled with the name PETER, as the saints Peter and Paul share the same feast day.

Paula, Paulina, Pauline *f.*

The female forms of **PAUL**. The 4th-century St Paula founded several convents in Bethlehem, and thus established the name in the Middle Ages. Paulina and Pauline or **Paulette** are respectively the Latin and French forms. **Polly** is sometimes used as a pet form.

Payal *f.*

An Indian name meaning 'anklet'. It is also spelt **Paayal**.

Pearl *f.*

This name first became common in the 19th century, with other gem names such as BERYL and RUBY. It has also been used as a pet name for MARGARET, which is derived from the Greek for 'pearl'.

Peg, Peggy *see* **Margaret**

Penelope *f.*

In Greek legend Penelope was the name of Odysseus's faithful and astute wife, who waited ten years for her husband to return from the Trojan Wars. The name has been used regularly since the 16th century. It is often abbreviated to **Pen** or **Penny**.

Percy, Percival *m.*

Percy is an English aristocratic family name, ultimately from a village in Normandy, which became popular in the 19th century, partly due to the fame of the Romantic poet Percy Bysshe Shelley (1792–1822). It is also a short form of Percival (**Perceval**), the name, in the medieval story, of one of King Arthur's knights, although as a surname it also comes from a village in Normandy. Both can be shortened to **Perce**; and Percival can become **Val**.

Perdita *f.*

This is from the Latin meaning 'lost'. It was coined by Shakespeare for the heroine of *A Winter's Tale*, who was lost at birth.

Peregrine *m.*

From the Latin *peregrinus*, meaning 'stranger' or 'traveller' and hence 'pilgrim'. There was a 7th-century saint of this name who was a hermit near

Modena in Italy. The name has been used in the UK since about the 13th century, but it has always been rather uncommon. **PERRY** is used as a short form.

Perry *m.*

This name sometimes occurs as an abbreviation of **PEREGRINE**, but it is also a surname used as a first name. It was the surname of two 19th-century American admirals, one of whom inflicted a defeat on the British while the other led the expedition that opened up Japan to the west. Their exploits probably encouraged the use of the name in the US. The singer Perry Como, who helped spread the popularity of the name, was born Pierino, a pet form of **PETER**.

Persephone *see* Corinna

Peter *m.*

From the Greek *petras*, meaning 'rock'. *Cephas* is the Aramaic equivalent which Jesus gave as a nickname to Simon bar Jonah, to symbolise steadfastness in faith. Peter was chief of the Apostles and became the first Bishop of Rome. He was a favourite saint of the medieval church and his name was very popular throughout Christendom. In England the name is first recorded in the Domesday Book in the Latin form, Petrus. The Normans brought over the French form, **Piers** (or **Pierce**), which was usual until the 14th century, when Peter became predominant, although Piers is now quite fashionable once again. The name was unpopular after the Reformation because of its association with the Papacy and did not return to fashion until 1904, when James Barrie's *Peter Pan* was published. A short form is **Pete**. **Peta**, **Petra** and **Petrina** are modern female forms of the name.

Petronella, Petronilla *f.*

These are derived from Petronius, a Roman family name. Petronilla, a 1st-century martyr, came to be connected with St **PETER**, and was even thought by some to be his daughter; because of this the name was popular in the Middle Ages and used as Peter's female equivalent.

Phebe *see* Phoebe

Phelim *see* Felix

Philip *m.*

From the Greek meaning 'lover of horses'. It was common in the Middle Ages on account of Philip the Apostle. However, in Elizabeth I's reign Philip of Spain was the arch enemy of England, and the name suffered accordingly. It was revived in the 19th century. **Phil** is now the most usual short form, although **Pip** and **Flip** are sometimes used. **Phillip** is a variant spelling reflecting the form usually found in surnames.

Philippa *f.*

This is the female form of **PHILIP**, but originally was only used to distinguish women (who shared the name Philip with males in the Middle Ages) in Latin records. Its use as a separate name dates from about the 19th century. Often abbreviated to **Pippa**, an Italian form, it can be found as **Phillippa** and **Philipa**. **Philippine** is a much rarer female form of Philip.

Phillis *see* *Phyllis*

Philomena *f.*

This name comes from the Greek for 'beloved'. It used to be a popular name in Ireland, but is now rather out of fashion. It was thought that there were two saints of this name, but when it was realised that the word Philomena on the inscription on their graves was an address to the reader and not their names the cult was suppressed; hence the name's fall from favour.

Phoebe *f.*

From the Greek meaning 'the shining one'. It is one of the titles given to the Roman moon goddess, **DIANA**. It occurs as a personal name in St Paul's Epistle to the Romans and, perhaps for this reason, was adopted after the Reformation, reaching its peak of popularity in the 17th century. It is currently enjoying another rise in popularity and sometimes spelt phonetically **Phebe**. It can be used as a pet form of **EUPHEMIA**.

Phyllis, Phillis *f.*

From the Greek meaning 'leafy'. In legend it was the name of a girl who died for love and was transformed into an almond tree. **Phyllida** is an alternative form which is sometimes found.

Pia *f.*

From the Latin meaning 'pious'. It was not used by English speakers until well into the 20th century.

Pierce, Piers *see* Peter

Pip *see* Philip

Pippa *see* Philippa

Polly *see* Mary, Paula

Pooja *f.,* Poojan *m. and f.*

This Hindi name, which can also be spelt **Puja** and **Pujan**, means 'worship'. **Poojit** (*m*) and **Poojita** (*f*), also found as **Pujit** and **Pujita**, mean worshipped.

Poonam *f.*

A Hindi name which refers to the 'full moon'. The spelling **Punam** is also used.

Poppy *f.*

The flower used as a name. It was particularly popular at the end of the 19th century and the beginning of the 20th.

Portia *f.*

Portia is an old Roman family name with the
unfortunate meaning of 'pig'. However, Portia,
wife of Brutus, became famous for her stoicism and
bravery, which probably inspired Shakespeare to
choose this name for the heroine of *The Merchant of
Venice*. This Portia is beautiful, rich, wise, witty and
charming, and it is thanks to her that the name has
come into use as a modern girl's name.

Pratik *m.*

A Hindi name which means 'a symbol'.

Priscilla *f.*

The Latin diminutive of *prisca*, meaning 'ancient'.
It was the name of a woman mentioned in the Acts
of the Apostles and as with other New Testament
names it was a favourite with the 17th-century
Puritans. It also appears as **Prisca** but this form is
very rare. **Pris** and **Prissy** are sometimes found as
short forms, but **Cilla** is the most used form.

Priya *m.*, Priyal *f.*

An Indian name from the Sanskrit for 'beloved'.
The girls' versions also include **Priyam**, **Priyanka**
and **Priyasha**.

Prudence *f.*

Prudence first appears as a name in Chaucer's
books, and it was one of the first abstract virtues to

be adopted by the Puritans. It is usually abbreviated to **Prue** or **Pru** (see also PATIENCE).

Prunella *f.*

Probably from the Latin *prunus*, meaning 'little plum'. It is also the name of a kind of silk and the Latin name for a wild flower, the self-heal, and a bird, the hedge sparrow or dunnock. The actress Prunella Scales has made the name more widely known. It shares short forms with PRUDENCE.

Puja, Pujan, Pujit, Pujita *see* Pooja

Punam *see* Poonam

Punit *m.,* Punita *f.*

A Hindi name which means 'pure'.

Qasim *m.*

The name of a son of the Prophet Muhammad, this comes from the Arabic and refers to a 'distributor', one who distributes food and money among the people.

Quanisha *see* **Kanisha**

Queenie *f.*

This name is sometimes given independently, but it is really a pet name for **Regina**, which is Latin for 'queen'. This name also appears as **Reina** in Spanish, **Regine** or **Reine** in French and **Raina** (**Raena**, **Rayna**) in Polish, all forms which are showing signs of increasing popularity in the USA. Regina was used from the Middle Ages, possibly with reference to the Virgin Mary, Queen of Heaven. Queenie was also used as a nickname for girls christened **VICTORIA** during Queen Victoria's long reign.

Quentin, Quintin *m.*

From the Latin for 'fifth', originally a name for a fifth son. Quentin was the French form which the

Normans introduced to England. It became obsolete after the Middle Ages except in Scotland, although it revived in the 19th century, possibly due to Walter Scott's historical romance *Quentin Durward* (1823). **Quinton** and **Quinten** are other forms of the name.

Quiana *see* Kiara

Quincy *m.*

A surname taken from a French place name. Its use in the US may have been due to the prominent New England family of that name in colonial times. John Quincy Adams (1767–1848), the 6th President, may have received his middle name in honour of this family or it may have been taken from Quincy, Massachusetts, where he was born. It can also be found as **Quincey**.

Quinn *m. and f.*

Quinn is an old Irish family name, literally meaning 'descendant of Conn' (see **CONOR**), but used to indicate 'chief, leader'. It has recently come into use for both sexes in the USA.

Rab, Rabbie *see* Robert

Rabiah *f.*

An Arabic name which means 'garden'.

Rachel *f.*

From the Hebrew for 'ewe', a symbol of gentleness and innocence. In the Book of Genesis, Rachel was 'beautiful and well-favoured', and **JACOB** laboured seven years to win her (Gen. XXIX, 20). In Britain the name was adopted after the Reformation and was very popular in the 17th and 19th centuries and is popular today. The usual pet forms today are **Rach**, **Rachie**, **Rae**, **Rai** and **Ray**, and it can be spelt **Rachael** or **Racchel(l)**. The actress **Raquel** Welch shows the Spanish form of the name. From Rachel have developed the forms **Rachelle** (sometimes pronounced with a 'sh' sound) and **Rochelle**, the French for 'little rock', a place name taken from Brittany to the US where the name has been popular. **SHELLEY** is a short form.

Radha *f.*, Radhakrishna *m.*

Radha is the name of the cowherd loved by Krishna. It derives from the Sanskrit for 'success'.

Another form of this Indian name is **Radhika**. Radhakrishna is a blend of this and **KRISHNA**, and is meant to symbolise the male and female nature of the supreme god. In southern India it appears as **Radhakrishnan**.

Rae, Rai *see* Rachel, Raymond

Raelene *see* Darlene

Rafael, Rafaella, Rafaelle *see* Raphael

Rafe *see* Ralph

Rahil *f.*

An Arabic form of **RACHEL**. It is also found as **Raheel** and **Raheela**.

Rahim *m.*, Rahima(h) *f.*

From the Arabic meaning 'merciful' and 'compassionate'. The fuller form of the male name is AbdurRahim 'servant of the Merciful', a reference to one of the attributes of Allah. The spellings **Raheem**, **Raheema** and **Raheemah** are also found.

Raina *see* Queenie

Raja *m.*

An Arabic name which means 'hope'.

Rajan *m.*

An Indian name derived from the Sanskrit word for 'king'. Similar names include **Rajesh** and **Rajendra**.

Rajani _f._

From the Sanskrit meaning 'the dark one' or 'night'. This is one of the names of the Hindu goddess **DURGA**.

Rajni _f._

An Indian name from the Sanskrit for 'queen', this name can also be a contracted form of **RAJANI**.

Rajnish _m._

This Indian name derives from the Sanskrit words meaning 'ruler of the night', the reference being to the moon. **Rajneesh** is a variant spelling of the name.

Ralph _m._

From the Old Norse words meaning 'counsel' and 'wolf'. In its earlier form, Radulf, this name was fairly common in England before the Norman Conquest, and it was reinforced by French use. The medieval spellings were **Ralf** and **Rauf** which were pronounced with the same vowel sound as the word 'ray'. **Rafe** was the common form in the 17th century and Ralph appears in the 18th century. The current usual pronunciation with a short 'a' and pronouncing the 'l' is 20th-century practice. **Raoul** is the French form of the name, and **Raul** the Spanish.

Rama *m.*

From the Sanskrit for 'pleasing'. As the seventh incarnation of Vishnu, Rama is widely worshipped in India. Rama's full name is **Ramachandra**, or **Ramachander** in southern India.

Ramona *see* Raymond

Ranald *see* Ronald

Randolph *m.*

From the Old English Randwulf, meaning 'shield wolf', which in the Middle Ages became **Ranulf** and **Randal(l)**. The short form, **Randy** (**Randi**), has been used as a name in its own right, particularly in the USA, where it can also be a short form of the girl's name, **Miranda**.

Raphael *m.*

This is the name of an archangel, meaning 'God heals' in Hebrew. It is often found in the Spanish spelling **Rafael** in the USA. Use is currently increasing. Feminine forms are the Italian **Raphaelle** (**Rafaella**), and **Raphaelle** (**Rafaelle**).

Raqib *m.*

A Muslim name from an Arabic word meaning 'guardian' or 'supervisor', especially in religious matters.

Raquel *see* Rachel

Rashad *m.*

This Arabic name means 'integrity' or 'maturity'.

Rauf, Raul, Raoul *see* Ralph

Raven *f. and m.*

The name of this large, sleek, black bird has been intensely used by Afro-American parents since 1989, when an actress of that name appeared in TV's *The Cosby Show*. Other bird names such as **Finch**, **Lark** and **Swan** have occasionally been used in the past. **MAVIS**, a poetical name for the song thrush, enjoyed a spell of popularity, and **Robin** has long been in use. **JAY** can also be interpreted as a bird name.

Ravi *m.*

The Indian name of the sun god, from the Sanskrit for 'sun'. **Ravindra** is another boy's name based on the same word.

Ray *see* Rachel, Raymond

Raymond *m.*

From the Old German meaning 'counsel protection'. The Normans brought the name to Britain and it was particularly popular in crusading times. Two 13th-century saints bore the name. One of them spent much of his life rescuing Spaniards captured by the Moors. **Redmond** or

Redmund is a form of the name which developed in Ireland. The short form, **Ray**, is sometimes given independently. There is a feminine form **Raymonde** which also has the short forms **Ray**, **Rai** and **Rae**. The Spanish female form is **Ramona**.

Rayna *see* Queenie

Razina *f.*
A Muslim name from the Arabic for 'contented'.

Reagan *see* Ryan

Reanna, Reanne *see* Rhiannon

Rebecca *f.*
In the Old Testament **Rebekah** (the name's Hebrew form) was the wife of **ISAAC** and was famous for her beauty. It was a favourite name among Puritans, who took it to North America. It is occasionally spelt **Rebekka** and is currently very popular. **Becky** is the short form.

Redmond, Redmund *see* Raymond

Reece, Reese *see* Rhys

Regina, Regine *see* Gina, Queenie

Reginald *m.*
From the Old English Regenweald, meaning 'power force'. It was not a common Anglo-Saxon name but

was reinforced at the time of the Norman Conquest by the French equivalent **Reinald** or **Reynaud**, and developed into **Reynold** or **Reynard**. It can be abbreviated to **Reg**, **Reggie** or **Rex** (see also **Ronald**).

Reilley *see* Riley

Reina, Reine *see* Queenie

René, Renée *m. and f.*

These are the French boys' and girls' names derived from the Latin *renatus*, meaning 'reborn'. The Latin form was sometimes used by Puritans in the 17th century, and the French forms have been used in Britain in the 20th century. The Latin feminine form, **Renata**, is also used occasionally.

Renie *see* Irene

Reshma *f.*

An Indian name which means 'silken'.

Reuben *m.*

From the Hebrew meaning 'behold a son', it appears in the Bible as the name of a son of Jacob, the founder of one of the tribes of Israel. The form **Ruben** is also found.

Rex *m.*

This is the Latin for 'king' which has been used as a

first name only in recent times. It is also found as an abbreviation of **REGINALD**.

Reynard, Renaud, Reynold *see* Reginald

Rhiannon *f.*

The name of an important figure in medieval Welsh literature. There is evidence that she was originally a Celtic goddess connected with horses. The name means 'great queen, goddess' and is spreading outside Wales. The old form was **Riannon**, and a new form **Rhianna** (also **Reanna**) is also found. **Reanne**, **Rhian(n)e** and **Riann** are also used, although some forms shade into feminines of **RYAN**.

Rhoda *f.*

Derived from the Greek for 'rose', this is a New Testament name (see Acts X, 11-13) that was taken into use in the 17th century. It was popular in the early years of the 20th century.

Rhodri *see* Roderick

Rhona *see* Rowena

Rhonda *f.*

This is a simplified spelling of the Welsh place name, Rhondda, which has been used as a first name since the early part of this century.

Rhonwen *see* Rowena

Rhydderch see **Roderick**

Rhys *m. and f.*

An old Welsh name meaning 'rashness, ardour'. It has had many famous bearers, including a Prince Rhys who checked the Norman advance into Wales. The name's popularity increased rapidly in the mid 1990s, with the alternative spelling **Reece** overtaking Rhys itself. Currently use for girls is mainly restricted to the USA, usually spelt **Reese**.

Ria see **Mary**

Rian see **Ryan**

Riann, Riannon see **Rhiannon**

Richard *m.*

This name first appears in Anglo-Saxon as Ricehard meaning 'strong ruler', which was later developed into Ricard. It was the Normans who spread the present form of the name, the softer, French Richard. The short form **Dick** appears as early as the 13th century, and this is still very common, though **Rich(ie)**, **Dickie**, **Rick(ie)**, **Ricky** and **Dickon** have been used at various times. Female forms of the name include **Richelle**, **Richenda** and **Ricarda**.

Rick, Rickie, Ricky see **Derek, Eric, Richard**

Riley *m. and f.*
   Riley (**Rilley**, **Reilly**) is an Irish surname of unknown meaning, currently fashionable for both sexes in the USA and spreading to the UK. For girls it is also found as **Rylee** or even **Ryleigh**.

Rio *f. and m.*
   This is a recent addition to the store of names, its spread probably helped by a 1982 Duran Duran hit song. It comes from the Spanish word for 'river', and is also the short form of the glamorous Brazilian city of Rio de Janeiro. In the USA **River**, as in the late River Phoenix (1970–93), is more usual.

Riona *see* **Catriona**

Rishi *m.*
   An Indian name which means 'sage' or 'wise man'.

Rita *f.*
   This is an abbreviation of **Margarita** (see **MARGARET**). However, it is used much more often as a separate name, and some of its popularity in the 20th century may have been due to its use by the film star, Rita Hayworth (1918–87).

River *see* **Rio**

Robert *m.*
   This name is derived from the Old German meaning 'famous and bright'. Although there was

an equivalent Anglo-Saxon name, it was the French form which took hold in Britain after the Norman Conquest. King Robert the Bruce popularised the name in Scotland where it has the local short forms **Rab** and **Rabbie**. **Rob**, **Robbie**, **Bob**, **BOBBIE** or **Bobby** and **BERT** are used in England. **Robin** or **Robyn**, a French pet form of Robert, is now popular in its own right (see also **RUPERT**). **Roberta** and **Robina** are female forms, particularly used in Scotland. **BOBBIE** and **Robin** or **Robyn** are also used for girls.

Rocco *m.*

This is a name that has become fashionable since it was chosen by the singer Madonna for her son. It is the Italian form of the name of the 14th-century saint, patron of the sick from his work with plague victims, called St **Roch**. It has also been anglicised to **Rock**, a source of the name **Rocky**. It means 'rest'.

Rochelle *see* Rachel

Roderick *m.*

From the Old German meaning 'famous rule'. The Goths took the name to Spain where it became Rodrigo, and it was established there at least as early as the 8th century. In Britain the name is commonest in Scotland where it was first used to transliterate the Gaelic name, **Ruairi**. In Wales it is used as an English form of **Rhodri**, meaning

'crowned ruler' or **Rhydderch** ('reddish-brown').
Short forms are **Rod**, **Roddy** and **RORY**.

Ro(d)ge *see* Roger

Rodney *m.*

This means 'reed island', and was originally a
surname. It was not used as a first name until
Admiral George Rodney gave it heroic associations
in the 18th century. Short forms are **Rod** and **Roddy**.

Roger *m.*

Hrothgar, meaning 'famous spear', was an Anglo-
Saxon form of this name. It became famous as the
name of a legendary king, but it was the Normans
who gave us the present form, which was derived
from Old German. Roger was a favourite name in
the Middle Ages, but from the 16th to the 19th
centuries it was thought of as a peasant name and
consequently fell from esteem. The ancient short
form Hodge, once a type-name for a farm labourer,
has been replaced by **Ro(d)ge**.

Rohan *f. and m.*

This name comes from a Sanskrit word which can
mean either 'ascending' or 'medicine', although
some like to interpret the meaning as 'sandalwood'.
In Sri Lanka it is the name of a sacred mountain,
also known as Adam's Peak, which has on its
summit a mark like a footprint which features, with
different interpretations, in the legends of all three

of the island's great religions – Muslim, Hindu and Buddhist.

Roisin *see* Rose

Roland *m.*

From the Old German *Hrodland*, meaning 'famous land'. Roland was the most famous of Charlemagne's warriors, and the Normans brought the name to England. **Rowland**, is both the medieval spelling and the form of the surname which comes from this name. They are shortened to **Roly** or **Rowley**. **ORLANDO** is the Italian version of the name.

Rolf *m.*

From the Old German meaning 'famous wolf'. **Rollo** is a Latin form and Rollo the Ganger ('Walker') was a 9th-century Norwegian exile who, with his followers, founded the Norman race. Rolf developed in Normandy and came to Britain at the time of the Norman Conquest. It was soon absorbed into **RALPH**, but revived in the late 19th century.

Romey, Romy *see* Rosemary

Rona *see* Rowena

Ronak *m.*

This Indian name is from a Sanskrit word meaning 'radiance, embellishment'.

Ronald _m._

Ronald and **Ranald** are Scottish equivalents of
Reynald and **REGINALD**, but they are from the
Norse (Viking) not the Old English forms. Ranald is
still almost exclusively Scottish but Ronald is now
widespread. Short forms commonly used are **Ron**
and **Ronnie**.

Ronan _m._

An Irish and Scottish name meaning 'little seal',
borne by a number of early saints. **Ronat** is the
feminine form, although **R(h)ona** (see **ROWENA**) is
also used.

Rory, Rorie _m._

From the Irish and Gaelic **Ruairi**, meaning 'red-
haired'. The name became popular in Ireland due
to the fame of the 12th-century King Rory
O'Connor. It is also widely used in the Scottish
Highlands, and is sometimes found in England as
an abbreviation of **RODERICK**. It can also be spelt
Ruari and **Ruaridh**.

Rosa, Rosabel, Rosabella, Rosalba _see_ Rose

Rosalie _f._

From Latin _rosalia_, the name of a Roman festival
when garlands of roses were draped on tombs.
Its use as a first name is due to St **Rosalia**, a 12th-
century hermit, the patron saint of Palermo in
Sicily. Rosalie is the French form.

Rosalind *f.*

The origin of this name is the Old German Roslindis, either made from elements meaning 'horse' and 'serpent' or 'fame' and 'shield' – the experts disagree. When the Goths took it to Spain it was interpreted as *rosa* and *linda*, 'pretty rose', and it was with this meaning that it came to England in Elizabeth I's reign. It was used by Shakespeare for the heroine of *As You Like It* and in another form, **Rosaline**, in two other plays. Largely due to this literary association it has been popular ever since. It developed a number of different forms such as **Rosalyn**, **Rosalin**, **Rosalinda**, **Roslyn** and **Rosaleen**, which is used in Ireland as an alternative form of **Roisin** (see **ROSE**). A short form is **Roz**.

Rosamund, Rosamond *f.*

This comes from the Old German words meaning 'horse' and 'protection', but it has generally been associated with the Latin *rosa munda*, meaning 'pure rose' or *rosa mundi*, 'rose of the world'. The Normans brought the name to England. A short form is **Roz**.

Rose *f.*

This flower, the symbol of the Virgin Mary, has been the most popular of all flower names which are used as personal names. The Normans brought the name to England and it has been consistently popular, giving rise to many derivatives, like **Rosalba** ('white rose'), **Rosetta**, ('little rose'), and **Rosabel(la)** ('beautiful rose'), as well as **Rosina**, **Rosita** and the pet form **Rosie** or **Rosy**. **Rosa** is a Latin form which has been used occasionally since the 19th century. In Ireland **Roisin**, sometimes spelt **Rosheen** to reflect its pronunciation, is popular. It means 'little rose'. Rose is used as a short form of all the girls' names which begin with its sound.

Roseanne *f.*

This is one of the many developments of **ROSE**, here combined with **ANNE**. Variants include **Roseanna**, **Rosanna**, **Rosanne** and **Rosannah**, as in Rose + **HANNAH**.

Rosemary *f.*

This is generally considered to be a plant name, although it is sometimes analysed as a combination of **ROSE** and **MARY**. The plant name is derived from the Latin *ros marinus*, meaning 'dew of the sea' which describes the misty blue-green of its leaves. It can be spelt **Rosemarie**, and **Romy** or **Romey** and **Rosie** are short forms.

Rosetta, Rosheen, Rosina, Rosita *see* Rose

Roshan *m. and f.,* Roshni *f.*

A name from the Persian for 'shining' or 'famous',

used by both Muslims and Hindus in India. **Roxana** or **Roxan(n)e** is the English form of the name, usually interpreted by users as meaning 'dawn light'. It was the name of one of Alexander the Great's wives.

Rosie *see* Rose, Rosemary

Roslyn *see* Rosalind

Ross *m.*

From the Gaelic for 'of the peninsula', and the name of a Scottish clan. Its use as a first name has spread throughout the English-speaking world.

Rosy *see* Rose

Rowan *f. and m.*

From the Irish **Ruadhan**, meaning 'little red-(haired) one'. It was the name of an Irish saint. Once used exclusively for boys, it is now also found as a girl's name, in which case it can take the form **Rowanne**.

Rowena *f.*

Probably best thought of as a form of the Welsh **Rhonwen**, meaning 'fair (woman) slender as a lance'. Rowena was the daughter of the Saxon chief Hengist and her beauty bewitched the British king Vortigern, bringing about his downfall; she may have had a truly Saxon name, but her story is transmitted through Welsh-speaking British writers and seems to have taken on a Welsh form. Its modern use is due to Sir Walter Scott, who gave this name to the heroine of his novel *Ivanhoe* (1819). **Rowina** is another spelling. **Rhona** or **Rona** has been claimed as a short form of Rhonwen, although it is also the name of a Scottish island.

Rowland, Rowley *see* Roland

Roxana, Roxan(n)e *see* Roshan

Roy *m.*

From the Gaelic *ruadh*, meaning 'red'. A well-known example of the name is the famous Highlander Robert Macgregor, commonly known as Rob Roy because of his red hair, who was involved in the Jacobite Rising of 1715. Walter Scott's novel about him may have contributed to the name's popularity.

Roz *see* Rosalind, Rosamund

Ruadhan *see* Rowan

Ruairi, Ruari, Ruaridh *see* Roderick, Rory

Ruben *see* Reuben

Ruby *f.*

This is one of many jewel names introduced during

the 19th century. Other precious substances used as first names include **Diamond**, AMBER, BERYL and PEARL.

Rudolf, Rudolph *m.*

From the Old German Hrodulf, meaning 'famous wolf', the same name that gives us ROLF. Rudolf is the Modern German form of the name. The spread of this name was undoubtedly helped by the widespread adoration of Rudolf Valentino (1895–1926), the American film star. Another American, the singer **Rudy** Vallee (1901–86) made the pet form, found in Germany as **Rudi**, well known.

Rufus *m.*

This is a Latin word meaning 'red-haired'. William Rufus was the second son of William the Conqueror, and became King William II of England. It gained popularity as a given name during the 19th century.

Rupak *m.,* Rupli *f.*

An Indian name from a Sanskrit word meaning 'beautiful'. Other boys' names based on the same word are **Rupesh**, **Rupchand** ('as beautiful as the moon') and **Rupinder** ('of the greatest beauty'). Names for girls which have a basic meaning of 'beauty' include **Rupashi** and **Rupashri**.

Rupert *m.*

This name has the same origin as **ROBERT** and means 'bright fame'. In Germany it became Rupprecht, and Rupert is an English form of this. Prince Rupert of the Rhine was the nephew of Charles I, and a brilliant general. He came to England to support the Royalist cause during the Civil War, and was much admired for his dashing bravery. It was because of him that the English form of the name was coined and became popular.

Rupesh, Rupinder *see* Rupak

Russell *m.*

This is primarily a surname and is derived from the Old French *rousel*, which means 'little red (haired) one'. It was a surname which came into use as a first name along with other family names in the 19th century. **Rus(s)** and **Rusty** are pet forms.

Ruth *f.*

A biblical name which came into common use just after the Reformation on account of the Old Testament heroine who gave her name to the Book of Ruth. The name is also associated with the abstract noun, ruth, meaning 'sorrow' or 'pity'. **Ruthie** is a pet form.

Ryan *m.*

A common Irish surname perhaps meaning 'little

king', now used as a first name. Its spread was greatly helped by the success of the film star Ryan O'Neal (b. 1941). It is also found as **Rian**. It is now beginning to be used for girls, often in forms that are difficult to distinguish from developments of **RHIANNON**. As a surname its history is confused with that of **Regan** or **Reagan**, which, despite being the name of a deeply unpleasant character in Shakespeare's *King Lear*, is now being used in the USA as a girl's name, presumably inspired by President Ronald Reagan.

Rylee, Ryleigh, Ryley *see* Riley

Saagar *see* Sagar

Sabah *f.*

An Arabic name which means 'morning' or 'dawn'. The Lebanese singer of this name has made it well known in the Arab world. In India it is often **Saba**.

Sabina *f.*

A Latin name meaning 'a Sabine woman'. It has been used in Ireland for the Irish **Sadhbh**; **Sive** in its phonetic spelling, meaning 'sweet'. There is also a French form, **Sabine**.

Sabrina *f.*

This is a very ancient name, used for the River Severn before the Romans came and probably the name of the goddess of the river. The poet John Milton (1608–74) used it as the name of the nymph of the Severn in his masque *Comus*, and subsequent uses of it as a first name probably stem from this, although nowadays it is probably better known from the television series *Sabrina The Teenage Witch*.

Sacha *f. and m.*

A Russian short form of **ALEXANDER**. Although

originally a man's name, the 'a' ending has led to its use for girls. **Sasha** is an alternative form.

Sade *f.*

Made famous by the British-Nigerian singer, Sade is a pet form of the Yoruba name Falasade, meaning 'honour bestows a crown'. Phonetic spellings such as **Shardai** or **Sharday** are also found.

Sadhbh *see* Sabina

Sadie *see* Sarah

Sa'eed *m.*

Sa'eed or **Sa'id** is an Arabic name meaning 'happy, lucky'.

Saffron *f.*

The name of the golden-yellow crocus pollen used as a spice, which has come to be given as a first name in modern times.

Sagar *m.*

An Indian name from the Sanskrit meaning 'ocean'. The spelling **Saagar** is also used. **Sagarika** means 'wave' and is used for girls.

Sage *f. and m.*

This is one of the most recent plant names to come into fashion as a first name, its use boosted by several American entertainers choosing it for their children. The aromatic plant sage gets its name from the ancient reputation tea made from its leaves had for boosting memory and wisdom. The spelling **Saige** is occasionally used.

Sahil *m.*, Sahila *f.*

An Indian name from the Sanskrit for 'guide'.

Sajan *m.*

This Indian name comes from the Sanskrit for 'beloved'.

Sajjad *m.*

This Muslim name refers to one who 'prostrates' himself, or worships God. The name is sometimes spelt **Sajad** or **Sajid**.

Salah *m.*, Saliha(h) *f.*

A popular Muslim name from the Arabic for 'goodness, righteousness'. The boy's name is sometimes spelt **Saleh**.

Salima *f.*, Salman *m.*

An Arabic name which means 'safe' or 'unharmed'.

Sally *f.*

Originally a pet name for **SARAH**, but one that is nowadays used independently. It is shortened to **Sal**.

Salma *f.*

From an Arabic word meaning 'peaceful'. The word
for 'peace' is much used as a greeting in the Middle
East, as in the Arabic salaam or the Hebrew shalom.
The latter forms the basis of names like **SALOME**
and **SOLOMON**, both of which mean 'peaceful'.

Salome *f.*

The Greek form of an Aramaic name meaning
'peace'. In the New Testament Salome was one of
the women at Jesus' tomb on Easter Sunday.
However, it is better known from the story of the
Salome who danced the dance of the seven veils
and, at her mother's insistence, asked Herod for
John the Baptist's head as a reward.

Sam, Sammy *see* Samantha, Samuel

Samantha *f.*

Probably an 18th-century coinage, meant to be a
feminine version of **SAMUEL**. It first became popular
in the 1950s, when it appeared in the film *High
Society* and in the title song, *I Love You, Samantha,*
and is well used once again. It shares short forms
Sam and **Sammy** with **SAMUEL**.

Samimah *f.*

From the Arabic for 'true' or 'sincere'. The name is
also spelt **Sameema** and **Sameemah**.

Samir *m.*, Samira(h) *f.*

An Arabic name which means 'one whose conversation in the evening or at night is lively', thus an entertaining companion. The spellings **Sameer**, **Samara**, **Sameera** and **Sameerah** are also used.

Samuel *m.*

From the Hebrew meaning 'heard by God'. In the Old Testament the prophet Samuel was the leader of the Israelites who chose Saul and later David as their kings. In Scotland and Ireland it was for a long time used to transliterate the Gaelic **Somhairle**, a name anglicised as **Sorley**; this derives from the Old Norse term meaning 'summer wanderer', that is, 'Viking'. Currently a popular choice, Samuel shares short forms **Sam** and **Sammy** with SAMANTHA.

Sana *f.*

This Arabic name means 'resplendence' or 'brilliance'. **Saniyya** has the same meaning.

Sanchia *f.*

A Provençal and Spanish name derived from the Latin *sanctus*, meaning 'holy'. The name came to England in the 13th century when the Earl of Cornwall married Sanchia, daughter of the Count of Provence.

Sandip *f.*

This Indian name means 'beautiful'.

Sandra *f.*

This is a short form of Italian **Alessandra**, now used as a name in its own right (see **ALEXANDRA**). **Sandie** or **Sandy** (also used for **CASSANDRA**) are pet forms. It also appears as **Sondra**, and the designer **Zandra** Rhodes uses an unusual alternative form.

Sandy *see* Alexander, Sandra

Saniyya *see* Sana

Sanjay *m.*

From a Sanskrit word which means 'triumphant', but referring specifically to the charioteer of King Dhritarashtra in classic Hindu epics. The name was made familiar by Sanjay Ghandi, son of the former Indian Prime Minister, and, more recently, through a character in the TV series *EastEnders*,

Sara(h) *f.*

Sarah comes from the Hebrew, meaning 'princess', and was the name of Abraham's wife in the Old Testament. Sara is the Greek form found in the New Testament. **SALLY**, **Sal** and **Sadie** started life as pet forms. In Ireland Sarah has been used to render the Irish **Sorcha** ('sorr-ha', the 'h' as in Scottish 'loch') meaning 'bright', and **Saraid** ('sahr-it') meaning 'excellent'.

Sarika *f.*

An Indian name which refers to the 'koel' or 'black cuckoo'.

Sasha *see* Sacha

Saskia *f.*

This was the name of the wife of the Dutch artist Rembrandt (1606–69), whose paintings of her introduced the name to this country. It may be connected with the word for Saxon.

Saul *m.*

From the Hebrew meaning 'asked for (child)'. The name occurs in the Old Testament as that of the first King of Israel, and in the New Testament as St **PAUL**'s name before his conversion to Christianity. It was initially used as a first name in Britain in the 17th century.

Savannah *f.*

The name of a river and city in the state of Georgia. American parents are making increasing use of the name. The name comes from Spanish 'sabana', a treeless plain. It can appear with spellings such as **Savana** or **Savanna**.

Scarlett *f.*

The use of Scarlett as a first name is due entirely to the success of Margaret Mitchell's *Gone with the*

Wind. In the novel, Scarlett O'Hara is given her grandmother's maiden name as a middle name, but always called by it. **Scarlet** is also used.

Scott *m.*

This is a surname, meaning 'a Scot', used as a first name.

Seamas *m.*

This is an Irish form of **JAMES**. It is also spelt **Seamus** and the Gaelic form is **Seumas** or **Seumus**. **Shamus** is a modern phonetic version of the name (see also **HAMISH**).

Sean *f. and m.*

The Irish form of **JOHN**, developed from the French Jean. It is also spelt as it is pronounced, **Shaun** or **Shawn**. **Shane** is a variant form. Shawn and Sean are used now for girls, along with **Shawna** and **Shawndelle** (see also **SHANAE**).

Sebastian *m.*

From the Latin *Sebastianus*, meaning 'man of Sebasta'. The name of this town in Asia Minor was derived from the Greek meaning 'majestic' or 'venerable'. St Sebastian was executed by being shot with arrows, and his martyrdom was a particularly popular subject for paintings. The name took hold in Spain and in France, where it was shortened to

Bastien, and taken by fishermen across the Channel
from Brittany to the West Country, where the form
Bastian took root. The name did not spread to the
rest of Britain until modern times, but Sebastian is
now reasonably common, having the short forms
Seb and **Sebbie**.

Seeta, Seetha *see* Sita

Sejal *f.*

This Indian name means 'river' or 'water'.

Selina *f.*

The etymology of this name is disputed. One
possible derivation is from **Selene**, the Greek moon
goddess; another is from the Latin name Coelina
from *caelum*, meaning 'heaven', through the French
form **Céline**. **Celina** and **Selena** are also found.

Selma *f.*

Selma is the name of a castle in James Macpherson's
18th-century poems about Scottish legendary
heroes. When the poems were translated into
Swedish the translator failed to make the meaning
clear, and it was understood by many Swedish
readers to be a personal name; some then used it for
their children. Immigrants took the name to the US,
where it is still more common than in Britain.

Seonaid *see* Sheena

Serena *f.*

This is a Latin word meaning 'calm, serene (woman)'. **Serenity** is also used for girls.

Seth *m.*

This is a biblical name meaning 'appointed' which was given to the third son of Adam and Eve.

Seumas, Seumus, Shamus *see* Seamas

Shahid *m.,* Shahida(h) *f.*

An Arabic name which means 'witness' or 'martyr'.

Shahin *m.*

An Arabic name which means 'falcon'. **Shaheen** is a variant spelling.

Shaina *f.*

From a Yiddish word meaning 'beautiful', Shaina is also found as **Shayna**, **Sheyna** or **Cheyna**.

Shakir *m.,* Shakira *f.*

This is an Arabic name meaning 'grateful'. Shakira has come to be used outside the Muslim community, publicised firstly by the actress Shakira Caine, and more recently by the Spanish-language singer Shakira. **Zshakira** is an alternative form.

Shakil *m.,* Shakila *f.*

These are Arabic names meaning 'beautiful, handsome'. They can also be spelt **Shakeel**,

Shakeela, and among English speakers take forms
such as **Shaquil(le)** and **Shaquilla(h)**.

Sham *see* Shyam

Shamina(h) *f.*

An Arabic name from a word meaning 'scent' or
'flavour'.

Shanae *f.*

An Afro-American name, making use of the now
fashionable prefix 'Sha-'. It seems to be an invented
name of no special meaning, its sound being more
important. It is also spelt **Shanay** and **Shanaye**.

Shane *see* John, Sean

Shanel(le), Shannel *see* Chanel

Shani *see* Sian

Shania *f.*

Although this is regarded by some as a feminine
form of **SEAN**, the singer Shania Twain, who has
popularised the name, regards it as from the Native
American Ojibwa language, meaning 'I'm on my
way'. **Shainya** is also found.

Shanice *f.*

An Afro-American blend of the fashionable
'Sha-' prefix and Janice. The name has been given

publicity by singer Shanice Wilson, who uses only her first name as her stage name. Spellings such as **Chaniece** or **Chanise** are also found. **Shaniqua** (**Shanika**) is a similar blend of Sha- and **MONICA**.

Shannon *f.* and *m.*

This is the Irish river and place name, meaning 'the old one', which has become a popular first name in recent years. It is less common for boys. **Shanna** can be seen as either a variant of this or of **SEAN** or **SHANAE**.

Shante, Shanti *see* Ashanti

Shaquil(le), Shaquilla(h) *see* Shakil

Shantal *see* Chantal

Sharad *m.*, Sharada *f.*

From an Indian word for 'autumn'. An alternative feminine form is **Sharadini**. **Sharadchandra** (*m*) means 'autumn moon'. **Sharadindu**, also for boys, has a similar meaning.

Sharif *m.*, Sharifa(h) *f.*

This Arabic name means 'eminent' or 'honourable'. It is also used as a title for descendants of the Prophet Muhammad.

Shardai, Sharday *see* Sade

Sharlene *see* **Charlene**

Sharlott *see* **Charlotte**

Sharmaine *see* **Charmaine**

Sharon *f.*

In the Bible Sharon, which means 'the plain', is an area of rich natural beauty and to compare a woman to it came to be a great compliment. It has been used as a first name only since the 20th century. It is occasionally spelt **Sharron**. **Shari** is a pet form.

Shaun(a), Shawndelle, Shawn *see* **Sean**

Shayla, Shaylee, Sheela *see* **Sheila**

Shayna *see* **Shaina**

Shea *f. and m.*

An Irish surname meaning 'descendant of the fortunate one' now used as a first name. **Shay** is also used.

Sheba *see* **Bathsheba**

Sheena *f.*

This is a phonetic form of **Sine**, the Gaelic for **JANE**. An alternative form of Jane is **Siubhan**, which in Irish becomes **Siobhan**, with phonetic spellings **Shevaun** and **Chevonne**. **Shona**, the Scottish form of **JANET**, comes from the same root and is a phonetic form of **Seonaid**, in Irish **Sinead** (shin-aid).

Sheila *f.*

A phonetic spelling of **Sile**, the Irish form of **CECILIA**. It can also be spelt **Shelagh**, **Shiela** and **Sheela**. In the USA it has developed the forms **Shayla** and **Shaylee**.

Shelby *f.*

An English place name and surname. The original meaning was probably 'settlement with willow trees'. Its use as a first name started in the USA and was sparked by a character in the 1989 film *Steel Magnolias*.

Shelley *f.*

This is a pet form of **MICHELLE** and **RACHEL** as well as being a variant of the name **SHIRLEY**. From the 1940s the name was brought to public attention by the actress Shelley Winters.

Sheree, Sherrie, Sherry *see* Cherie

Sheril, Sheryl *see* Cheryl

Shevaun *see* Sheena

Sheyna *see* Shaina

Shiela *see* Sheila

Shirley *f.*

This was originally a place name meaning 'shire meadow'. From this it became a surname in Yorkshire and elsewhere. It was primarily a boy's name until Charlotte Brontë started the fashion for it as a girl's name in 1849, when her novel *Shirley* appeared (see also **SHELLEY**).

Shiva *m.*

The name of the Hindu god, from the Sanskrit meaning 'benign'. Similar names are **Shivaji**, **Shivesh**, **Shivlal**, **Shivraj** and **Shivshankar**, which mean 'Lord Shiva'.

Shona *see* **Sheena**

Shree, Shri *see* **Sri**

Shrikant *see* **Srikant**

Shyam *m.,* **Shyama** *f.*

From the Sanskrit for 'dark', but identified with **KRISHNA**. In some parts of India the male form becomes **Sham**. The feminine form, **Shyama**, is a name of the goddess **DURGA**. Similar names for girls, with a basic meaning of 'dusky', include **Shyamal**, **Shyamala**, **Shyamalendu**, **Shyamali**, **Shyamalika**, **Shyamalima**, **Shyamari** and **Shyamasri**.

Shyann *see* **Cheyenne**

Sian *f.*

This is the Welsh form of **JANE**, properly spelt **Siân**. **Siani** is a pet form which may appear as **Shani**.

Sibyl, Sibylla *see* Sybil

Sidney, Sydney *f. and m.*

This is a surname used as a first name from at least the beginning of the 18th century. The spelling Sydney did not appear until the 19th century, and the city in Australia was named after Viscount Sydney, who was then Secretary of State. The short form is **Sid**. In the 18th century girls were given surnames as first names more often than was usual until very recently, and Sydney as a girl's name may date from this. Alternatively, it may be a form of the Latin name **Sidonia** ('woman of Sidon'), which became **Sidonie** in French and **Sidony** in English. In the US Sydney is more common as a female name, and can appear as **Sydnee** or **Sidni(e)**.

Sienna *f.*

Like **FLORENCE**, this is the name of an Italian city that has come to be used as a first name in recent years. The Italian spelling, **Siena**, is also used.

Sierra *f.*

The Spanish word for a mountain range used as a first name in the USA, although possibly, because of its association with automobiles, not destined to spread to the UK. The situation is complicated in the USA by the fact that **Ciara**, a feminine form of **KIERAN**, is a brand of perfume there which is used as a first name and pronounced in the same way as Sierra. Spellings such as **Cierra** are also found.

Sigourney *f.*

The actress Sigourney Weaver chose to call herself Sigourney while still a child, inspired by the character Sigourney Howard in Scott Fitzgerald's 1925 novel *The Great Gatsby*. Fitzgerald in turn is thought to have been inspired by the name of Lydia Huntley Sigourney (1791–1865), one of the earliest American women to earn her living by writing, although the name was already in use when Fitzgerald was writing, and it may be no coincidence that there was a prominent New York socialite at the time called Sigourney Thayer.

Silas *see* **Silvester**

Sile *see* **Sheila**

Silvester, Sylvester *m.*

The Latin for 'wood-dweller'. There have been three popes of this name, which was quite common in both forms in the Middle Ages. The New Testament name **Silas** is probably a form of Silvester. Like so many names popular with the Puritans, Silas is showing signs of coming back into fashion. **Sylvestra** and **Sylvana** are rare female forms.

Silvia, Sylvia *f.*

This is the Latin word meaning '(woman) of the wood'. Rhea Silvia was the mother of Romulus and Remus, the founders of Rome. This may have been the reason why the name was adopted during the Renaissance in Italy. Like other classical names, it came to England in Elizabethan times. Shakespeare used it in *Two Gentlemen of Verona*, and this probably gave rise to its use in Britain. The diminutive form is **Silvie** or **Sylvie**.

Simon *m.,* Simone *f.*

This is the better-known English form of the New Testament **Simeon**, the name of the man who blessed the baby Jesus in the Temple. The popularity of Simon in the Middle Ages was due to Simon **PETER**, the Apostle, whose popularity was great at that period. The short form is **Sim**. Simone is the feminine form taken from the French.

Sine, Sinead, Siobhan *see* Sheena

Sion *see* John

Sis, Sisley, Sissy *see* Cecilia

Sita *f.*

From the Sanskrit for 'furrow', the reference being to the goddess who personifies agriculture and is wife to Rama. **Seeta** and **Seetha** are other spellings of the name.

Siubhan *see* **Sheena**

Sive *see* **Sabina**

Skye, Skyler *f. and m.*

Skye is the name of the Scottish island used as a fashionable name, comparable to the older use of **IONA**. The name's associations with the word 'sky' may have helped its rise, and it is sometimes found as **Sky**. The same sound may have helped make the Dutch surname **Skyler**, 'scholar', a popular first name in the USA, for it is often shortened to Sky. This, in the original Dutch form **Schuyler**, has been in use since at least the late 19th century. It is the surname of a family prominent in New York since the mid-17th century, and was originally used in honour of Philip Schuyler (1733–1804), congressman, senator and hero of the American Revolution.

Sneha(l) *f.,* **Snehin** *m.*

From a Sanskrit word which originally meant 'oil', but later came to mean 'friendly affection'. **Snehal** is another form with the meaning 'friendly'. The male form, **Snehin**, means 'friend'.

Sol *see* **Mary**

Somhairle *see* **Samuel**

Sonal *f.*

An Indian name meaning 'golden'. **Sonali** and **Sonika** are variants.

Sondra *see* Sandra

Sonia *f.*

This is a Russian pet form of **SOPHIA**, and its use in Britain is modern, perhaps a result of the novel of this name by Stephen McKenna, published in 1917. **Sonya** and **Sonja** are other spellings of the name.

Sonika *see* Sonal

Sophia, Sophie *f.*

From the Greek meaning 'wisdom'. *Hagia Sophia* ('Holy Wisdom') is a common dedication for Orthodox churches as in the case of the great cathedral at Constantinople. This led to Sophia's use as a name in Greece. The name spread through Hungary to Germany and then to England when George I became king. Both his mother and his wife had the name. Sophie is the anglicised form which is currently the more popular. The forms **Sophy** and **Sofia** are also used (see **SONIA**).

Sorcha *see* Sarah

Sorley *see* Samuel

Spencer *m.*

This name, originally a surname given to the steward

of a great household, but later an aristocratic surname, was made famous by the actor Spencer Tracy.

Spring see Autumn

Sri *f.*

This Indian name is from the Sanskrit meaning 'light' or 'beauty', later developing into 'majesty' and used as a title as well as a name. Sri is one of the names of Lakshmi, goddess of prosperity and beauty. **Shree**, **Shri** and **Sree** are variants.

Srikant *m.*

From the Sanskrit words meaning 'beautiful throat', a name applied to the god Shiva. **Shrikant** is an alternative spelling.

Stacey, Stacy *f. and m.*

This is a pet form which has become popular as an independent name. For men it was a short form of **EUSTACE**; as a woman's name it was originally short for **ANASTASIA**. Currently, it is mostly given to girls, sometimes in the form of **Stacie**.

Stanley *m.*

This was originally a surname derived from an old Anglo-Saxon place name meaning 'stony field'. It was used as a first name from the mid-19th century partly because of its association with Sir Henry Morton Stanley, the famous explorer. It has the short form **Stan**.

Stefan, Steffan *see* Stephen

Stella *f.*

This is the Latin word for 'star'. Its use stems from its literary associations. An early use was in Sir Philip Sidney's *Astrophel and Stella* (1591). Then, in the early 18th century, Jonathan Swift used it as a pet name in letters to Esther Johnson. The French form **Estella** was popularised by Charles Dickens, when he used it for the main female character in his *Great Expectations* (1861). **Estelle** is another French form. These share the short forms of ESTHER.

Stephen, Steven *m.*, Stephanie *f.*

From the Greek *stephanos* meaning 'crown' or 'wreath'. The laurel wreath was the highest honour a man could attain in the classical world. Stephen was a common personal name in Ancient Greece, and was borne by the very first Christian martyr. Steven is the alternative spelling. **Steve** and **Stevie** are the modern pet forms. There is a Welsh form, **Steffan**, and also a Continental form, **Stefan**. The female form, Stephanie, has variants such as **Stefanie**, **Steffany**, and the Italian **Stefania**.

Stuart *m.*

From the Old English *sti weard*, an official who looked after animals kept for food. Though it has changed its meaning somewhat, it survives as 'steward' today. The co-founder of the Scottish royal house of Stewart or Stuart in the 14th century was William the Steward who married the king's daughter and whose son later became king. **Stewart** is a common alternative and **Stuert** is also used.

Suhayl *m.*

An Arabic name which refers to a bright star, Canopus, in the southern constellation Carina. **Suhail** is a variant.

Sujan *m.*

A Hindi name which means 'honest'.

Sumayyah *f.*

A Muslim name of uncertain meaning, borne by the first martyr in the cause of Islam. It also occurs as **Sumaya**, **Sumayah** and **Sumayya**.

Summer *see* Autumn

Sunil *m.*

This is a rather puzzling name, as it comes from an obscure, ancient Sanskrit word meaning 'very dark blue'. Its use as a first name is modern. It has become a popular choice for parents in India and is sometimes interpreted as 'sapphire'. The form **Sunila** can be used for girls.

Sunita _f._

This name comes from the Sanskrit for 'of good conduct' or 'righteous' and was the name of a princess in epic poetry who was the daughter of the King of Bengal. **Suniti** is another form of the name.

Sunni _see_ **Surinder**

Suraj _m._

This Hindi name means 'the sun'.

Surinder _f. and m._

This is a development of the name **INDRA**, and can be interpreted as meaning 'mightiest of the gods'. It is also found in the form **Surendra**. It is less often used for girls than for boys, and as a boy's name can be shortened to **Sunni**.

Susan, Susanna(h) _f._

Shushannah is Hebrew for 'lily' and Susanna(h) was the earliest form of this name in England, occurring in the Middle Ages and becoming quite common after the Reformation. Susan was adopted in the 18th century. In the 20th century the French forms, **Suzanne** and **Suzette**, have also been used in Britain, and spellings such as **Susana** and **Suzanna** have been found. **Sue**, **Sukey**, **Susie** and **Suzy** are pet forms.

Swan _see_ **Raven**

Sybil *f.*

In classical times the Sibyls were prophetesses, and some of them were supposed to have foretold the coming of Christ. Because of this, **Sibylla** came to be used as a first name, the Normans bringing it with them to England. Sybil or **Sibyl** had a revival in the second half of the 19th century after Disraeli had published his political novel of that name (1845). The actress **Cybill** Shepherd has introduced another form of the name.

Sydney *see* Sidney

Syed *m.*

This is a common way of spelling the Arabic name **Sayyid**, meaning 'noble' or 'master'. Its feminine form is **Sayyida**.

Sylvana, Sylvester, Sylvestra *see* Silvester

Sylvia, Sylvie *see* Silvia

Syril *see* Cyril

Tabitha *f.*

This name derives from the Aramaic word for 'gazelle'. In the New Testament it is the name of a Christian woman of Joppa who showed great charity towards the poor, and was raised from the dead by St Peter. The Greek translation of her name is **Dorcas**. **Tabatha** is a modern spelling of the name.

Tadhg *see* **Timothy**

Taffy *see* **David**

Tahir *m.*

An Arabic name which means 'pure' and 'virtuous'.

Taja *see* **Anastasia**

Talia *see* **Natalie**

Taliesin *see* **Ceridwen**

Tallulah *f.*

This name is well known from the American actress Tallulah Bankhead (1903–68). She was named after her grandmother, who was in turn named after a place, Tallulah Falls in Georgia. The place name is said to come from a Native American word meaning 'terrible'. The name was given further publicity by a character in the 1976 film and musical *Bugsy Malone*.

Tally, Talya *see* Natalie

Tam *see* Thomas

Tamara *f.*

Tamara is the Russian form of the biblical name **Tamar**, which means 'date palm'. Tamara was the name of a famous Russian queen, and remains a popular name in Russia. A pet form is TAMMY.

Tammy *f.*

A pet form of TAMARA and TAMSIN, now used as an independent name. In 1957 a film called *Tammy* and a song of that name, which was the bestselling record in the USA, started a vogue for the name's use. It is also a Scottish form of **Tommy** (see THOMAS). **Tamia** (**Tamya**) is probably a blend of Tammy and TANYA.

Tamsin *f.*

This is a West Country female form of THOMAS. It can also be found as **Tamsine**, **Tamzin** and **Tamzen**. It comes from **Thomasin** or **Thomasine** which have been used since the Middle Ages. **Thomasina** is an old latinised version which was revived in the 19th century. TAMMY is a short form of these names.

Tanisha *f.*

This name is used almost exclusively by Afro-Americans and seems to be a Hausa name from West Africa, meaning 'girl born on Monday'. It comes in a variety of forms, including **Taneisha**, **Tanesha**, **Taniesha**, **Tenecia**, **Tenesha** and **Tenisha**.

Tanith *f.*

The name of a Phoenician goddess of love that has recently come into occasional use as a first name. It can also take the form **Tanit**.

Tanner *m.*

A surname, from the job, used as a first name.

Tansy *see* **Anastasia**

Tanya *f.*

Tanya or **Tania** is a pet form of **Tatiana**, which has been popular in Russia for many years, inspired by St Tatiana, a martyr revered by the Orthodox Church. **Tonya** is also found although, properly, this is the Russian pet form of **ANTONIA**.

Tara *f.*

Tara is the name of the hill where the ancient High Kings of Ireland held court and which plays an important part in Irish legend. It has been used as a first name only since the end of the 19th century.

It is occasionally used for boys. As an Indian name it means 'star'.

Taryn *f.,* Tarun *m.*

These are part of a group of names with varied origins. Taryn, as a girl's name, was coined by the actors Tyrone Power and Linda Christianson for their daughter, also an actor, Taryn Power in 1953, and use spread after she started appearing in films in the 1970s. Tarun is an Indian boy's name, from the Sanskrit for 'young, tender'. In addition, the American author Lloyd Alexander coined the name **Taran**, (probably based on TARA), for the hero of his Celtic fantasy novels *The Chronicle of Prydain*. Many other variants of these names have appeared in recent years.

Tasha *see* Natalie

Tashan *m. and f.,* Tashana *f.*

While Tashan is a common Turkish surname, as a first name these appear to be new creations, in use since about the 1970s. Tashan has been given publicity as the name of an American singer.

Tasia, Tassia *see* Anastasia

Tasnim *f.*

An Arabic name meaning 'fountain of paradise'. It is also found as **Tasneem**.

Tatiana *see* **Tanya**

Tatum *f.*

This name, which seems to have been coined for the actress Tatum O'Neal (b. 1963), comes from a surname which in turn comes from an Old English place name meaning 'homestead of a man named Tata'.

Tavia, Tavie, Tavian, Tavius *see* **Octavia**

Taylor *f. and m.*

This English surname, indicating an ancestor who was a tailor, has been made familiar as a first name by the American author (Janet Miriam) Taylor Caldwell, who chose to use it as her pen name in order to obscure her gender. The more exotic spellings it takes shade into forms of **TYLER**.

Tea *see* **Tia**

Ted, Teddy *see* **Edmund, Edward, Theodore**

Tegan *f.*

This is an old Cornish name meaning 'lovely little thing' or 'ornament'. The name first got more general exposure in the 1980s in the television series *Dr Who*, when it was used for an Australian air hostess who became involved in the doctor's adventures. The name seems to have reappeared in the form **Tiegan** in the Australian soap *Home and*

Away. Tegan is pronounced with a short 'e' sound, but Tiegan with the sound of 'tea' hence the common US spelling **Teagan**. The word 'teg', meaning 'pretty, fair', is found in Welsh as well as Cornish, for they are closely related, and there are a number of Welsh names that use it, of which **Tegwen**, 'pretty and fair', is the most common.

Tejal *f.*

A Sanskrit name meaning 'lustrous'.

Tenecia, Tenesha, Tenisha *see* Tanisha

Terence *m.*

This is from the Latin Terentius, the name of a famous Roman comic playwright. Short forms are **Terry** and **Tel**. It is now also found in the forms **Terance**, **Terrance**, **Terrence** and **Terrell** (although this could also be from the name of an American city). It is a comparatively modern name, having come from Ireland, where it was used to transliterate the native **Turlough** ('tar-loch', pronounced as if Scottish), meaning 'instigator' (see also **THEODORIC**). Terry as an independent name can also come from Theodoric (see **DEREK**).

Teresa, Theresa *f.*

The meaning of this name is obscure. The first recorded Theresa was the wife of the 5th-century St Paulinus, and was responsible for his conversion.

The name was for a long time confined to Spain until the fame of St Teresa of Avila (1515–82) spread the name to all Roman Catholic countries, but it did not become common in the UK until the 18th century. It is often abbreviated to **Tess**, **Tessa** or **Tessie**. The form **Teri** or **Terry**, shared with some boys' names, is also found. A variant is **TRACY**. The French form, **Thérèse**, is also found occasionally.

Tevin m.

This recent name is probably a development of **KEVIN**, although some would link it to a French surname, Thevin, which comes from an old form of **STEPHEN**.

Thea see Dorothy, Theodora

Thelma f.

Like **MAVIS**, this name was introduced in the 19th century as a character in a novel by the writer Marie Corelli, and spread quickly throughout the country. There is a Greek word *thelema* meaning 'will', which may have had some influence on its development.

Theodore m., Theodora f.

From the Greek meaning 'gift of God'. There are 28 saints called Theodore in the Church Calendar. In England the name did not become general until the 19th century, but in Wales it has long been used as a form of **Tudur** or **Tudor**, which in fact probably comes from a Celtic name. The usual abbreviation in North America is **Ted** or **Teddy**, as in the case of President Theodore Roosevelt who gave his name to the teddy bear. In England **Theo** (sometimes used as an independent name) is a more common abbreviation. The feminine form has been used since the 17th century. It is usually abbreviated to **Theo** (sometimes used as an independent name), **Thea** and **DORA**. The rarer **Theodosia** has a similar meaning.

Theodoric *see* Derek, Terence

Theophania *see* Tiffany

Theresa, Thérèse *see* Teresa

Thomas *m.*

From the Aramaic nickname meaning 'twin'. It was first given by Jesus to an Apostle named Judas to distinguish him from Judas Iscariot. The abbreviation **Tom** appears in the Middle Ages. **Tam** and **TAMMY** are the Scottish pet forms. The use of **Tommy** as a nickname for a British private soldier goes back to the 19th century, when the enlistment form had on it the specimen signature 'Thomas Atkins'. Thomas has been one of the three top boys' names for some years.

Thomasin, Thomasina, Thomasine *see* Tamsin

Thora *f.*

From the Norse meaning 'Thor-battle'. Its earlier form was **Thyra**. Thor was the god of thunder in Norse mythology, and he also gave his name to 'Thursday'. Thora is a rare name in Britain, but well known from the actress, Thora Hird.

Thurstan *see* Dustin

Thyra *see* Thora

Tia *f.*

Tia is a Spanish word for 'Auntie'; but although its use in such contexts and the liqueur named Tia Maria may have helped its spread, it is probably best regarded as a pet or short form of such fashionable names as **Tiana** and Tiara (see **KIARA**) or **Tierra**; or of names ending in -tia. It appears in numerous spellings, including **Téa** (which can also be a pet form of Teodora, in Italian form of **THEODORA**) and **Tya**.

Tiesha *see* Letitia

Tiffany *f.*

Originally a pet form of the name **Theophania**, from the Greek meaning 'the manifestation of God'. Tifainé was the Old French form, and this name was given to girls born at the time of the Epiphany, the words having the same meaning. The names were fairly rare until recently when Tiffany became popular.

Tiegan *see* **Tegan**

Tilak *m.*

An Indian name which refers to the *tika* or *tilak*, the red mark worn as a caste-mark or decoration by Hindus. It is also placed as a blessing on the forehead of an honoured guest.

Tilda, Tilly *see* **Matilda**

Timothy *m.*

Timotheos is an old Greek name meaning 'honouring God'. Its use as a first name is due to Timothy, the companion of St **Paul**. It was not used widely until the 16th century when many classical and biblical names were introduced. **Tim** and **Timmy** are the abbreviations. **Timothea** is a rare female form. In Ireland Timothy has long been used as an equivalent for the native **Tadhg** ('tieg') which means 'poet'.

Tina *f.*

Originally a short form for girls' names ending in '-tina', commonest of which is **Christina** (see **Christine**). It is now used in its own right.

Titus *m.*

This is a Latin name of unknown meaning. Two well-known holders of the name were a follower of St Paul and, in contrast, the infamous Titus Oates, an English conspirator and perjurer in the 17th century. It is probably best known today as the name of the hero of Mervyn Peake's *Gormenghast* books.

Toby *m.*

Toby is the English form of the Greek **Tobias**, itself derived from the Hebrew name which means 'the Lord is good'. The story of *Tobias and the Angel*, which is told in the Apocrypha was a favourite one in the Middle Ages. Punch's dog Toby is named after the dog that accompanied Tobias on his travels.

Tod, Todd *m.*

Originally a surname meaning 'fox', now used as a first name.

Toinette *see* **Anthony**

Tom, Tommy *see* **Thomas**

Toni, Tonio, Tony *see* **Anthony**

Tonya *see* **Antonia, Tanya**

Torcall *see* **Torquil**

Tori, Toria, Torie *see* **Victoria**

Tormod *see* **Norman**

Torquil *m.*

This is the English rendering of the Norse name

Thorketill ('Thor's cauldron'). The first element is the name of the Norse thunder god, Thor. The original became **Torcall** in Gaelic, which was anglicised into Torquil. It is used in Scotland, especially in the Outer Hebrides and among the Macleod family, and it has occasionally been given in England.

Totty see Charlotte

Toyah see La Toya

Tracy *f. and m.*

This popular girl's name seems to have started life as a pet form of TERESA. It is also found as **Tracey** and **Tracie**. Its beginnings as an independent name were probably helped by the use of the surname Tracy (from a French place name) as a boy's name, particularly as at the time when it first became popular Spencer Tracy (1900–67) was a well-known film star. **Trace** is used as a boy's name, and as a pet form of the girl's.

Travis *m.*

A surname, notably that of William B. Travis (1809–36) US commander at the Battle of the Alamo, used as a first name. It comes from the French word *traverser*, meaning 'to cross' and would have been given originally to a toll-collector.

Trevor *m.*

From the Welsh **Trefor**, meaning 'great homestead'. Trevor is the English spelling. **Trev** is the short form.

Trey *m.*

Trey is an old word for 'three' in card games, and has been used, particularly in the USA, as a pet name for the third bearer of the same name, to distinguish him from his grandfather and father (often called 'Junior'). More recently it has been used as a given name, when it can also appear as **Tre** and (sometimes for girls) **Trea**.

Tricia, Trisha *see* Patricia

Trinity *f.*

This vocabulary word has recently become fashionable as a girl's name in the USA.

Triss *see* Beatrice

Tristan, Tristram *m.*

This is a name of obscure origin, possibly Pictish. It appears as the name of the noble hero of the medieval love stories of Tristram and **ISOLDA**. When Tristram is escorting Isolda to be married to his uncle they unknowingly drink a magic love-potion intended for the newly-weds, and are doomed to adulterous love until their tragic deaths. **Tristran** is also found. It is currently popular in the USA, where it also appears as **Tristen**, **Tristian**, **Tristin**, **Triston** and **Trystan**.

Trixie *see* Beatrice

Troy *m.*

Troy was the ancient city in Asia Minor besieged by the Greeks for ten years. Its use as a first name was boosted in the 1960s by the actor Troy Donahue (1936–2001, given name **MERLE** Johnson). It has been popular in Australia and is well used in the USA.

Trudi, Trudie, Trudy *see* Gertrude

Tudor, Tudur *see* Theodore

Tulsi *m.*, Tulasi *f.*

This Indian name is from the Sanskrit word meaning 'sacred basil', a plant which symbolises Vishnu. Tulasi, the girls' form, is also the name of a goddess based on the same word.

Turlough *see* Terence

Tya *see* Tia

Tyler *f. and m.*

A surname, from the job, used as a first name. It has been popular in the USA for some years and can be shortened to **Ty**. **Tyla** is a feminine form.

Tyrone m.

The name of the Irish county, which means 'Eoghan's land', used as a first name. It was used in the past by the actor, Tyrone Power (1913–58) in the USA and by the British theatre director, Sir Tyrone Guthrie (1900–71). **Ty** is the short form, although Guthrie was known to his friends as Tony. **Tyree**, another Celtic district name, is also used. **Tyra** is used as a female equivalent (see also **TARYN**).

Ulick *see* **Ulysses, William**

Ulysses *m.*

This is the Latin name for the Greek hero **Odysseus**, whose tale is told in Homer's *Odyssey*. Though little used in England, Scotland or Wales, it has been used in Ireland as an equivalent for **Ulick**, an Irish form of **WILLIAM**. James Joyce's most famous novel bears this name. In the USA, where it also appears as **Ulises**, use of the name probably comes from the fame of General Ulysses S. Grant (1822–85), hero of Appomattox and the 18th American President.

Uma *f.*

A Sanskrit name of a goddess, meaning 'flax, turmeric', which has been made internationally famous by the actress Uma Thurman.

Umar *see* **Omar**

Una *f.*

The etymology of this ancient Irish name is obscure. It is also found in the forms **Oonagh** or **Oona** (pronounced 'oo-na'), both of which are also found in Scotland. **Juno**, influenced by the name of the Roman queen of the gods, is another Irish form, best known from Sean O'Casey's play *Juno and the Paycock* (1924). The Elizabethan poet Edmund Spenser took the Irish name Una and gave it its Latin sense, 'one, unity', in his epic poem *The Faerie Queene*.

Unice *see* Eunice

Unity *f.*

This is one of the abstract virtue names that became quite common among Puritans after the Reformation. It is rarely found today.

Ursula *f.*

From the Latin meaning 'little she-bear'. The name was fairly common in the Middle Ages on account of St Ursula, a 5th-century Cornish princess who, along with her companions, was murdered near Cologne while on a pilgrimage. The name had a revival after Mrs Craik chose it for her heroine in her popular novel, *John Halifax, Gentleman* (1856).

Uthman *m.*

A Muslim name from an Arabic word meaning 'baby bustard'. Uthman was the son-in-law of the Prophet Muhammad. The Turkish form of the name, **Usman**, is also much used, though often westernised as **Osman**. The name of the Ottoman Empire derived from this name's Latin and Italian plural form.

Val *see* **Perceval, Valentine, Valerie**

Valentine *f. and m.*

From the Latin *valens*, 'strong' or 'healthy'. St Valentine was a 3rd-century Roman priest martyred on 14 February, the eve of the celebrations of the pagan goddess Juno, when lots were drawn to choose lovers. The feast was absorbed into the Christian calendar. **Valentina** is an alternative girl's form, **Valentin** a continental masculine. **Val** is a common diminutive, shared with **VALERIE**.

Valerie *f.*

This is the French form of the Roman family name **Valeria**, and was taken into use in Britain in the late 19th century. It comes from a word meaning 'to be in good health'. It has the short form **Val**.

Vanda *see* **Wanda**

Vanessa *f.*

A name invented in the early 18th century by the writer Jonathan Swift as a pet name for **ESTHER** Vanhomrigh. He took the first syllable of her surname and added Essa, which was probably a pet form of Esther.

Vanna *see* Gianna

Vaughn, Vaughan *m.*

From the Welsh *fychan*, meaning 'small one'.

Velma *f.*

A name of unknown origin, first used in the 1880s in the United States.

Venetia *f.*

The Latin name for the Italian city of Venice, used as a first name. It was previously thought to have a connection with **Venus**, the Roman goddess of love, which is very occasionally used as a first name.

Vera *f.*

This name has two possible derivations. One source is the Russian for 'faith', another is the Latin meaning 'true'. It was used in English literature in the 19th century, and became popular in Britain at the beginning of the 20th. It is sometimes used as an abbreviation of **VERONICA** (see also **VERENA**).

Verena *f.*

The name of a rather obscure 3rd-century saint. Its meaning is not known, but may well come from the same source as **VERA**. St Verena lived in Switzerland and her name is popular there, but use among English speakers probably owes something to the name's prominence in Henry James's novel *The Bostonians*.

Vergil *see* **Virgil**

Verity *f.*

From the old English word for 'truth'. It was first used by the Puritans in the 17th century, and has been quite common ever since. The variant **Verily** ('truly') is also found occasionally.

Vernon *m.*

Richard de Vernon was a companion of William the Conqueror. The surname comes from a French place name which means 'alder grove'. It was not used as a first name until the 19th century, when many such aristocratic names were taken into general use.

Veronica *f.*

Traditionally, this name is thought to derive from the Latin *vera icon*, meaning 'a true image'. St Veronica wiped the sweat from Christ's face on his way to Calvary, and a 'true image' of his face was said to have been left on the cloth. It is more likely, however, that the name is a form of **BERENICE**. **Véronique** has long been popular in France, and from there the name reached Scotland in the late 17th century. It does not appear much in England before the late 19th century (see also **VERA**).

Veva *see* **Genevieve**

Victor *m.*

This is the Latin for 'conqueror'. Although it occurs in medieval England it was not common until the 19th century when it was used as a boy's form of **VICTORIA**. The commonest short form is **Vic**.

Victoria *f.*

From the Latin for 'victory'. This name was hardly used in Britain until the reign of Queen Victoria, who was named after her German mother. In the recent past the name has been very popular and is often found in one of its short forms, **Vicky**, **Vickie**, **Vikki** and **Tori**, **Torie** or **Toria**. **Vita** and **Viti** and the nickname **QUEENIE** are also found.

Vida *see* **Davida**

Vijay *m.,* **Vijaya** *f.*

This Indian name is from a Sanskrit word meaning 'victory'. The feminine form, Vijaya, is also applied to the goddess **DURGA**, wife of Shiva.

Vikesh *m.*

A Hindi name which means 'the moon'.

Vilma *see* **William**

Vina *see* **Davida**

Vinay *m.*, Vinaya *f.*

An Indian name which means 'educating to act in a proper way'. For Buddhists it suggests the modest behaviour appropriate to a monk.

Vincent *m.*

From the Latin for 'conquering'. There was a 3rd-century Spanish martyr of this name and it occurs in English records from the 13th century. But the 17th-century St Vincent de Paul popularised the name when he founded the Vincentian Order of the Sisters of Charity. It became quite common in the 19th century. Its usual short form is **Vince**. The Continental forms **Vincente** and **Vincenzo** are also found.

Viola, Violet *f.*

Viola is Latin for 'violet'. Although it does occur in the Middle Ages, the modern use of this name comes from Shakespeare, who gave it to the heroine of *Twelfth Night*. **Violette** and **Violetta** have also been used.

Viral *m.*

This Indian name comes from the Sanskrit for 'priceless, rare'.

Virgil *m.*

The name of the great Roman poet. The original spelling of his name was **Vergil**. The name has been more used in the USA than in Britain.

Virginia *f.*

Although there was a Roman family called Virginus, the modern use of this name dates only from 1587. Sir Walter Raleigh had called his newly founded colony in North America Virginia, after Elizabeth I, the 'Virgin Queen', and the name Virginia was given to the first child born to the settlers there. **Ginny**, **Gini** or **Jinny** is a common pet form.

Vishal *m.*, Vishala *f.*

An Indian name which means 'immense, spacious'. For girls **Vishalakshi** is also used, with the meaning 'wide-eyed'.

Vita, Viti *see* Victoria

Vitus *see* Guy

Vivian, Vivien *f. and m.*

From the Latin *vivianus*, which means 'lively'. Vivian is now used for both sexes, but was originally the masculine form, with Vivien, **Vivyan** or **Vyvyan** mostly used for girls. The French **Vivienne** is always female as is **Viviana**. **Viv** is used for short.

Vonda *see* Wanda

Wallace *m.*

From the surname of Sir William Wallace, the great Scottish patriot of the 13th century. The use of his surname as a first name started about a hundred years ago. The surname comes from the same root that gives us the word 'Welsh', but which was once used of the British in the north as well. Another spelling of the name is **Wallis**, found in North America where it is used for both sexes. The short forms, **Wal** and **Wally**, are shared with **WALTER**.

Walter *m.*

From the Old German Waldhar, meaning 'army ruler'. The name was very popular among the Normans, and quickly became established in England. Sir Walter Raleigh is a very well-known later example and he used the short form **Wat** for his son. **Walt**, **Wal** and **Wally** are more popular short forms in use today, and Walt is used as an independent name in North America.

Wanda *f.*

This is a Polish girl's name which is probably connected with the word 'vandal'. Its wider use may have started when a novel of the same name by Ouida was published in 1883. **Vanda** and **Vonda** are both variants.

Waqar *m.*

This Arabic name means 'dignity' or 'soberness'.

Warren *m.*

From the surname, which can either be from an old German tribe name, Varin, or from a Norman place name meaning 'a game-reserve'. The Normans introduced the forms Warin and Guarin to England and these led to the surnames Warren, Waring and Garnet.

Warwick *m.*

The name of the English town which means 'houses by the weir', used as a surname and then as a first name. **Warrie** is a pet form.

Wasim *m.*, Wasimah *f.*

An Arabic name which means 'handsome' or 'graceful'. The feminine form, **Wasimah**, also means 'pretty'.

Wat *see* Walter

Wayne *m.*

This is a surname meaning 'cart' or 'cart-maker'. Its use as a first name is mainly due to the popularity of actor John Wayne (1907–79).

Wendy *f.*

This name was first used by James Barrie in *Peter Pan* (1904). The name started as 'Friendy-Wendy', a pet name for Barrie used by a child friend of his, Margaret Henley. **Wenda** has been described as a variant of Wendy, but is more probably a form of **Gwenda** (see **GWEN**).

Wenonah *see* Winona

Wesley *m.*

John and Charles Wesley were the founders of Methodism, and the name came to be used as a first name in their honour. As a surname it means 'west meadow'. **Wes** is a short form.

Whitney *f. and m.*

This name, made famous by the singer Whitney Houston, was originally a surname meaning '(living) at the white island'. Its use as a first name in the USA may be due to its being the surname of both a wealthy family prominent in national politics and arts, and of Josiah Dwight Whitney (1819–96), geologist and surveyor, after whom the USA's highest mountain outside Alaska, Mount Whitney in south California, is named.

Wilbur *m.*

This name is used in North America but is practically unknown in Britain. The most famous example was Wilbur Wright, who, with his brother **ORVILLE**, made the first successful powered flight in 1903.

Wilfred, Wilfrid *m.*

From the Old English Wilfrith, meaning 'desiring peace'. St Wilfrid was an important figure in the 7th century, and his name was particularly popular in Yorkshire where he preached and founded the bishoprics of Ripon and Hexham. The name did not survive the Norman Conquest but was revived by high-church Anglicans in the 19th century. It has the pet form **Wilf**.

William *m.*, Wilma *f.*

From the Old German, meaning 'desiring protection'. William was always a popular name with the Normans, who brought it to England, and, until the 13th century when it was ousted by **JOHN**, it was the commonest of all names in England. **Will** or **Willie** are the old short forms but **Bill** and **BILLIE** are more usual today. **Gwilym**, shortened to **Gwill**, is the Welsh form of the name, and **Liam** a short form which has spread from Ireland; **Ulick** (see **ULYSSES**) is another Irish form. Feminine forms which have been used occasionally are **Wilhelmina** and **Wilma**. Their pet forms include **Willa** or **Vilma**, **Minnie** and **Minna** and **Elma** (see **ELMER**). These feminine forms are more popular in America where German immigrants have spread their use.

Willow *f.*

A recent plant name, usually used for girls, but occasionally for boys. It is the name of a major character in the *Buffy the Vampire Slayer* television series.

Winifred *f.*

From the Welsh feminine name **Gwenfrewi**, anglicised as Winifred and later confused with the Old English male name **Winfrith**, meaning 'friend of peace'. St Winifred, a 7th-century saint, is said to have been decapitated by a Welsh prince when she rejected his advances, but then was restored miraculously to life. Although she was a popular saint in the Middle Ages, her name was not used much until the 16th century. It was a very popular name at the turn of the 19th-20th centuries. **Win**, **Winnie** and, less often, **Freda** are short forms. **Winifrid** is also used.

Winona *f.*

This is a Sioux word meaning 'eldest daughter'. It is also the name of a city in Minnesota. The name occurs as **Wenonah** in Longfellow's poem *Hiawatha* (1855), and can also be found as **Wynon(n)a**.

Winston *m.*

This is the name of a small village in Gloucestershire, which became a surname. The name has been used in the Churchill family since 1620, when Sir Winston Churchill, father of the 1st Duke of Marlborough, was born. His mother was Sarah Winston. It has come into use in honour of Sir Winston Churchill (1874–1965) to mark his contribution to world affairs.

Wyatt *m.*

The use of this surname, from medieval pet forms of both Guy and William, as a first name is mainly restricted to the USA, where it is well known from Wyatt Earp (1848–1929), famous from the gunfight at the OK Corral.

Wyn, Wynfor, Wynne *see* Gwyn

Xan, Xander *see* Alexander

Xanthe *f.*

From the Greek meaning 'yellow'. It has occasionally been used in Britain.

Xara *see* Zahra

Xavier *m.*

The surname of St Francis Xavier (1506–52) used as a first name. It is also occasionally spelt **Javier** or **Zavier** and there are rare feminine forms, **Xavia**, **Zavia**, **Xaviera** and **Xaverine**.

Xenia *f.*

The Greek word for 'hospitality'. It is only occasionally found. **Xena** is also used (see also **ZENA**) but it is too soon to tell if the international success of the television series *Xena, Warrior Princess* will affect usage.

Yasin *m.*

A name formed by the names of Arabic letters from an important passage in the Koran. Yasin features in a well-known Egyptian tale fighting social injustice.

Yasmin, Yasmina, Yasmine *see* Jasmine

Yehudi *see* Jude

Yessenia *f.*

Still mainly restricted to the Americas, this name of unknown meaning became popular with Spanish speakers as that of the titular gypsy heroine of a Mexican film (1971), later made into a television series.

Yolanda *f.*

From the Greek meaning 'violet flower'. The name of the Gilbert and Sullivan opera **Iolanthe** comes from the same root. **Yolande** is the French form.

Yseult(e), Ysolde *see* Isolda

Yusuf *m.*

Yusuf or **Yusif** is a popular boy's name, the Arabic equivalent of **JOSEPH**.

Yves *see* **Ivo, Ivor, Yvonne**

Yvonne, Yvette *f.*

These are French names meaning 'yew'. They are
female pet forms of the Breton boy's name, **Yves**.
The boy's name has never been common in Britain,
but the girls' versions are quite popular.

Zachary *m.*

The English form of **Zacharias**, the Greek for the Hebrew **Zachariah** or **Zechariah**, meaning 'the Lord has remembered'. Zachary was used occasionally in the Middle Ages, but did not become at all common until the Puritans adopted it in the 17th century. It has variant forms **Zachery** and **Zackery** and the short form **Zak** or **Zack**. **Zacchaeus** and **Zakki** are other forms of the name.

Zahid *m.*

An Arabic name which means 'abstinent'.

Zahra, Zara *f.*

A Muslim name which means 'to flower' or 'to achieve splendour'. It was the family name of the Prophet's mother and is traditionally used in her honour. The English form came to the attention of the British public in 1981 when Princess Anne, the Princess Royal, used it as her daughter's name. It is occasionally found as **Xara** or **Zaria**.

Zainab *see* **Zaynab**

Zak *see* **Zachary, Isaac**

Zake *m.*, **Zakiya** *f.*

An Arabic name meaning 'pure, chaste'. The feminine form can also be spelt **Zakiyah** and **Zakiyya**.

Zakki *see* **Zachary**

Zander *see* **Alexander**

Zandra *see* **Sandra**

Zane *m.*

The American author Zane Grey (1872–1939, given name **PEARL** Grey) took his pen name from his home town of Zanesville, Ohio. The town was named after its founder Ebenezer Zane; the meaning of his surname is not known.

Zara *see* **Zahra**

Zavia, Zavier *see* **Xavier**

Zaynab *f.*

A popular Muslim name, of uncertain meaning. Some scholars link it with a fragrant plant, and it was borne by several members of the Prophet Muhammad's family. It is frequently found as **Zainab**.

Zeb *m.*

This can be a short form of such Hebrew names as **Zebulun** ('exaltation') or **Zebedee** ('my gift'), or can simply be an attempt by parents to find an unusual name. Similarly **Zed** can be seen as a short form of **Zedekiah** ('justice of the Lord').

Zechariah *see* Zachary

Zed, Zedekiah *see* Zeb

Zeke *see* Ezekiel

Zelda *see* Griselda

Zena *f.*

One theory is that this name comes from a Persian word meaning 'woman'. Another makes it a pet form of various other names such as **Zinaida** which comes from Zeus, the Greek king of the gods, and is the name of two Russian saints; and another a variation of **XENIA**. It is also found as **Zina**.

Zenobia *f.*

This was the name of a great Queen of Palmyra (modern Syria) in the 3rd century AD. She was seen as a threat to the Eastern Roman Empire, and her aggressive foreign policy forced the Emperor Aurelian to invade. This he did successfully and put an end to her power, though he spared her life. The name appears in Cornwall from the 16th century but the reason for this is unknown.

Zillah *f.*

From the Hebrew for 'shade'. The name occurs in

the Old Testament (Genesis IV, 19-23) and was used occasionally after the Reformation.

Zina, Zinaida *see* Zena

Zita *f.*

The name of the last Empress of Austria who, although deposed just after the end of the First World War, died only in 1989. It comes from an Italian word for 'little girl' and was the name of a humble but good maid who became the patron saint of domestic servants.

Zoe, Zoë *f.*

This is the Greek word for 'life'. The Alexandrian Jews used it to translate the Hebrew equivalent for **EVE** into Greek. The name spread throughout the Eastern Church but has been used in Britain only in the last hundred years. It also appears as **Zoey** and **Zoie**.

Zorah *f.*

An Arabic name meaning 'light of dawn', also found as **Zora**. It can also be understood as a Hebrew name, taken from a place name of unknown meaning found in the Bible.

Zshakira *see* Shakir

Zubaida *f.*

An Arabic name, popular in India, meaning 'marigold'.

Zuleika *f.*

From the Persian meaning 'brilliant beauty'.
The name is known from Max Beerbohm's satirical
novel *Zuleika Dobson* (1911), whose heroine is so
beautiful that all the young men at Oxford University
kill themselves for love of her. The Arabic spelling
is **Zulekha**.

Top 50 boys' and girls' names in England and Wales, 2001

Boys

1	Jack		19	Jake	+3	37	Brandon	−2
2	Thomas		20	Alexander	+1	38	Owen	+8
3	Joshua	+1	21	Ethan	+11	39	Louis	+8
4	James	−1	22	Liam	−4	40	Aaron	−4
5	Daniel		23	Cameron	+1	41	Tyler	
6	Harry		24	Connor	+1		*New Entry*	+10
7	Samuel		25	Jordan	−6	42	Kyle	−3
8	Joseph		26	Mohammed	+1	43	Reece	−3
9	Matthew		27	Jamie	+1	44	Edward	
10	Lewis	+3	28	Dylan	+10	45	Alex	+3
11	Luke		29	Nathan	−4	46	David	−3
12	Oliver	+2	30	Jacob	−1	47	Robert	−6
13	William	−1	31	Ben		48	Harrison	
14	Benjamin	+2	32	Charlie	+1		*New Entry*	+8
15	Callum	−5	33	Michael	−3	49	Christopher	−7
16	George	+1	34	Kieran	−8	50	Joe	−1
17	Adam	+3	35	Max	+2			
18	Ryan	−3	36	Bradley	−2			

Girls

1	Chloe		6	Lauren		11	Ellie	+4
2	Emily		7	Charlotte	−3	12	Amy	+2
3	Megan		8	Hannah	+1	13	Katie	+3
4	Jessica	+1	9	Olivia	−1	14	Georgia	−3
5	Sophie	+2	10	Lucy		15	Rebecca	−3

16	Molly	+3	29	Jasmine	+3	41	Erin	
17	Bethany	−4	30	Courtney	−9		*New Entry*	+10
18	Emma	−1	31	Leah	−4	42	Millie	
19	Holly	+10	32	Amelia	+3		*New Entry*	+10
20	Ella	+6	33	Elizabeth	+1	43	Zoe	−2
21	Caitlin	+2	34	Anna	−3	44	Abbie	
22	Abigail	−4	35	Amber	+2	45	Nicole	−2
23	Grace	−3	36	Lily	+11	46	Paige	−4
24	Jade	+1	37	Laura	−7	47	Niamh	−7
25	Mia	+20	38	Sarah	−5	48	Daisy	+2
26	Shannon	−4	39	Rachel	−3	49	Natasha	−10
27	Eleanor	−3	40	Phoebe	−2	50	Alexandra	−2
28	Alice							

+/− indicates movement since 2000

Reproduced with permission of Office for National Statistics, 2002

Top 50 boys' and girls' names in Scotland, 2001

Boys

1	Jack		10	Jamie	−1	19	Jordan	−7
2	Lewis		11	Matthew	−4	20	Kyle	−3
3	Cameron	+1	12	Adam	+7	21	Michael	
4	Ryan	−1	13	Daniel		22	Ben	
5	James		14	Liam	−7	23	Thomas	
6	Callum	+4	15	Scott	+1	24	John	+3
7	Andrew	−1	16	Connor	−1	25=	Aidan	+11
8	Dylan	+12	17	Kieran	−3	25=	Craig	−1
9	Ross	+2	18	David		27	Sean	−1

28	Alexander	+3	36	Declan	−1	44	Mark	−7
29	Nathan	−4	37=	Aaron	−9	45=	Ethan	+16
30	Joshua	+4	37=	Ewan	+6	45=	Paul	
31	Calum	−2	39	Christopher	−9	47	Brandon	−1
32=	Robbie	+6	40	Reece		48=	Jay	+11
32=	William	+10	41	Robert	−9	48=	Samuel	+2
34	Luke	+5	42	Fraser	−2	50	Finlay	+1
35	Euan	−2	43	Josh	+6			

Girls

1	Chloe		18	Sarah	−1	35	Aimee	+2
2=	Amy		19	Morgan	+1	36	Jessica	+4
2=	Lauren	+1	20	Abbie	+7	37	Beth	−4
4	Emma		21	Niamh	+2	38	Charlotte	+3
5	Megan	+1	22	Anna	−3	39	Taylor	+8
6	Erin	+3	23	Eilidh	−2	40	Jennifer	−13
7	Hannah	+3	24	Olivia	+1	41	Jodie	+2
8	Rebecca	−3	25	Holly	+4	42	Heather	−6
9	Sophie	+2	26	Zoe	+8	43=	Abby	+17
10	Caitlin	−3	27	Laura	−3	43=	Samantha	
11	Rachel	−3	28	Courtney	−10	45	Robyn	−10
12	Emily	+1	29	Cara	+8	46	Louise	−14
13=	Katie	+2	30=	Eve	+19	47	Rachael	−5
13=	Lucy	−1	30=	Molly	+19	48	Bethany	−17
15	Nicole	+1	32	Jade	−2	49	Georgia	−4
16	Shannon	−2	33	Kirsty	−12	50=	Iona	−2
17	Ellie	+9	34	Leah	+5	50=	Kayleigh	+1

+/− indicates movement since 2000

Reproduced with permission of General Register Office for Scotland, 2002